The History of Civilization

A Thousand Years
of the Tartars

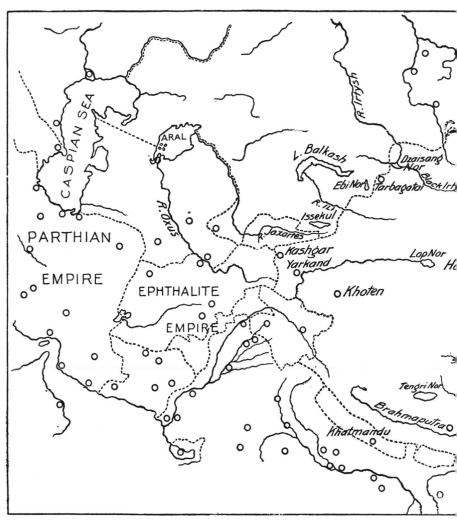

Rough adaptation based upon Varty's educational map of Asia.

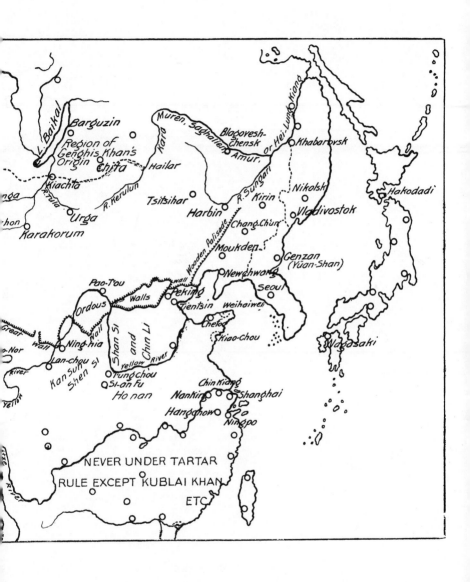

V. Baikal

Barguzin

Muren, Saghalien

Blagovesh-
Chensk

Amur.

Region of
Genghis Khan's
Origin

Khabarovsk

Chita

Hailar

or Hei-Lung Kiang

Kiachta

Kara

Nga

R. Kerulun

Tsitsihar

Nikolsk

Hakodadi

R. Sungari

Kirin

hon

Urga

Harbin

Vladivostok

Karakorum

Chang-Chun

Genzan
(Yüan-Shan)

Moukden

Pao-Tou

Wooden Palisade

Newchwang

Wall

Peking

Seoul

Ordous

Walls

Tientsin

Weihaiwei

Great

Wall

Ning-hia

Shen Si

Yellow River

Chefoo

Kiao-Chou

Wall

Lan-chou

Kan-Suh

Shan Si
and
Chin Li

Nagasaki

Nor

River

Tungchou

Yellow

Si-an Fu

Ho nan

Nanking

Chin Kiang

Shanghai

Hangchow

Ningpo

NEVER UNDER TARTAR

RULE EXCEPT KUBLAI KHAN

ETC

River

A Thousand Years of the Tartars

By
E. H. PARKER
Professor of Chinese, Victoria University of Manchester

Second Edition, Revised

DORSET PRESS
New York

This edition published by Dorset Press,
a division of Marboro Books
Corporation.
1987 Dorset Press

ISBN 0-88029-136-2

The paper used in this book meets
the minimum requirements of the
American National Standard for
Permanence of Paper for Printed
Library Materials Z39.48-1948.

Printed in the United States of America

M 9 8 7 6 5 4 3 2 1

PREFACE TO SECOND EDITION

THIS unpretending work was originally written at K'iung-chou (Island of Hainan, South China), in 1893-4, the Prefect of that city having lent me the necessary original Chinese histories. I left China for good in 1894, and Mr. George Jamieson, then Acting-Chief Judge at Shanghai, kindly corrected the printers' proofs and saw to the publication there. Meanwhile the Russians had discovered near Urga a trilingual stone record, the Chinese and Syriac versions ultimately leading to the further discovery that the third language was Turkish. Professor V. Thomsen, of Copenhagen, was the first to establish this fact (by methods reminiscent of the Rosetta Stone); and Dr. W. Radloff, of St. Petersburg, followed by practically reconstructing the whole Turkish language in the form it existed 1,200 years ago. I had already in the *China Review*, vol. xx, attempted at length to show that the Hiung-nu, Scythians, Huns, and Turks were different phases of the same tribes ; and, since then, Chavannes, Hirth, and others have gone into the matter still more thoroughly.

E. H. PARKER.

14 GAMBIER TERRACE,
    LIVERPOOL.

ORIGINAL PREFACE

THE following pages are intended to give, in (it is hoped) readable form, the substance of all the Chinese have to say about the nomad Tartars previous to the conquests of Genghis Khan. Specialists and critics will doubtless find much which at first sight may seem to require further explanation; but when I say that I have translated, word for word, all the original Chinese authorities I can find, and that the explanatory references and manuscript notes attached to the translations reach to over seven thousand, it will be admitted that there is some ground for adopting the new course of omitting all justificatory matter whatever. There is one exception. As, in order to make the narrative more readable, I have endeavoured throughout to substitute Tartar sounds for Chinese transliterations of those sounds; and have almost uniformly used modern place-names instead of the names they bore at the time each event is described; I have thought it well to place the original Chinese sounds of all proper names in the margin, so that those who are competent to consult the originals may be able to search out the desired reference for themselves. I have done this in the Pekingese dialect. This, being a mere Tartar-corrupted jargon of standard Chinese, is about the worst that could have been chosen, so far as the chance of any resemblance to the Tartar sounds intended is concerned; but it is the dialect best known to those students in China who are likely to require the references. Cantonese would have been the best of all, but few Europeans know Cantonese. To explain the grounds upon which I arrive at my conclusions in this excepted department would require a separate treatise. I therefore enter into no further justifications. Armed with the original authorities, I am prepared to give satisfaction to all who can show that they merit it.

E. H. PARKER.

CONTENTS

CONTENTS

LIST OF ILLUSTRATIONS

BOOK I

THE EMPIRE OF THE HIUNG-NU

BOOK I

The Empire of the Hiung-nu

CHAPTER I

Earliest Notices of the Hiung-nu

THE real history of the nomads of Eastern Asia begins about the same time and very much in the same way as the history of the northern tribes of Europe. The Chinese Empire, like the Roman Empire, began a career of discovery and conquest, which resulted in closer and more frequent contact with and blending of races, incessant frontier wars, subversion of the Empire, and a general shifting of political centres. More ancient than the experiences of China and Rome were those of Greece and Persia; but the account of the Scythians given by Herodotus differs from the later Chinese and Roman records in being rather a vivid picture of life and manners than an exact political history. Yet there is very little in the descriptions of Herodotus which does not perfectly accord with the Chinese portrayal of the Hiung-nu on the one hand and the Roman narrative of the Huns on the other. Whether the Hiung-nu of China are to be etymologically connected with the Οὖννοι, Hunnen, and Huns of the west, is a question which is scarcely susceptible of positive proof either one way or the other. We confine ourselves to giving a plain record of facts as gathered from

Chinese history, leaving each reader free to form theories for himself, and avoiding speculation unless we are tolerably sure of our ground.

At the time when our narrative begins, nothing whatever was known by the Chinese of the Japanese, Burmese, Siamese, Hindoos, Turkestan races, or Southern Seas ; and there was only the very faintest knowledge of Corea, the Tungusic tribes, the Annamese, the various tribes south of the Great River or Yangtsze, the Tibetan nomads, or others. China's foreign relations were practically confined to the horse-riding freebooters of the north. In the oldest times they had been known by different names more or less similar in sound to the above-mentioned appellation so familiar to general history ; but it is a mistake to suppose, as most European writers have done, that the term Hiung-nu only dates from the second century before Christ. The historian Ma Twanlin, who died six hundred years ago, himself combats this idea, and cites two instances to prove not only that, long previous to this, the national designation was in use, but also that under the same name the power in question had already become a considerable one. In nearly every case the Chinese trace the political beginnings of their frontier kingdoms to some Chinese exile or adventurer who, accommodating himself to local circumstances, and doubtless easily gaining paramount influence through his acquaintance with the all-important art of writing, succeeded in welding a series of homogeneous tribes into a nation. It is quite certain that this was later the case in Corea, Foochow, Canton, Yün Nan, Kan Suh, and Formosa ; and, this being so, there seems no good reason for rejecting the traditions that the same thing took place with the nomadic races of Tibet, Mongolia, and Manchuria. The Chinese themselves do not make too much of the Hiung-nu tradition, (which, however, is there,) to the effect that about B.C. 1200 a royal personage, who had most probably been misconducting himself, fled to the nomads of the north and founded among them a sort of dynasty (cf. end of Bk. I). But, although for many centuries previous to B.C. 200 the northern states of the Chinese Empire had trouble with these nomads, there was never any record of the generations and successions of the latter, and the amount of knowledge possessed concerning them was about on a par with that recorded in the pages of Herodotus concerning the Scythians. As yet nothing positive was known of the Tungusic or eastern branch of nomads, with whom the Chinese were not brought into close contact until several centuries later. It was only the great and predominant nomad nation of the Hiung-nu of which they had any satisfactory knowledge. In later times the word "Turkish" or "Turko-Scythian" has been applied to distinguish the various homogeneous tribes which formed the Empire of the Hiung-nu ; but this word Türk was totally unknown previous to the fifth century of our era, and it would therefore be an anachronism for us to speak of "Turks" just yet. So with the word "Tartar"—which, singularly enough, is also used by the Chinese in the same vague way as with us ; —this word was certainly unknown to history in any form previous to the second century of our era, and even then, as in the subsequent case of "Turk," it was at first only applied to one petty tribe. So, whatever we may think of the identity between the word Hiung-nu and the word Hun, it is quite as certain that the Chinese had no other name for the horse-riding, flesh-eating, and kumiss-drinking nomads of North Asia as it is that the Europeans had no other name for the horse-riding, flesh-eating, and kumiss-drinking nomads of North Europe, who only appeared there after the ruling castes of the Hiung-nu power had been driven from China. Moreover, the Scythians of Herodotus who were brought into contact with the Greeks and Persians seem to have possessed exactly the same manners as the Hiung-nu of China and the Huns of Europe, so that we may reasonably conclude, apart from any stray pieces of definite evidence, that each of the three had some ethnographical connection one with the other.

The Hiung-nu lived on horseback; "their country was the back of a horse." They moved from place to place with their flocks and herds, always in search of fresh pasture. Horses, cattle, and sheep were their usual possessions; but they also occasionally had camels, asses, mules, and other peculiar breeds of the equine family which it is not easy for us now to identify; probably one was the onager of Assyria and Central Asia. They had no cities or towns of any description; but, though their residence in one place never lasted long, each tribe had reserved to it a certain range of territory; and, though they had no agricultural occupations, each tent or household seems to have had a share of land for its own exclusive use. They possessed no written character, and all orders and administrative acts were conveyed by word of mouth only. When mere babies, they were taught to ride on sheep and to shoot rats or birds with a tiny bow and arrow; as they grew older, they practised their skill upon foxes and hares. Every grown-up man strong enough to bend an ordinary bow was a trooper. Every one, from the highest to the lowest, fed upon flesh and milk; used the skins of the animals slaughtered as clothing; and wore an overcoat of felt made out of the hair. The fighting men were always conceded the best entertainment; the old and feeble were despised, and had to pick up what was left. A universal custom, which, as we shall see, extended for a thousand years over the whole of Tartary, was for the son to take over his deceased father's wives, (with the exception of his own natural mother), and for younger brothers to take over the widows of their elder brethren. It does not appear quite certain whether the son or the brother had first choice : perhaps the brother only took when there was no son : possibly *vice versa*. In times of peace, besides tending their herds, they kept their hands in training by hunting and shooting; at other times every man was ready for a fight or a raid. It was not considered shameful to retreat before an enemy : in fact, their system of warfare seems to have been one of

sudden ill-concerted rushes, feints, and ambushes. They
were, the Chinese thought, destitute of any considerations
of mercy or justice : force was their only law ; and, when
hand-to-hand combats did take place, they possessed swords
and daggers as well as their bows. Some of the oldest accounts
seem to show that in winter there were cave-dwellers amongst
them : but perhaps this statement has special reference to
the Tungusic Tartars of the East.

It is unnecessary to go into the earliest accounts of Tartar
wars, which are of the vaguest description. Suffice it to
say that from B.C. 1400 to B.C. 200 there are laconic notices
of Chinese fights with the nomads, with approximate dates
given in each case, so that they may fairly be accepted as
history ; but it must be remembered that even Chinese history
is only dated, year by year, from B.C. 828. The Northern
parts of the provinces now known as Shen Si, Shan Si, and
Chih Li were then in possession of the nomads. For many
centuries, during what is known as the " Conflicting State
Period," the nomad power stood on terms of equality with
China. Both the Emperor of China and his restless vassal
kings at different times formed marriage alliances with the
nomad powers, and at least one Chinese king deliberately
adopted the Tartar costume and mode of life. Another
etymological question now appears, and that is whether
the Chinese word *Tung-hu* or " Eastern Tartars ", (a term
which is as regularly applied to the ancestors of the Cathayans
or Kitans, Manchus, and Coreans as the term Hiung-nu
is regularly applied to the ancestors of the Turks, Ouigours,
Kirghiz, etc.), has any etymological connection with the European word Tungusic or Tunguz. I have not the means of tracing
back a careful enquiry into this point, which is discussed
again in Book II : if the two words are in no way connected
by etymology, it is a remarkable instance of coincidence,
for they both serve, in Russian and in Chinese respectively,
to indicate exactly the same idea. There is another incident
mentioned which tends to show that the frontier states of

China must have been deeply impregnated with Tartar ideas. One of the vassal princes had a beaker fashioned out of the skull of a rival satrap, a proceeding as contrary to Confucian ideas of propriety as it is consonant with all we know of Hiung-nu and Scythian customs. Towards the end of the third century before Christ, and just before the menacing Western power of Ts'in succeeded in destroying the old feudal system and reducing the whole of China under one direct imperial sway, the vassal state which then ruled over the Northern parts of what are now called Shan Si and Chih Li carried out a systematic policy of resistance, on Fabian principles, to the nomad incursions, and at last succeeded in decoying the Tartar king into the open, where he was utterly defeated with the loss of 100,000 men. After Ts'in had amalgamated this state together with the others, the celebrated general Mêng T'ien was sent at the head of several hundred thousand men to attack the Tartars; the whole line of the Yellow River was recovered, including the Loop portion now known as the Ordous country. The Tartars were driven away to the north of the Great Desert; enormous numbers of criminals and other unfortunate people were drafted northwards, in order to construct a military road and do garrison duty; over forty citadels or fortified towns were built along the line of the frontier; and, finally, the so-called Great Wall was carried continuously from the sea to a point near the modern provincial capital of Lan-chou Fu in Kan Suh. This Great Wall still exists in a more or less complete state throughout nearly its entire length; and, as it is distinctly marked upon almost every modern map of China, the reader of the following pages will find his task much facilitated if he keeps this line well before his mind; for it not only enables us to dispense with the necessity of introducing multitudinous strange Chinese names of places,—names, too, which often vary as to locality with each succeeding dynasty,—but it marks in a vivid way the blood-line along which millions of human skeletons are to lie bleaching without intermission during a thousand years' struggle. It is proper, however, to remark that Mêng T'ien with his half million of slaves did not do more than improve and consolidate already existing walls ; for we are told that the Chinese king who adopted Tartar costume had already built a Great Wall from north-east Shan Si to the westernmost extremity of the Loop country ; and a little before that the rising power of Ts'in had built another wall still further west. To the east, again, the frontier state of Yen, which roughly speaking may be taken to represent the plain of modern Peking, had constructed a Great Wall from about the longitude of Peking to the sea, so that it is evident very little remained for Mêng T'ien to do but to improve and strengthen the already existing fortifications. In later times, too, various northern dynasties added to or laterally extended the line of the Great Wall in the east, more especially near Peking ; so that the magnificent and almost perfect structure which modern visitors make a point of going to see at a distance of about thirty miles from that capital is very far from being the ancient Great Wall of two thousand years ago, most of which is in a ruined condition the farther west you travel.

CHAPTER II

The Reign of the Conqueror Baghdur

AS we have seen, the Hiung-nu were obliged to retire before the formidable power of the great Chinese Imperator, who was a man of the most uncompromising and grandiose ideas. It is not improbable that his eternally execrated act of destroying all the literature and learned men he could lay his hands on worked some good in an indirect way ; for the necessity of reproducing this literature and of having some handier means of written communication for the immediate necessities of government probably stimulated the Chinese to invent objects less cumbrous than the old bamboo tablets, bamboo varnish brushes, and iron styles, and something more potentially rapid of production than the clumsy old characters of innumerable strokes. Be that as it may, Mêng T'ien has not only the reputation of having been the original builder of the Great Wall, but also the equally unmerited one of having been the original inventor of the modern hair writing pencil: but competent Chinese critics prove that the utmost he did, when short of the usual materials, was to improve the bamboo or bristle pencil which had already been in use for some time. The Hiung-nu had to contend with another formidable power as well as with the Chinese. This was a nomadic nation known to the Chinese as the Yüeh-chï, and then in possession of the western half of the long straggling province now known as Kan Suh. The Chinese seem to have been almost totally ignorant of this people previous to the absorption of the feudal states in the new Empire of Ts'in; and indeed this is no wonder; for, previous to that important event, the state of Ts'in was the only one which could have conveniently had any relations with the West at all. At the time the Hiung-nu were forced to retire before the all-pervading power of the Imperator, the nomad Emperor (or Jenuye as he styled himself) was called Deuman, and with the Jenuye Deuman the recorded history of the nomad empires may be said to begin. The new Chinese Universal Empire fell to pieces almost immediately after the death in B.C. 210 of its able founder, who, however, besides being of bastard birth, really owed most of the consolidating work to the 56-year-long reign of his great-grandfather, practically his immediate predecessor; and, during the four years' anarchy which followed the collapse, Deuman was able to recover and develop his reduced power. The northern frontier was necessarily neglected during the mortal struggle which took place between rival Chinese military adventurers aiming at the imperial succession. Deuman gradually moved southwards from his inaccessible stronghold north of the Desert, and ended by crossing the northernmost bend of the Yellow River, repossessing himself of the Ordous territory, and resuming his old boundaries with China : in other words, he once more occupied the eastern part of modern Kan Suh province. Deuman was now an old man, and unfortunately in the hands of a much-beloved young queen. Listening to the voice of this female charmer, he allowed himself to be persuaded into accepting her son as his heir, to the prejudice of the legitimate aspirant, who was an able captain named Baghdur. In order to encompass Baghdur's destruction, Deuman sent him as a hostage to the neighbouring state of Yüeh-chï, and then attacked that power, hoping that in their indignation the Yüeh-chï would murder his son. But Baghdur was too alert for them, and, mounting one of their fleetest steeds, succeeded in making his way safely home. Deuman was so pleased at this act of prowess that he at once placed his valiant son in command of ten thousand troopers. Baghdur, however, was by no means so ready to forgive the uxorious father's initial display of feebleness and treachery ; so he carefully matured a scheme for Deuman's destruction. First of all he invented a new species of " singing-arrow,"—the *nari-kabura* of the early Japanese,—the use of one of which by him upon any victim was to be a signal for all his attendants to fire instantly at the same object. After having tried their mettle, first upon his best horse, and next upon his favourite wife, with the result that several troopers were in each case executed for disobedience, he watched his opportunity one day when old Deuman was out hunting, and fired a singing-arrow at him. The result was that the Jenuye fell dead pierced through and through, and Baghdur was immediately proclaimed in his place. A general massacre of his late father's family and household followed, but Baghdur seems to have reserved at least one paternal widow, according to custom, to be his own wife.

At this time it would appear that the Tunguses were

a consolidated power, little inferior to the Hiung-nu, and that a 300 mile stretch of desert lay between the two dominions as a sort of neutral zone. Hearing of Baghdur's unfilial behaviour and usurped succession, they sent envoys to him to demand a present of the finest horses as the price of their non-interference. Baghdur, who was as wary a diplomat as he was dashing a captain, affected to censure those of his council who were in favour of war, and feigned anxiety to conciliate the Tunguses by granting their request. As he had anticipated, the latter now grew more presuming, and demanded one of his favourite wives. But Baghdur's policy was to give them plenty of rope before hanging them with it, and so off the demanded queen went too, much to the consternation of the warlike council. The Tunguses now began to mass troops on their western frontier, and, having come to the conclusion that Baghdur had not the courage of his position, boldly demanded the cession to them of the hitherto neutral strip. Baghdur's councillors were some of them inclined to give up what they termed a useless piece of land, but they paid the penalty of their failure to penetrate their master's deep policy with their heads, and war was promptly declared. Immediate decapitation was to be the lot of every able soldier in the kingdom who should fail to present himself promptly at headquarters. Baghdur's sagacious calculations were perfectly successful : the Tunguses, having come to the conclusion that he was a craven spirit, had neglected all precautions ; their nation was utterly broken in one short campaign ; their flocks and herds were driven off, and the majority of the population were made slaves. A miserable remnant of them took refuge in the now Mongol plateaux north-east of modern Peking, where, as we shall see later on, they gradually developed into a formidable power. It is as well here to direct attention to a phenomenon in nomad history which at once explains how each successive dominion of Huns, Tunguses, Turks, Ouigours, Kitans or Cathayans, Mongols, and Manchus were formed, and at the same time proves how utterly impossible it is to provide a definite locality for or clothe with an exclusive nationality any particular horde. The result of a great battle was that many of the women passed over to new masters ; the captive youths became warriors, usually under their own chiefs, but subject to the supreme control of the conqueror ; the old men were turned out to tend the flocks and herds, and the flocks and herds simply changed masters for a few years until another revolution occurred. Slave and master lived very much in the same way, the only difference being that one did the menial work whilst the other enjoyed himself : meanwhile the women, habituated to the idea of passing from one man to the other, even in their own tribes, only had to undergo the rough excitement of an extra embrace from a man who was not of their own particular choice. Under such circumstances, though the main distinctions of Hiung-nu and Tungus are always preserved, it is not to be wondered at that languages got intermingled, tribes hopelessly mixed up, and customs interchanged. For the present the Tungusic power utterly disappears. Up to this date the Chinese knew little of it as apart from that of the Hiung-nu, and for a couple of centuries at least this ignorance of their manners and customs continues. The Tunguses had no relations with China of any kind, and we are told so.

Baghdur was one of the great conquerors of the world's history, and may fairly be called the Hannibal of Tartary. It is the practice even amongst our most highly educated men in Europe to deliver sonorous sentences about being " master of the world," " bringing all nations of the earth under her sway," and so on, when in reality only some corner of the Mediterranean is involved, or some ephemeral sally into Africa, Persia, or Gaul. Cyrus and Alexander, Darius and Xerxes, Cæsar and Pompey all made very interesting excursions, but they were certainly not on a larger scale or charged with greater human interest than the campaigns which were going on at the eastern end of Asia. Western civilization possessed much in art and science for which China never cared, but on the other hand the Chinese developed a historical and critical literature, a courtesy of demeanour, a luxury in clothing, and an administrative system of which Europe might have been proud. In one word, the history of the Far East is quite as interesting as that of the Far West. It only requires to be able to read it. When we brush away contemptuously from our notice the tremendous events which took place on the plains of Tartary, we must not blame the Chinese too much for declining to interest themselves in the doings of what to them would appear insignificant states dotted round the Mediterranean and Caspian, which, at this time, was practically all the world of which we knew in Europe.

Baghdur, having thus disposed of the Tunguses, now turned his attention to the Yüeh-chï, who found it necessary to move farther away to the south and west. He recovered all the disputed territory which had been annexed by Mêng T'ien, and also considerably advanced his frontiers farther east in the direction of modern Kalgan and Jêhol. As he had 300,000 troopers under his command, it would be fair to estimate his population at about the same number of tents. All the northern tribes in the neighbourhood of Lake Baikal and the Amur were under his sway; but, as the Chinese knew nothing of these remote peoples at the time, we can only judge by slender indications that the Kirghiz, the future High Carts or Ouigours, and the Orunchun or Fishskin Tartars were certainly amongst those he had subdued. It is certain the Kirghiz were.

A few words regarding the Hiung-nu administrative system will not be uninteresting. The full title of the king or Emperor was Tengri Kudu Jenuye, which we are distinctly told means "Heaven's Son Immense." The word *tengri* is still both Turkish and Mongol for "heaven," but it is for Turkish scholars to exercise their wits upon the word *kudu*. The next in rank to the Jenuye were the two Dugi, one for the East and one for the West, the Jenuye himself ruling the central portion of the nomad Empire. The Chinese tell us that the word *dugi* (Turkish *doghri*) meant " virtuous " or " worthy," and as East and West are equivalent to Left and Right in Chinese parlance, they almost invariably translate instead of using the Tartar words, and say " Left and Right Worthy Princes." Of the two the Eastern Dugi was of the higher rank, and was usually heir to the throne. Then came the Left and Right Rukle, Left and Right Marshals, Left and Right Chamberlains, and Left and Right Kuttu (cf. Bk. IV, Ch. II) Marquesses with a few others in similar pairs. The Left Rukle ranked before the Right Dugi. There were twenty-four in all who had deca-chiliarch rank, that is, the right to command ten thousand troopers. The Right and Left Dugi and Rukle formed the " Four Horns." Then came three other pairs called " Six Horns." All these were agnates of the Jenuye, and the " white horn " of Genghis Khan and the Great Mogul is perhaps in some way connected with the idea. I cannot even guess at the (imaginary) word *rukle*, but the word *kuttu* which, in this form and the form *kutuluk*, endures through the history of the Turks for a thousand years, is undoubtedly the same etymologically as the modern Turkish word *kutluk*, " felicitous." We are told that the two Kuttu Marquesses were specially charged with the administrative business of the state, and that each of the twenty-four officers of the first rank had his own area within which to wander after pasture, and had besides the right to appoint his own chiliarchs, centurions, decurions, etc. The Jenuye's queen had the native title of Inchi, and she might be taken from any one of the three or four great clans which, with the Jenuye's own private clan, formed the aristocracy of the state. It is not necessary to enumerate all the minor titles, but we may fitly mention that of *Tsugu*, which, as we shall see later on, is the connecting link between the Hiung-nu and the later Turks. Every new year the Jenuye held a great religious festival at what the Chinese call Dragon City : it was evidently much the same kind of affair as the Mongol *couroultai* of Marco Polo's time. Sacrifices were then offered to ancestors, Heaven, Earth, the spirits, and the genii. This fact, together with the Jenuye's title "Son of Heaven," distinctly points to a community of early religious ideas between the Tartars and the Chinese. In the autumn another great meeting was held for the counting of the population and the taxing of property and cattle. Crimes in the state were remarkably few, and were summarily disposed of at one or both of these great meetings. Horse-racing and camel-fighting under the Jenuye's patronage were indulged in at the same time. Death or ankle-crushing were the punishments for offences against the person, whilst the members of a man's family were delivered over into slavery as compensation for attacks upon property. The Jenuye rose every morning to greet the sun, and in the evening performed a similar obeisance to the moon. The east or left side was most honourable, as with the Chinese. It is only proper to mention, however, that some texts say the right was most honourable, and it is certainly puzzling to be told that the Jenuye sat facing north, while, as we all know, the Chinese Emperors faced south : but it is at any rate certain that the Left Dugi was the more honourable of the two. There were also certain superstitions regarding the position of the sun, and touching certain days in the calendar. In all important undertakings the state of the moon was taken into account, the waxing period being selected for commencing operations, whilst the waning period was considered favourable for retiring homewards. It appears that individual bravery was encouraged by each man's being allowed to keep as his own property, or as slaves, all that he captured with his own hand ; besides which a goblet of strong drink was the special reward for cutting off the head of an enemy. There are several other doubtful passages which seem to reward a man for carrying off a friend's body from the battle-field by bestowing all the deceased's possessions upon the rescuer, and which send all

a man's servants, wives, and intimates after his coffin (perhaps
rather as mourners than as victims to be buried with him,
though Gibbon mentions such sacrifices by the White Huns
of Sogdiana, and the semi-Tartar Ts'in dynasty certainly
did so). Valuable objects were buried with the dead, but
no mourning was worn, and no mound, tablet, or tree was
erected over the grave, the native name for which was *dörok*.

Baghdur was now clearly recognized by his own people
as being a very great man, and he strengthened his position
considerably by securing the person of one of the best generals
of the new Han dynasty, who surrendered his army to the
Hiung-nu, together with one of the strong frontier cities in
North Shan Si. The founder of the celebrated Han dynasty,
himself a great captain, had just disposed of his chief rivals, and
was no sooner (B.C. 202) firmly seated himself upon the
Chinese throne, than he at once marched in person to the
relief of the other great towns in the region then chiefly
menaced by the Tartar hordes. It was a terribly cold and
snowy winter, and about a quarter of the vast Chinese host
had their fingers frozen off. Baghdur, seeing his opportunity,
had recourse to the usual Hiung-nu tactics ; feigned defeat
and flight, kept his best troops well out of sight, and enticed
the Chinese army, numbering 320,000 men, mostly infantry,
on a wild-goose chase northwards. The Chinese Emperor
reached a strongly fortified post only a mile distant from
the modern Ta-t'ung Fu in Shan Si some time before the bulk
of his army could arrive, on which Baghdur let loose 300,000
of his best troopers, surrounded the Emperor, and cut off all
communications with the rest of the imperial army during
a period of seven days. It must have been a very picturesque
affair, for we are told that the white, grey, black, and chestnut
horses of the Tartars were all massed in four separate bodies,
one at each point of the compass. Like Attila at the battle
of Châlons six centuries later, Baghdur seems to have lost
a grand opportunity through fears that a trap was being
laid for him ; and meanwhile Chinese cunning took advantage

of his hesitation to get the Emperor out of his desperate straits. Exactly how it was done history does not tell, but it is clearly hinted that some discreditable negotiations were carried on by the Emperor with the Inchi, the result of which was that Baghdur was persuaded to leave one corner of his beleaguering lines unguarded; the Emperor made a successful sally through this weak point, and managed to join his main army in safety. Baghdur abandoned further attempts at conquest for the moment, and a Chinese ambassador was sent to offer him a lady of the blood in marriage, with an annual subsidy payable in silk piece-goods, refuse-silk for wadding garments, rice wine, and choice eatables. The man who had recommended this prudent policy to the Emperor was himself selected as envoy, and the idea was at some future date to utilize the offspring of the Chinese Inchi in the interests of the Empire; but, as we shall see, this dangerous diplomatic tool could cut both ways, and had the contrary effect 500 years later of placing a series of Hiung-nu Emperors upon the throne of China as the sole surviving " legitimists."

During the rest of the Han founder's reign Baghdur continued his raids and incursions, which, however, were moderated in consideration of the annual subsidy. In his old age the Han Emperor imitated the uxorious Deuman, and was nearly persuaded by a bewitching concubine to set aside the legitimate successor in favour of her own son; but the Empress-Dowager, a woman of masculine vigour, not only succeeded in placing her own son on the throne, and in cruelly putting her rival to death, but actually ruled for nearly a decade herself as a regularly recognized legitimate monarch. Baghdur, evidently prompted by one of the numerous Chinese renegades in his employ, sent the Dowager Empress a flippant letter placing his hand and heart at her disposal. This created a tremendous flutter in the imperial council, and the question now was whether to send back the envoy's head or a civil answer. Braggart generals were not wanting to fan the Empress' fury; but she cooled down a little when one cautious old statesman reminded her that the lads in the public streets were still singing a popular song about her late husband's narrow escape from the beleaguered town. A very diplomatic reply was therefore sent, thanking the Jenuye for the honour, but pointing out that the condition of the Dowager's teeth and hair was unequal to the task of securing his affections; two royal carriages and teams of horses were at the same time humbly offered to his Majesty. Baghdur seems to have felt rather ashamed of himself, for he sent an apology for his previous want of politeness, together with a present of Tartar horses. Things now went on quietly until the accession (B.C. 180) of the philosophic but concubine-born Emperor Wên Ti, the Marcus Aurelius of Chinese history. Baghdur evidently thought that the accession of an irregular or illegitimate monarch was a favourable moment for renewing his depredations. The old king of Canton, a Chinese adventurer ruling over Annamese tribes, took the same view; but by his courteous yet firm diplomacy the Emperor Wên Ti succeeded in subduing both his rivals, and his letters remain on record still as models of astute diplomatic fencing. In one of his despatches to the Emperor, Baghdur took the opportunity of explaining that he had succeeded in welding all the Tartars,—or " all the nations who use the bow from horseback " as he calls them,—into one dominion : the power of the Yüeh-chï had been annihilated, and the three tribes of Tarbagatai, Lob Nor, Sairam Nor, together with twenty-six other neighbouring states, had all been reduced. In other words, he was in full possession of what was until 1911 the Chinese Empire beyond the Great Wall, except Tibet. He added that, if the Emperor did not wish the Hiung-nu to trespass beyond the Great Wall, he must not allow the Chinese to come actually up to the Great Wall : moreover his own envoys must not be kept in detention, but must always be sent back at once. This haughty standpoint taken by Baghdur was naturally very distasteful to the Chinese, and several councils were held to deliberate the question of peace or war.   It ended in the Chinese Emperor, who was dissuaded by his consort from taking the field in person, "respectfully asking after the health of his Jenuye Majesty," and sending him a number of magnificent robes, buckles, hair-pins for plaited hair, fine cloths, and other things. Shortly after this (B.C. 173) Baghdur died, after a very successful reign of 36 years, and was succeeded by his son Kayuk.

CHAPTER III

The Period of Contest for Mastery with China

KAYUK was generally known by the nickname of the "High Old Jenuye." On learning of his accession, the Emperor of China sent him another princess, in whose suite was a palace eunuch or private chamberlain. This man did not at all like the idea of Tartar life, and protested vigorously against the indignity. The Emperor, however, insisted ; but the eunuch was heard to mutter as he started something about being "a thorn in the side of China." As soon as ever he reached the Tartar headquarters he abandoned his Chinese nationality, and before long became a great confidant of the Jenuye, whom he harangued as follows :—
"Your whole horde scarcely equals in numbers the population "of a couple of Chinese prefectures, but the secret of your "strength lies in your independence of China for all your "real necessities.   I notice an increasing fondness for Chinese "productions. Reflect that one-fifth of the Chinese wealth "would suffice to buy your people all over.   Silks and satins "are not half so well suited as felts for the rough life you lead, "nor are the perishable delicacies of China so handy as your "kumiss and cheese."   The eunuch went on to instruct the Jenuye in the elements of account-keeping by means of tallies, and suggested that in his reply to the Chinese Emperor's

letter he should use a tablet one-fifth longer than before, and that the envelope should be one of imposing size. The Jenuye was also advised to style himself, " The Great Jenuye " of the Hiung-nu, born of Heaven and Earth, the equal of " the Sun and Moon, etc., etc." One of the Chinese commissioners having made some remarks criticising the Tartar custom of despising the aged, the eunuch asked him :— " When the Chinese armies set out, do not their relatives " by contribution deprive themselves of some good thing " for the sustenance of the army ? " " Yes." " Well, " then," said the eunuch, " the Tartars make war a business : " the weak and aged cannot fight, so the best food is given " to their protectors." " But," argued the commissioner, " the same tent is used by father and son ; the son marries " his step-mother, and the brother his sisters-in-law : the " Hiung-nu have no manners and no ceremonies at all." The eunuch replied :—" Their custom is to eat the flesh " and drink the milk of their flocks and herds, which move " about after pasture according to season. Every man is " a skilful bowman, and in times of peace takes life easily " and happily. The principles of government are simple ; " the relations between ruler and people are to the point and " durable ; the administration of the state is as that of the " individual ; and, though wives are taken over by sons and " brethren, it is done in order to retain kith and kin all in the " family : it may be incest, but it keeps up the clan stock. " In China, on the other hand, though (nominally at least) " sons and brothers are not incestuous, the result is estrange- " ment, feuds, and the breaking up of families. Moreover, " rites and rights are so corruptly managed that class is set " against class, and one man is forced to slave for another " man's luxury. Food and clothing can only be got by tilling " the land and rearing the silkworm. Walled towns have " to be built for personal safety. Thus in times of danger " no one knows how to fight, whilst in times of peace every " man exists only by the sweat of his brow. Don't talk to

" me, you caged-up man-milliners ! What is the use of that
" trumpery hat of yours ? " This style of language, (which
bears a wonderful resemblance to that of Attila's favourite,
the Roman deserter, freedman of Onegesius, who harangued
the assistant envoy Priscus upon the vices of the Roman
Empire), was repeated whenever any Chinese envoy showed
disposition to carp at his Tartar surroundings. The eunuch
would say :—" You envoys should talk less, and confine
" yourselves to seeing that we get good quality and good
" measure of silk, floss, rice, and spirits in our annual subsidies.
" Talking is superfluous if the supplies are satisfactory ; and
" we shall not talk at all, but raid your frontiers, if the contrary
" is the case." Thus the eunuch kept his word, and, by
carefully teaching the Jenuye where his true interests lay,
was really a thorn in the Chinese side.

After he had been on the throne about seven years, the
Jenuye Kayuk at the head of 140,000 men made a raid upon
the valley of the River King, which flows south-east to the
old Chinese metropolis in South Shen Si : his scouts advanced
almost up to the walls of the capital city of Ch'ang-an (Si-an Fu),
and immense numbers of people and cattle were carried away.
Great preparations were made to drive the invaders off,
but they always disappeared before the Chinese troops could
come up with them ; and for several years the whole line
of the Great Wall was kept in a state of ferment and uneasiness.
Resort was once more had to diplomatic negotiations, in the
course of which the principle is distinctly laid down that
" all north of the Great Wall is the country of the bowmen,
" whilst all south of the Great Wall is the country of hats
" and girdles,"—or, as the Romans would have said, " of
the toga."

It was during the reign of Kayuk that the Yüeh-chï were
finally driven from their ancient seat between Lob-nor and
Koko-nor : they passed the great Celestial Range near the
modern Kuldja, after having to fight their way past their
congeners, the Wu-sun of modern Cobdo and Ili, who were

also emigrants from Kan Suh : thence they seem to have worked their way past Issekul and Tashkend to the Sea of Aral. Turning south-east, they appropriated the realm of the Tocharoi. For some time their capital is distinctly stated by the Chinese to have been north of the Oxus.

The last of the Greek rulers of Bactria, Heliocles, died about this time, and the Parthians and Yüeh-chï would seem to have divided his kingdom between them. The latter gradually extended their empire down to the Pamir, Kashmir, and the Punjaub, and, abandoning their nomadic habits, soon formed a powerful state, known in the West as the Empire of the Haithals, Viddhals, Abdals, Ephthalites, or Hephthalites. European, Persian, and Chinese writers are perfectly at one upon this point. In fact, the histories of the Manchu dynasty state in as many words that the Affghanistan of to-day is the Ephthah of the 5th century, and that the Ephthah were the ancient Yüeh-chï (see end of Bk. III). Their congeners of Cobdo are not so easily identified. Arguing solely from the similarity of sound, some European writers suggest Eusenii ; others Edones ; the latest Chinese writers suggest Russians, which is absurd, except in so far as the modern Ferghana of Russia was the Wu-sun of old in parts. I should be inclined to say that Awsen or Orson was the sound the Chinese wished to imitate 2,000 years ago ; whoever they were, they soon disappeared from Chinese records, and never exercised any appreciable influence upon her history. We may discuss the question again when we come to treat of Chinese relations with countries west of the Pamir, but in the present work our concern is only with Central and Eastern Tartary, and Tartary west of the Celestial Mountains, so that it will suffice here simply to notice the fact that it was Kayuk who finally crushed the Yüeh-chï, and, in good old Tartar fashion, made himself a wine-goblet out of their king's skull.

Kayuk was succeeded by his son Kyundjin in the year B.C. 162. The eunuch continued in his post of adviser to the new Jenuye, and therefore it is not to be wondered at that raiding went on as before. China's position was the more difficult in that after the death of the Emperor Wên Ti intestine troubles broke out, both in the interior and on the frontier, and one of the founder's grandsons even entered into traitorous alliance with the Huns. But the Emperor King Ti encouraged frontier trade, sent liberal presents to the new Jenuye, and gave him a fresh princess in marriage : the result of this conciliatory policy was that, though during the sixteen years of his reign there were petty frontier robberies, there was no raiding on a grand scale. This desirable state of affairs would probably have continued indefinitely, and the two empires might have learned to live in peace alongside each other, had not the counsellors of the youthful Emperor Wu Ti, shortly after his accession in B.C. 140, imprudently attempted a disgraceful act of treachery. It was in this wise. Frontier trade was going on quite flourishingly between the two peoples, and there were plenty of facilities for passing to and fro. A Chinese merchant was sent to offer the Hiung-nu for a consideration a city known as Ma Ch'êng, or " Horse City," a place which always had been, and was for many centuries destined to be, one of the most contested places on the frontier : it was not far from the spot where sixty years earlier the founder had been nearly captured by Baghdur. The idea was to entice the Jenuye into a tight place, and then get rid of him and his best troops by a general massacre ; so with this object in view, 300,000 soldiers were set in ambush to await the arrival of the Tartars. The Jenuye, whose cupidity had been aroused by the prospect of plundering so rich a town, had already passed through the Great Wall with an army of 100,000 troopers, and was within thirty English miles of Horse City, when he noticed that the herds of cattle scattered about over the plain had no one to tend them. His suspicions being aroused, he made for the nearest Chinese watch-tower, and soon captured the warden, who, to save his own life, disclosed the whole plot. The Jenuye lost no time in retiring from so dangerous a situation, and of course the scheme fell through, while the general who had recommended it had to commit suicide. The warden who had proved such a godsend to the Jenuye was rewarded with the title of " God-sent Prince " and carried off to fill a high position in Tartarland. The result naturally was that, though the frontier trade was still kept up in the interests of both parties, raids became very frequent, and the Hiung-nu now made no attempt to palliate or dissemble their hostile acts, which were openly declared to be in retaliation for Chinese treachery. For the next few years there was incessant war, entailing campaigns on the Chinese side followed again by cruel raids on the part of the Hiung-nu : a recital in detail of the events which occurred in succession would be as wearisome to read as monotonous to compose. It will be enough to say that things were about as bad as they could be when Kyundjin died in B.C. 127. He was succeeded by his younger brother Ichizia, who set himself up in defiance of the rights of the late Jenuye's son, and drove the latter into the arms of the Chinese.

With the assistance of the Chinese officers who fell into his hands, the Jenuye Ichizia continued to make things very uncomfortable on the frontier. Large Chinese armies one after the other made deep sallies into the nomad territory, cut off innumerable heads, captured large numbers of sheep and cattle, and gradually pushed forward their fortified posts. The greater part of what is now called Kan Suh province was added to the Chinese dominions, and it was at the conquest of the Kan-chou Fu of to-day that " a certain gold man used by the Tartar Prince in the worship of Heaven " was taken amongst the plunder.

By some Chinese authors it is considered that this was an image of Buddha ; by others that the introduction of Buddhism into China two centuries later owing to an imperial dream was indirectly connected with this conquest, in that the Emperor's vision of a golden man was inspired by the historical fact just recounted. In any case it was directly owing to these conquests that a knowledge of Affghanistan, India, and Buddhism was first brought into China ; and here it is important to bear in mind that the earliest Buddhism entered China, not by way of Burma or Yün Nan, (as yet almost totally unknown countries) ; nor by way of Tibet, which, besides being unknown, had not yet any political existence ; but by way of the Punjaub, the Pamir, and the Kashgaria-Sungaria main roads to the east. It is worth while digressing here in order to describe precisely how all this happened.

When the Yüeh-chï were driven westwards by the Hiung-nu, there was nothing to prevent the horse-riding nomads of the north from allying themselves with the sheep-driving nomads of Tibet and keeping up a perpetual war of raiding and cattle-lifting along the whole line of the Chinese frontier. Hence it became a matter of vital importance to "amputate the Tartars' right arm", and push forward a long line of posts westward, which should keep the two nomad agglomerations apart from each other. It must have been about B.C. 136 that the world-renowned traveller Chang K'ien made his first discoveries in the West, for we are told that it was some time after the Yüeh-chï king lost his head that this intrepid adventurer volunteered to proceed on a diplomatic mission in search of the dispossessed people. He was stopped on the way and detained in captivity for ten years. The Wu-sun having successfully freed themselves from Hiung-nu vassalage, Chang K'ien took advantage of the circumstance to effect his escape to modern Kokand, then a settled or citied state, having nothing nomadic about its constitution. Thence he passed by way of Samarcand to what is now styled Affghanistan, then the headquarters of the Yüeh-chï, beyond whom were the Arsac monarchs, or Parthians. He found the widow of the Yüeh-chï king administering the kingdom, and that the Tocharoi of the Pamir—a people of the same manners as the Kokandese—were already tributary to her. Unsuccessful in his attempts to induce the Yüeh-chï to co-operate with China, he spent a year with the Tocharoi, and was once more arrested by the Hiung-nu as he was endeavouring to make his way back to China by the Khoten Lob-nor road. After a second year's captivity he succeeded in reaching home, and related to the Emperor what he had seen of the above places, and what he had heard of India, Parthia, etc. The Chinese authors are careful to explain that nothing whatever was yet known of the nature of Buddhism. When amongst the Tocharoi, Chang K'ien had noticed certain articles of Chinese produce which he found had come from India. His idea was that it would be better to avoid the Tibetan mountains on the one hand, with the risk of capture by the Western Hiung-nu of Lob-nor and Koko-nor on the other, and to strike direct for India through modern Sze Chuen—as, indeed, to this day our modern travellers have been successfully trying to do. The Emperor appointed him chief of a roving commission with this object in view; but it was found impossible to get past the petty kingdoms of modern Yün Nan. Now it was that his services were requisitioned as a guide for the Chinese armies. He was also sent on an embassy to the Wu-sun of Kuldja, with a view of inducing that tribe to re-occupy its old territory north of Lob-nor and to co-operate against the Hiung-nu. He was with the Chinese armies in B.C. 121 when the "right arm was lopped off," and seems to have superintended further minor missions, both to the settled Kokandese and Tocharoi and to the nomad Samarcandese and Yüeh-chï, previous to his death a year or two later. Further embassies were later on despatched to Parthia, India, and other states not yet satisfactorily identified belonging to the Transoxianian system,—probably Keria was also one. This led to a Chinese war with Kokand, and to struggles with the Hiung-nu for the possession of modern Harashar. The object here, however, is merely to show how, both now and later on, the Tartars were the channel through which the earliest Buddhism found its way to China. Further consideration of this and other Turkestan matters has since been made in papers contributed to the *Asiatic Quarterly Review*. In the spring of B.C. 120 a tremendous expedition was organized against the Hiung-nu, who, in accordance with the advice of one of the renegade Turkestan Begs or *Jabgu* in their employ, moved to the north of the Desert in the direction of the River Kerulon. Hearing that the Chinese had resolved to cross the Desert, the Jenuye sent all the women and heavy baggage to a secure and distant place, himself awaiting the Chinese onslaught with the flower of his troops,—herein following out exactly the same strategy as that recounted by Herodotus of the Scythians, who with the swiftest of their horsemen went forth to meet the Persians at a place three days' distance from the Danube. The Hiung-nu were utterly defeated, and the Jenuye only just succeeded in effecting his escape with a few unencumbered horsemen. The slaughter was tremendous, and for some time the Jenuye, who could not be found, was replaced by his relative the Right Rukle. On this occasion it seems clear that the Chinese armies got as far as the modern Urga, now the seat of a high Buddhist functionary ; they also left records of their prowess carved in stone upon the side of a mountain north of the Ordous country not far from the spot marked in modern maps as Kara Narin : as we shall soon see, towards the end of the 19th century the Russians found a trilingual stone tablet near the Orkhon River, treating of Turkish affairs seven or eight centuries later. After this great campaign there was no centre of Hiung-nu government south of the Desert ; the Alashan or Eleuth country west of the Yellow River was annexed by China ; and half a million agricultural colonists were drafted to the western frontiers so as to secure a thorough hold upon the newly conquered territory. The Hiung-nu had lost 90,000 men during the year, but the losses of the Chinese were considerable too, numbering about 25,000 men and 100,000 horses. At the advice of the renegade Beg (who had formerly been employed by China) the Jenuye now sued for peace, and it was a question in the imperial council whether the advantage should be further pushed so as to completely crush and subject the enemy, or whether his peace proposals should be entertained. The former course was decided upon in effect, and an envoy was sent to demand homage. The Jenuye was so highly incensed at this presumption that he detained not only this special envoy, but a number of previous envoys, corresponding to the number of Tartars of rank who had, after the Hiung-nu defeat, elected to stand by China. Another campaign on a vast scale was just being prepared for when China's greatest general died, and the expedition fell through. Ichizia also died three years afterwards and was succeeded, B.C. 114, by his son Achvi.

Just at this time the Chinese Emperor was making preparations for a grand tour of inspection throughout other parts of his empire, and, being engaged in subduing the two then foreign states now amalgamated with China under the names of Canton and Foochow, was unable to give much attention to his northern neighbours. Three years later, when these two southern coast states had been thoroughly subdued, the Emperor himself came as far as the Alashan Mountains, and reviewed a fine force of 150,000 cavalry, so as to give weight to the diplomatic overtures he was about to open. Like the much later Roman envoys to Attila, and like the still later Rubruquis on his way to Caracorum, the Chinese envoy sent to conduct the negotiations declined to discuss with minor functionaries the nature of his mission, but demanded to be conducted into the Jenuye's presence,— somewhere near Urga and Caracorum. Here he at once commenced to boast of the doughty deeds which had been done in the south, and challenged the Tartar monarch to sally forth and give battle to the Emperor, who was waiting for him on the frontier. The Jenuye's reply was imprisonment of the envoy and decapitation of the court chamberlain who had introduced him : the envoy was sent to do ignominious service in the neighbourhood of Lake Baikal. Yet the Jenuye was chary of venturing south across the Desert just yet : he preferred to feed up and recruit his horses and men until a suitable moment should arrive. Meanwhile he sent individuals skilled in the arts of diplomacy to temporise with the Chinese, who on their part sent spies in the guise of ambassadors to watch what was going on in Tartarland : these envoys were not allowed to enter the royal tent unless they conformed to the local etiquette by blackening their faces and leaving outside their stick of office. [Perhaps this is like the " purifying by fire " undergone by Zimarchus, envoy of Justin II, before he was admitted into the tent of Dizabul the Turk.] Meanwhile the energetic Emperor Wu Ti had effected the conquest of part of Corea, and was busily engaged with those western embassies and intrigues which led to the war with Kokand mentioned in advance above (p. 25): the Chinese outposts now extended nearly as far as modern Tarbagatai (which, however, was still a Hiung-nu princedom), and all along both the northern and southern roads to Kashgar and Yarkand. Another envoy was sent to see if the Jenuye could be induced to carry out his promises and formally declare himself a vassal ; but this envoy had to conduct his negotiations outside the tent, as he would not conform to the prescribed etiquette. The Jenuye was quite ready to receive his princesses, his silk piece-goods, and his other good things, but he showed no disposition whatever to send hostages as security for the observance of the treaty of peace ; like Attila in Europe, he demanded that envoys of the highest rank should be sent to treat with him, and he asserted a policy of strict retaliation for injuries received : in short, " *do ut des* " and " tit for tat " were the only terms upon which he would treat at all, and even then on the most thoroughgoing terms of equality. At the same time he was lavish of soft words which cost him nothing, and protested his desire to see the Emperor face to face and to make an alliance with him. But with all this he kept on the safe side of the balance sheet by detaining Chinese envoys where there was any doubt about the safety of his own, and by raiding the Chinese frontiers wherever any tempting opportunity occurred.

CHAPTER IV

THE PERIOD OF DEFEAT AND DECLINE

THE Jenuye Achvi died in B.C. 105, after a reign of ten years, and was succeeded by his son Chimsiru, nick-named " the Boy Jenuye," a young man of restless and bloodthirsty disposition. The Hiung-nu seem at this period to have lost their hold upon the Tungusic part of their dominions, and to have concentrated themselves into two main bodies, the eastern one of which did not reach farther than the Chinese frontier at modern Ta-t'ung Fu in Shan Si, whilst the western one came into contact with the Chinese at the great junction of roads east of Lob-nor, thus leaving the Harashar and Khoten roads to Kashgar both in possession of the Chinese, and themselves manœuvring along the Caracorum, Uliasutai, and Cobdo road. It was during the Boy Jenuye's reign that the already mentioned war with Kokand took place ; but the opportune arrival of a great snow-storm, which carried off a great number of the Hiung-nu sheep and cattle, prevented them from doing very much injury to the Chinese. Still, the frontier war went on ; the Chinese armies once more fought their way to the Tula and Orkhon rivers, and the nomads found themselves unable to make any impression upon the line of Chinese posts north of the Yellow River Loop and the Ordous country. Chimsiru only lived three years, and, as his son was too young to be of any use, his uncle Kulegu, brother of Achvi, was elected to fill the vacant throne. The Chinese attempted to hold a line of fortified posts all the way north to the River Kerulon, and there was a good deal of fighting along this road ; but without any satisfactory results for the Hiung-nu. Kulegu's idea was to attack the successful Chinese army on its way back after its brilliant action in Kokand ; but no good

opportunity occurred, and Kulegu sickened and died the next
year, B.C. 101. He was succeeded by his younger brother
Zütegeu. The successful war with Kokand had so raised the
Chinese prestige that the Emperor began to think it a fit
moment to crush the Hiung-nu power once for all ; on the
other hand, the latter, feeling the danger of their position,
adopted a more conciliatory style in their correspondence
(managed of course by Chinese) ; the Jenuye was contented
with the junior political status of " son " or " son-in-law "
to the Emperor, and all the Chinese envoys who had resolutely
refused to accept Tartar nationality, office, or favours were
sent back. It was now that the celebrated Su Wu was sent
to negotiate with the Jenuye, who in spite of the liberal gifts
sent to him, assumed very arrogant airs. Su Wu, whose
name is quoted to this day as a pattern of fidelity for envoys
abroad, was kept in detention and put to the menial duty of
tending flocks near Lake Baikal. But his political virtue
does not appear to have been proof against the charms of
Tartar maidens, for, when he ultimately returned to China,
he brought a wife and a brood of hybrid children with him.

[It may be mentioned here parenthetically, by way of
illustration, that two thousand years later a Chinese envoy
held in detention by the King of Burma was officially declared
by the Manchu Emperor to be superior even to Su Wu because
he had (according to his own story) spent his time at Ava
in a monastery, and had refused to solace himself with
a Burmese wife. On the other hand, only forty-five years
ago the unhappy Ch'unghou was held up to derision by the
statesman Chang Chï-tung and gibbeted as a painful contrast
to Su Wu because (it was alleged) he allowed himself to be
coaxed by the Russians into betraying his august master's
interests in the Kuldja region.]

During the rest of Zütegeu's reign, severe fighting went on
between the two nations, chiefly in the region known as the
" Mouth of the Desert," a little north of the Yellow River
Bend,—and west of Marco Polo's Tenduc, the modern Kuku-

hoton or Kwei-hwa Ch'êng. The Hiung-nu again thought it
prudent to retire to the valleys of the Tula and Orkhon Rivers,
and on the whole the advantage seems to have remained
almost entirely with the Chinese. Zütegeu only reigned
five years, after which he was succeeded in B.C. 96 by his son
Hulughu. Hulughu had been not only the Left Dugi, and
as such the heir-presumptive to the throne, but he had been
specially designated as heir-apparent by his father. As
Hulughu was out of the way when the demise of the crown
took place, another prince was declared Jenuye, much against
his own will ; and after some diplomatic fencing between
the two it was agreed that Hulughu should have the throne
now, but that his successor should be the son of the prince
who had resigned in his favour. Soon afterwards the father
of this prince designate died, and the Jenuye, instead of making
his son Senghendjen Left Dugi, as would have been expected
under the family agreement, made his own son Left Dugi,
and conferred quite an inferior title upon the son of the deceased
prince. As will be afterwards seen, this breach of faith led
to serious civil war later on. In the seventh year of Hulughu's
reign raiding was renewed, and several distinguished generals
once more made their way to the Caracorum and Barkul
regions of modern times. Though these places cannot all
retrospectively be exactly identified now, they can be positively
associated with places known to have been near the ancient
localities, and which were in the possession of Turks and
Ouigours a thousand years later. Moreover oäses and watered
valleys then, as now, must have always been chosen for nomad
encampments. At the time we write about, all the present
roads to the west except two were undoubtedly known to
the Chinese. The two which were probably not yet known
to them were the northernmost road from Urga and Caracorum
by way of Uliasutai to Kuldja, and the road cutting north-west
across the desert from Shan Si to Uliasutai. These two last roads
are those which were followed in the 13th century by the Mongol
armies moving westwards, and by the embassies, whether

from China to Genghis in Persia, or from Europe to the later
Khans at Caracorum ; and consequently we know more,
at least from non-Chinese sources, about the roads which
the Chinese did not use 2,000 years ago than about those
which they have been steadily using during the past 2,000
years. The road, now disused, from Etzina to Caracorum
was, however, probably travelled by Chinese armies. In
the campaigns of B.C. 90 it is quite certain that the Chinese
had possession for a time of both Karahodjo and Pidjan,
then the capitals of two petty kings of agricultural and settled
tribes. In fact, as far back as history goes, we find a string
of cities from Harashar to Kashgar and from Kashgar to
Khoten governing "Sart" populations of cultivators,
apparently of old Persian stock, and probably ethnologically
very much like what they are now. The Chinese were again
victorious in this last campaign, and the Hiung-nu were
driven far away to the north. The Chinese then, as now,
had an unfortunate habit of decapitating generals and envoys
who were unsuccessful in war or diplomacy. The consequence
was that some of their ablest officers, men who had suffered
a reverse in the field or a check in diplomacy, were always
to be found in the enemy's employ, having taken refuge with
him in order to save their lives. In later times several Turkish
and Kirghiz tribes or ruling families traced back their origin
to this or that renegade Chinese general : the historian Sz-ma
Ts'ien was emasculated by the Emperor (B.C. 98) for attempting
to palliate one general's offence. In the present instance China's
best general, the one who had conquered Kokand, hearing
that his wife and children were under arrest, was advised
to go over to the Hiung-nu. The man was really no traitor
at heart, and after some hesitation decided to attempt a grand
coup in order to reinstate himself. Owing to the treachery
or lukewarmness of his own lieutenants, who had no similar
motive for running extra risks, he suffered on the contrary
a great defeat, and fell into the enemy's hands : he was well
received, and along with another renegade became one of the

chief advisers of the Jenuye, who now sent an ambassador
to China with the following letter :—" South is the great
" house of Han ; north are the powerful Tartars. The Tartars
" are Nature's wanton boys, who do not care to trouble
" themselves with petty formalities. I now propose to have
" frontier trade with China on a large scale, to marry a Chinese
" princess, and to receive annually 10,000 firkins of spirits,
" 10,000 pieces of assorted silks, and besides all the rest as
" provided by previous treaties : if this is done we will not
" raid the frontiers." The Chinese ambassador sent to talk
matters over was taunted with the fact that the Chinese
heir-apparent was giving his father trouble, notwithstanding
the much vaunted Chinese proprieties. The envoy retorted
by comparing the incestuous Tartars (and more especially
the former Jenuye Baghdur) to so many wild beasts : he was
put into gaol, but managed to escape after three years'
detention. The Jenuye's mother being ill, the Jenuye,
like Attila his remote successor, consulted the haruspices.
The two Chinese renegades were intriguing against each other
for favour, and it ended in the conqueror of Kokand being
served up as a sacrifice to the gods. But the gods were not
appeased : for several months in succession there were heavy
falls of snow ; beasts and their offspring perished ; the people
suffered from epidemics, and the millet harvests would not
ripen. In addition to all this there was defeat in the field,
the best generals were killed, and the Hiung-nu were so
discouraged that for several years they kept quiet. Meanwhile the Emperor Wu Ti, who in his old age repented him
of his foolish superstitions, involving the murder of his son
and heir, and of his conquests and concomitant waste of human
life, died, and in B.C. 83, three years later, Hulughu died also.
The Tartar hordes were in favour of setting up his younger
brother, a man of high character ; but the Dowager-Inchi,
who desired the succession for her own son, had the brother
murdered. The story now becomes a little intricate, but it
appears that the son of another Inchi, who under the name

of Chwangü plays an important part for many generations, with the renegade's assistance succeeded in getting *her* son recognized as the Khuyente Jenuye. The son and remaining brothers of Hulughu thereupon went off to their governments, and declined to attend the usual ceremonies at Dragon City. It is not clear whether Khuyente was the son, brother, or cousin of Hulughu, or how many successive husbands Chwangü had had up to the time of Hulughu's death : it is certain that the new Jenuye was a very young man, and very much in the hands of the surviving Chinese renegade and of the queen-mother, who seems to have been the renegade's paramour. Various intrigues went on with the Chinese to the east and with the Wu-sun nomads of Kuldja to the west, besides which raiding went on whenever opportunity occurred. The chief renegade tried to persuade the Hiung-nu that it would be good policy for them to build fortified places and store them with provisions ; but others pointed out that the Tartars were not used to defensive fighting, and that the result would probably be to supply the Chinese armies gratuitously with well-stocked recruiting stations. The renegade now advised the unconditional return of all faithful Chinese envoys, and amongst them was the renowned Su Wu with his brood of hybrid children. The obstinate Tartars continued their reckless policy of raiding, notwithstanding the fact that they nearly always got the worst of it, and notwithstanding the renegade's earnest recommendation of a peaceful understanding. Still, the Jenuye's younger brother managed to use his influence in favour of law and order, and was a strong supporter of the renegade, who died about now. But, shortly after this, the well-disposed younger brother died also, and the wearisome story of incursions, murders, kidnappings, and punitory columns is repeated for several years to come. The leading Tungusic nation, first known in Chinese history as the Wu-hwan, were now at war with the Hiung-nu, and the Chinese learnt from captured prisoners that the Tungusic armies had succeeded in desecrating the tombs of the Jenuyes.

As the Wu-hwan were also giving the Chinese trouble to the east, it was endeavoured by the latter to set these two northern nations by the ears as much as possible with a view of subsequently attacking the weaker. The Wu-hwan came off second best in their fighting with the Hiung-nu, and the Chinese therefore fell upon the former. The Hiung-nu were now alarmed for their own safety, and tried to form an alliance against the Chinese with the nomads of Kuldja and the king of Ush, their object being to get possession of the Chinese princess who had been given in marriage to the king of Kuldja. He on his part sent a piteous appeal for assistance, and the result was that a great expedition in five columns, numbering considerably over 100,000 troopers in all, received orders to march out 600 English miles beyond the Great Wall. The king of Kuldja, at the head of his Begs and of half as many troopers again, was to co-operate from the west with the Chinese marching from the east. On this occasion it is quite clear that the Chinese advanced as far as the neighbourhood of Hamil and Barkul ; but the results were disappointing, for the Hiung-nu, receiving intelligence of the double expedition which was advancing, drove their families and their herds pell-mell northwards in hot haste, after the fashion so graphically described by Marco Polo in his chapter upon Charchan, leaving not a trace of their march behind. Several Chinese generals lost their heads or had to commit suicide in connection with this business, but one or two were more successful, and managed to come up with the enemy, who lost about 40,000 individuals of all ranks and 700,000 animals : the Jenuye's uncle, sister-in-law, and several other high personages were also taken. The Jenuye now tried to wreak his vengeance upon the nomads of Kuldja, but he had bad luck again with the snow, and not one-tenth of his army ever got back again. To make matters worse, their northern tribes—variously identified by the historians with the Telengut Kirghiz and Ouigours of later times— fell upon them from the north, and the Wu-hwan did the same

from the east, so that the political power of the Hiung-nu
was now completely broken ; one-third of their population
were starved to death, and one-half of their flocks and herds ;
their subject nations fell off from their allegiance and attacked
them ; the Chinese lost no opportunity of striking a blow ;
and thus it was that, when Khuyente died in B.C. 68, the
fortunes of the Hiung-nu were reduced to a very low ebb.
He was succeeded by his younger brother the Left Dugi,
who took the title of Hülügwengü. It seems that at this
time they were still strong enough to keep a hold on Karahodjo.
The new Jenuye dismissed the Inchi Chwangü, much to the
chagrin of her father, and gave the first place in his harem
to another lady. As he was too weak to carry on the old
policy of raiding, the Chinese on their part thought the time
had arrived for economizing a little, and the garrisons along
the extreme north line of the Yellow River were withdrawn.
The Jenuye, who was peacefully inclined, was pleased at this
news, and took council with his nobles as to the desirability
of cultivating a friendly understanding ; but other counsels
prevailed, and a struggle took place for the possession of
Karahodjo, the people of which place, inclining to a Chinese
alliance, were moved eastwards, whilst the Hiung-nu
endeavoured to drive out the Chinese military colonists
and to put pressure upon the Kuldja and Kashgarian states.
The modern Urgendj, one of the Hiung-nu westernmost
principalities, was engaged in this war, which on the whole
was unsuccessful ; any way, before the Jenuye had time to
modify his strategy, he was seized with blood-vomiting,
and died. The jealous ex-queen Chwangü and her brother
lost no time in communicating with the Right Dugi before
the usual council or *couroultai* could be summoned, and
managed to get him proclaimed at once under the title of
Okyenküte. It is not very clear whose son this Jenuye
was : all that is certain is that he was Achvi's great-grandson,
and that his father had been Right Dugi before him. He at
once made overtures to China, and sent his younger brother

to have audience of the Emperor. Unfortunately for the stability of his empire, he was a prince of most brutal instincts, and inaugurated his accession by a series of bloody massacres, placing himself entirely in the hands of Chwangü and her brother. The legitimate heir to the throne, Kegeushar, son of Hülügwengü, took refuge with his wife's father, who was prince of a petty foreign state somewhere between Samarcand and Kuldja, and had thrown himself under Hiung-nu protection in order to escape the tyranny of his neighbours of Samarcand. This was in the time of Hulughu, who had given him a niece in marriage : this niece was the sister of Senghendjen, who had, as above related, been unfairly deprived of the succession, and who now went over with his horde to the Chinese. In consequence of this the Jenuye murdered Senghendjen's brothers, and a general civil war broke out, during which the tyrannical Jenuye's unpopularity went on daily increasing. The Tunguses seized the opportunity to attack his eastern dominions, and the wretched Jenuye, finding himself gradually deserted, in his despair committed suicide : this was in the year B.C. 58. Kegeushar was now declared Jenuye with the title of Khughanja, one which, as we shall see afterwards, became more or less a hereditary one, and distinctive of the southern branch of Hiung-nu. Khughanja had a hard task before him, for Senghendjen and a number of other discontented princes each formed a cabal of his own, and before long the whole Hiung-nu dominions from Issekul to Manchuria were torn by the internecine struggles of no fewer than five rival Jenuyes, the most formidable of whom was the Jenuye's own elder brother, the Left Dugi, Chirche. It is not very easy to follow the tangled web of intrigue and war which follows ; but a great many Tartar princes found that their best safety lay in surrender to China, and Khughanja himself, after suffering a severe defeat at his elder brother's hands somewhere in the Caracorum region, came to the conclusion that this would be the best thing he could do too. He summoned a council

of his nobles and ministers to consider the question : almost
all of them disapproved of the idea, and it is interesting to
read the arguments which they advanced. They said :—
" Our natural condition is one of brute force and activity ;
" we are not suited to and we despise an inglorious condition
" of servitude and ease. Fighting from horseback is the
" essence of our political power, and it is by this that we have
" always been able to assert our predominance among
" barbarous nationalities. To die in battle is what every
" valiant trooper of us looks forward to. Even though we
" may engage in fraternal strife, if one brother does not succeed,
" well then, the other will, and dominion will thus always
" remain in the family, while the unsuccessful at least die
" a glorious death. Strong though the Chinese Empire is,
" it is incapable of conquering and assimilating us. Why
" should we abandon our ancient ways, do homage to the
" Chinese, disgrace the memory of the Jenuyes our ancestors,
" and make ourselves a laughing-stock in the eyes of other
" nations ? Though by doing so we may attain peace, yet
" our career of domination will be for ever at an end." One of
the princes favourable to surrender argued :—" Not so. All
" nations have their opportunities and their vicissitudes.
" China is in the hey-day of her power at present. Kuldja
" is fortified, and all the other states in that quarter are
" China's humble servants. Ever since Zütegeu's time we
" have been losing ground, and we cannot recover it. We
" have been beaten along the whole line, and it is surely
" better to bend our pride a little than to go on fighting for
" ever. If we do homage to China, we preserve our lives
" in peace. If we do not, we perish in the most dreadful
" way. Surely the better course is plain." The Hiung-nu
Jenuyes must have possessed very absolute power, for we
are told that, notwithstanding the determined opposition
which all the leading men continued to offer to the scheme,
Khughanja decided to send one of his sons to the Chinese
court as a hostage-page. His rival and elder brother Chirche

did the same thing. In the following year Khughanja presented himself at the Great Wall of modern Shan Si and offered to come to court in person. A strong and brilliant escort was sent to bring him to the imperial lodge, and he was received by the Emperor in a most distinguished manner : he was given precedence over all the imperial and feudal princes, introduced into the presence without having to undergo the usual degrading ceremonies, and was allowed to use the simple term " your liege " without having to add his own personal name—as required by Chinese etiquette. The Emperor made him a number of exceedingly valuable presents, including a gold seal with purple ribbon, a state sword and chariot ; clothes, stuffs, horses, saddles, and so on. After the audience, a special envoy was sent to conduct the Jenuye to the hotel placed at his disposal, whilst his suite were permitted to witness the magnificent spectacle of the Emperor's return in state to his own lodge. After a stay of one month the Jenuye received his dismissal and returned to his own country. These important events, which may be said to have closed the period of Hiung-nu independence, took place in the year B.C. 51 of the Emperor Süan Ti.

CHAPTER V

The Period of Semi-Independence

K HUGHANJA offered to make his headquarters outside the Great Wall in the Ordous country in order to guarantee the Surrender Cities in time of danger. This name, which continues in use throughout later Turkish history, is given to a line of fortified posts extending from the modern Kwei-hwa Ch'êng in Shan Si (the Tenduc of Marco Polo) to the extreme north-west corner of the Great Bend, and designed to prevent the nomads from crossing the Yellow River. As has been mentioned above, many of the Chinese garrisons had recently been withdrawn from motives of economy. An escort of 16,000 troops conducted the Jenuye beyond the Great Wall, and the officers in command were ordered to assist him in punishing the refractory, and in seating him firmly on the throne. About a thousand tons of grain and other provisions were sent to the frontier in carts to keep the party well supplied in their new settlement.

The rival Jenuye Chirche thought that he might as well have some of these good things too, so he also sent an envoy to the Chinese court, where he was treated with great liberality. The following year both Jenuyes sent ambassadors, and Khughanja's was treated with special distinction. The year following (B.C. 49) that again, Khughanja came once more in person, and was welcomed with exactly the same forms and with even more presents than on the first occasion ; but, as he had an encampment of his own this time, no corps of cavalry was collected on this occasion to escort him back. The jealous Chirche kept a watchful eye upon all these proceedings, and came to the conclusion that Khughanja must feel his own power to be very weak if he was so ready to debase himself before China, and that he was evidently not coming back to the West. He therefore marched his whole horde westwards, and after some fighting with rival pretenders settled himself in what was called the Right Land (or West Land), at the same time making overtures to the nomads of Kuldja. So far from welcoming Chirche's ambassador, the king cut off his head and declared war, thinking to best please China by acting in this way. But Chirche defeated him, went on to subdue modern Tarbagatai in the north, and then, continuing his march west, reduced the Kirghiz and another group of cognate Tartars—who cannot easily be identified on account of there being an eastern and a western branch. For want of a better word we shall call them Kankali (meaning " Carts "). It is interesting to learn that the Kirghiz headquarters were 2,300 English miles west of the Jenuye's state residence (apparently Urga or Caracorum), and 2,000 miles north of the Turfan and Pidjan of to-day, so that their general area or position two thousand years ago must been very much what it is now. To resume, in B.C. 48 a new Emperor came to the throne, and one of his first acts was to respond to an appeal of Khughanja by sending him 20,000 measures of grain for his impoverished horde. Chirche thereupon evinced his envious displeasure by recalling his son the page, and had the meanness to assassinate the envoy sent by China to escort the lad safely home. Of course China put this dastardly act down to Khughanja, whose supposed offence was, however, pardoned in order to keep things quiet. *His* son was also sent back in charge of a couple of ambassadors. These ambassadors, keeping their eyes open, were surprised to find that Khughanja's horde was in a remarkably flourishing condition, and quite strong enough to match Chirche. Being afraid lest he should accept the advice which his nobles were now offering that, having killed off all the game near the Wall, he should move northwards to the old Jenuye head-quarters near Caracorum, the envoys took upon themselves to make the following treaty with him :—" Peace shall continue " between China and the Hiung-nu for ever, and they shall be " united as one family. Neither party shall deceive or attack " the other. If robberies take place, the complaining party " shall notify the other, who will punish the offenders and " cause compensation to be made ; and if any raiding takes " place each side will do its best to suppress it. Whichever " first breaks this treaty, may Heaven do to him and his " heirs as he shall have done with the treaty ! " The sanction of the treaty was applied in the following way. The Jenuye and the Chinese ambassadors mounted a hill, a white horse was slaughtered, the Jenuye held in his hands a jewelled sword or dagger, and, mixing blood and gold together in the skull of the Haithal king (evidently preserved by Kayuk (see p. 21) as a state heirloom), together with the envoys took a draught of this mixture.

All this is very remarkable, and tends to connect the Scythians of Herodotus with the Huns and Mongols in one unbroken line. Herodotus mentions skulls covered with leather and lined with gold used as drinking cups. He also mentions the making of oaths by pouring wine into a bowl, mixing it with the blood of those that swear, and dipping a scimitar into the bowl. Besides this he mentions the sacrifice to the sun of a horse by the Massagetae of the Caspian, (a Scythian race wrongly identified by some, regardless of time and place, with the Haithals of the Oxus who came five centuries later). The Chinese frequently mention the sacrifice of white horses by the Tungusic rulers of China in the 5th century of our era ; whilst Genghis Khan, as stated by Gibbon, used the skull, enchased in silver, of the Khan of the Keraits, and ratified his first military league by the sacrifice of a horse. The Roman Emperor Nicephorus' skull, enchased with gold, was put to a similar use by the Bulgarians. The same thing is told of Cunimund of the Gepidae.

A storm of abuse awaited the ambassadors on their return, and, like the unhappy Ch'unghou on his return in 1879 from Russia, they were at once impeached for treason. It was argued that, Khughanja being a sort of " buffer " power, would not leave the frontier he had engaged to defend any weaker by the mere act of moving father north ; and that, in any case, the conduct of the ambassadors, in pledging the future good faith of China with a barbarous nomad and allowing the Jenuye to put unseemly words into their mouths, had exceeded their powers and disgraced the honour and prestige of China. It was recommended that other envoys should be sent at once to make the Jenuye solemnly cancel the treaty before Heaven with counter ceremonies of an equally binding kind with the contracting forms. However, the Emperor preferred to let matters stand. Khughanja actually did move north, and he organized a powerful dominion there.

Meanwhile Chirche was feeling uneasy about the murder he had committed, and soon conceived a strong desire to edge away further west. Just then the king of Samarcand was writhing under the tyranny of the nomads of Kuldja. He and his Begs in council came to the conclusion that it would be well to assist Chirche in his difficulties, and to enable him to recover the former Hiung-nu suzerainty over Kuldja, when any new chief or king who should be appointed would serve as a " buffer " state. They sent ambassadors accordingly to Chirche, who was then in his Kirghiz province, and the result was that Samarcand sent several thousand camels, asses, and horses to assist Chirche, who at once started off on his migration west. But the cold was so severe that nearly the whole horde perished, and only a dilapidated remnant succeeded in safely reaching Samarcand. Hither he was pursued by a detachment sent after him by the Chinese Proconsul for the West, who then had his residence at a place now by the Chinese called Tseter, between the River Kaidu and the city of Kuche as marked upon modern maps, probably quite close to Yanghishar. His head was promptly taken off (B.C. 36), much to the consternation of his brother Khughanja, who on hearing the news lost no time in renewing protestations of devotion to China : he laid at his brother's door the responsibility of his having himself failed to come to court to congratulate the Emperor Yüan Ti ; having, he said, been in constant dread of Chirche's attacks. In B.C. 33 he did come to court, and was received with the same ceremony and rewarded with the same presents as on the occasion of his second visit in B.C. 49. He applied for a wife, and one of the Emperor's prettiest handmaids who, owing to jealous feminine intrigues, had never yet once shared the imperial couch, courageously volunteered for the lively post of wife to a succession of vigorous Tartar monarchs. When she was marched forward for inspection, she looked so inviting that the Emperor, who had never before noticed her, would gladly have kept her back ; but the Jenuye was so manifestly

charmed with her appearance that withdrawal was out of
the question ; so off she went, and a very important political
personage she afterwards proved. The Jenuye in his delight
undertook to defend the whole frontier line westwards from
Shen Si to Lob-nor,—the main road in fact to the West ;
he promised that his descendants should carry on this duty
for ever, and suggested that the whole of the Chinese garrisons
might now be withdrawn. The imperial council was almost
unanimous in supporting this offer. But one old councillor
who had had plenty of local experience strongly protested
against this suicidal policy. He said :—" The well-wooded
" line of mountains which extends from Shen Si to Corea was
" once the stronghold of the conqueror Baghdur, whence he
" and his successors could always obtain game and material
" for his weapons, and whence he could choose his own time
" for raids upon China ; and they did so until the Emperor
" Wu Ti drove the Hiung-nu to the north of the Desert and
" fortified the whole line of the Great Wall. The character
" of the nomads is such that they will be as ready to take
" advantage of our weakness if we withdraw our posts as they
" are anxious to give us a wide berth when we show our teeth.
" Even civilized China needs punitory laws to secure obedience
" to restrictive rules : how then can it be expected that a pack
" of unsophisticated Tartars will be law-abiding without
" any display of power to compel it ? The frontier posts
" are as much needed for keeping Chinese traitors out of
" Tartarland as for keeping Tartars out of China ; not to
" mention that a large part of our own frontier population
" is of Tartar stock now in process of assimilation. Of recent
" years we have begun to hold relations with the Tibetans,
" who, it is sad to say, are justly incensed against us on account
" of the greed and rapacity of our officers. Great danger
" will follow any alliance of the Tibetans with the Tartars,
" and the free and easy nomad life has great temptations
" for restless people of our own who find their frontier duties
" irksome." The councillor proceeds with some remarks

which prove that the Emperor Wu Ti must have done as much as Mêng T'ien (see p. 18) towards completing the Great Wall. He says :—" It is now over a century since the Great Wall " was built. It is not by any means all of it a mere mud " rampart. Up hill and down dale, it follows the natural " configuration of the ground, is honeycombed with secret " passages, and bristles with fortified points. Is all this vast " labour to be allowed to go to rack and ruin ? And if ever " we have to reconstruct everything, where are the men and " the money to come from ? Besides, the more we dispense " with our own defences, the more we shall be beholden for " our safety to the Jenuye, whose pretensions will advance " in proportion. If we disappoint his expectations, it is " impossible to say what he may not do when once the thin " end of the wedge is inserted." The Emperor had the good sense to issue the following rescript :—" Let the proposition " drop." The next thing was to compose a diplomatic letter worded so as not to wound the Jenuye's susceptibilities. It ran :—" With reference to the Jenuye's offer to protect " the frontier, and his suggestion that the Chinese garrisons " might be withdrawn, China is much touched at the generosity " and courtesy with which so masterly an idea is advanced. " China, however, has frontiers not only in the north, but " on all other sides, the defences of which are kept up, not " only to ward off attacks, but also to restrain her own evil " characters from trespassing upon the rights of her neighbours. " Whilst appreciating therefore the Jenuye's kindly motives, " and assuring him of the entire absence of suspicion as to their " genuineness, China feels compelled to decline the offer, " and sends an envoy of high rank with this note to explain " matters in full to the Jenuye's complete satisfaction." Shortly after this the Jenuye expressed his thanks as follows :— " A simple individual such as I am is perhaps incapable of " evolving high notions of policy, but at the same time it is " a satisfaction to listen to the expression of such generous " sentiments from the mouth of the exalted envoy sent by

" the Emperor." From this it will be evident that Greece
and Rome had not by any means a monopoly of diplomatic
brains at that period, and that China's command of diplomatic
phraseology was far ahead of the Egyptian and Babylonian
style.

The Hiung-nu supporters of a " forward policy " never
forgave the councillor who had backed up the Jenuye's " policy
of scuttle," the more so as the said councillor was suspected
of presuming upon his services. Khughanja's jealousy was
ingeniously aroused by the " opposition," and the councillor,
afraid for his life, went over to China with his horde of about
a thousand individuals. When the Jenuye next came to
court he addressed the councillor, who had now become
a Chinese magnate, as follows :—" It is entirely owing to your
" noble conceptions, Prince, that I have been able to live in
" peace with China. I am afraid that it is solely my fault
" that you left us, and I should now like to apply to the
" Emperor for permission to take you back with me." The
councillor replied :—" Jenuye ! It was the will of Heaven
" combined with your own inspiration that guided you to place
" yourself under the Emperor's protection ; but, as I have
" become a Chinese subject, it would be a defection on my
" part to return : still, if you wish it, I will accept the post
" of Hiung-nu resident ambassador at the Chinese court."
Though the Jenuye tried very hard to recover his services,
it was without success.

Meanwhile the Chinese handmaid had given birth to a son
and been promoted to the rank of Inchi. Amongst the
Hiung-nu there does not appear to have ever existed the
Chinese notion under which the first formally-married woman
(*confarreatio*) alone has pre-eminent rank, no matter whether
in the family she be an Empress or a peasant. Khughanja
died in B.C. 31 after a reign of 28 years. He had first married
two daughters of the elder brother of the truant councillor
now in China. One of these, the elder, was Chwangü,
apparently the same woman as the mother of the Jenuye

Khuyente, who was clearly Khughanja's uncle : she bore Khughanja two sons.   The younger sister, who enjoyed rank as Chief Inchi, bore Khughanja four sons, two of whom were older than her sister's elder son, and two of whom were younger than her sister's younger son, from which it would appear that Khughanja must have married the younger sister first, and taken over the elder after she had run through the gamut of his predecessors.   There were also about a dozen other sons by minor queens, amongst whom no doubt were the Samarcand lady and Hulughu's niece mentioned towards the end of the last chapter (pp. 36–7).   Chwangü was the noblest wife so far as blood went, belonging as she did to one of the three clans which, as we have seen (p. 13), habitually inter-married with the Jenuye's clan, and her eldest son was Khughanja's favourite, and the one he wished to be his successor.   Unfortunately he was, in the opinion of his mother Chwangü, too young and inexperienced to cope with these troublous times, and she thought her younger sister's eldest son would suit better.   The Chief Inchi was equally magnanimous, and argued that the ministers could keep the state wheels going round notwithstanding this defect in years, and that a civil war would be sure to break out at some future time if the nobler blood were replaced by the more plebian. As the two sisters were both daughters of the same man, if not of the same woman too, it is a question for antiquaries to solve whether the elder sister derived her superior nobility from a different mother, (for, as we shall shortly see, the Tunguses and the Turks both gave a first place in genealogy to mothers), or whether she went on growing nobler in the ratio of the number of husbands she survived.   Be this as it may, it was desired by Khughanja on his death-bed that the elder son of Chwangü should be the immediate successor ; but the two queens successfully advised that the succession should first go to the eldest of the chief queen's four sons, and afterwards be transmitted in due course to the elder son of the elder sister Chwangü.   Accordingly the Chief Inchi's son succeeded with the title of Vughturoi-yokte. It must here be explained that *yokte* is a Hiung-nu word meaning " filial " or *pius*, a posthumous designation, like the Roman *divus*, which was given to all Chinese Emperors at this time. It is not clear whether or not the Jenuyes, who had no idea of post-humous honours, used this addition during their lives ; but at any rate from this time they all took the title in imitation of Chinese customs, a practice followed also later on by Corea, Japan, Annam, and the Shans, as each of them in turn began to appreciate the value of letters, and to yearn for Chinese pomp. Vughturoi made his next brother Left Dugi, and his two brothers by Chwangü Right Rukle and Right Dugi respectively. He also took over his father's Chinese wife, who bore him two daughters. To her credit it must be recorded that she at least went through the form of a protest to China before she re-married ; but the Chinese Emperor said " follow the national custom where you are."

These things being comfortably arranged, the new Jenuye sent an ambassador to pay his respects to the Emperor. This ambassador had his audience, and had not got very far from the metropolis on his way back when he suddenly turned to the envoy who was escorting him home and said :—" I " wish to become a Chinese subject, and will commit suicide " unless you will receive me. I dare not go back." This suspicious and startling incident was at once reported to the Emperor, and referred by him for an opinion to the Council members, most of whom thought the offer should be accepted in accordance (they said) with the usual practice. Two ministers, however, expressed themselves as follows :—" In old raiding " times, certainly, we used to offer inducements to renegades, " but now that the Jenuye has accepted the position of vassal " and ' buffer state,' a different policy should be pursued. " We cannot on the one hand accept his tribute, and on the " other harbour his deserters. What is the interest of one " individual compared with our duty to the Jenuye ? More- " over the new Jenuye may have prompted this offer himself

" in order to test the value of our alliance. Or perhaps
" he may only want a pretext for war, in which case we shall
" play straight into his hand if we take the man in. Honesty
" is our best policy, and we should be wary." The Emperor
at once saw the force of all this, and sent a general to ask the
envoy for further explanations. The ambassador joked the
matter off, and when he got back to the Jenuye's court was
careful to keep out of the Chinese envoy's way. The next
year the Jenuye came to court in person, and, besides receiving
special extra presents, was treated exactly as Khughanja
had been in B.C. 33 (p. 43). He died in B.C. 20 after a reign
of ten years, and was succeeded by the Left Dugi, from which
it seems evident that the family agreement must have con-
templated the *two* eldest brothers reigning before Chwangü's
son, as is plain also from the fact that the second had been
at once made Left Dugi. He now took the title of Seughie-
yokte. He reigned eight years, and died in B.C. 12 when on
his way to the Chinese court. He was succeeded by his next
brother the elder son of Chwangü, who styled himself Chega-
yokte. Four years later Chega died, and was succeeded by
his next brother Otyuru or Atiuru-yokte. Now, Otyuru
had taken over his father's Chief Queen, (his own mother's
sister) and made her his Second Queen. This arrangement
would seem to show that the Chief Queen was always one of
the first, if not the very first, married to the Jenuye in
possession of that title : possibly the first virgin married ;
or perhaps the first wife to have a son. Otyuru made her
two sons (his half-brothers) Left and Right Dugi respectively,
and sent his own son to the imperial court as a page. Meanwhile the Chinese dynasty of Han was on its decline, and the
Emperor Ch'êng Ti's maternal uncle was " running " the
government. Some meddlesome individual suggested that it
would be well to get hold of the well-wooded and well-stocked
territory towards the modern Kan-chou Fu which then, as
now, ran like a wedge into Chinese territory. The Emperor
expressed an opinion that, were it not for the risk of

a mortifying refusal, it would be best to apply frankly to the
Jenuye for its cession. The uncle took this to be a hint to
" go ahead," and instructed the Chinese envoys to put in
a request. Accordingly the leading ambassador delivered
himself as follows to the Jenuye :—" I have observed that you
" have a wedge of territory running into China : this
" necessitates China's keeping up three stations along the Wall.
" To spare these poor fellows their cold and irksome duty,
" and to save China the expense of supporting them, it would be
" a graceful return for the many favours you have received
" to offer this strip to the Emperor, who will certainly reward
" you very handsomely." Otyuru, who was evidently no
simpleton, asked :—" Am I to understand that it is the
" Emperor himself who sends this message ? If so, of course
" I will do it." The envoy replied :—" The Emperor has as
" good as said it, but it is I who suggest a good stroke of
" policy for the Jenuye." The Jenuye rejoined :—" Pius
" Süan and Pius Yüan were very kind to my father Khughanja
" and abandoned to him everything north of the Wall. The
" land you speak of is occupied by one of our princes, but,
" with your permission, I will send and find out what sort
" of land it is." The envoys returned to China and were
recommissioned. When they reached the Jenuye's court
they reopened the question. The reply was :—" During the
" reigns of my father and elder brothers no demand for
" this possession of ours was ever raised. Why should this
" particular piece be wanted now ? The prince in possession
" informs me that our vassal states in the west all derive
" from these forests the wood for their tents and carts. More-
" over I dare not give away the land of my ancestors." Not
content with this, the Jenuye wrote to the Emperor about it,
and the chief ambassador, who barely escaped with his head,
was removed to a post where he would have no further dealings
with the Hiung-nu for the rest of his life. The Jenuye's page
son, dying just now, was replaced by another.

The nomads of Kuldja soon after this made a predatory

raid upon, but were defeated by, the Hiung-nu, and hastened to propitiate them by sending a young prince as page to the Jenuye, who then explained the incident to China. The Emperor disapproved of the proceeding, and ordered the page to be sent back. The Jenuye offered to come to court to congratulate the Emperor Ai Ti upon the occasion of the new year's festivities of B.C. 2, but, as Ai Ti (who died next year) wás unwell at the time, some wiseacre suddenly discovered evil omen in these visits, which had on two occasions at least been immediately followed by an Emperor's death. The question of expense was also raised. The other side was championed by a statesman named Yang Hiung, whose name stands almost on a level with those of Mencius and Cincius as one of China's greatest philosophers. He recapitulated the whole history of China's relations with the Tartars ; how Mêng T'ien with his 400,000 men had failed to reach the point (near Tenduc) he aimed at, and had been obliged to build the Great Wall as a defensive frontier ; how the founder of the Han dynasty with a host of 300,000 had only barely escaped with his life, thanks to some unspeakably shameful trick ; how Baghdur had insulted the founder's widow ; how the ruse at Horse City had miserably failed, and had caused many years of cruel war ; and how, even after the Hiung-nu were driven vanquished to the north of the Desert, they had still scouted the idea of declaring themselves our vassals. Then followed our joint campaign with the nomads of Kuldja ; which, however, resulted in little for our peace and security. It was only when the five rival Jenuyes got to fighting together, and when Senghendjen with Khughanja threw themselves upon our protection, that a nominal subjection was achieved : but even then they only came to court when it suited their good pleasure to do so. Though we had succeeded in conquering Kokand, the Tunguses, the wandering tribes of Koko-nor, the Coreans, Canton, and Foochow, yet we had never been able to do more than scotch the monster of the north. The Jenuye is now in just that frame of mind we have always desired and striven for. True, it is a costly business to keep him in a good humour ; but look at the results ! Surely it cannot be supposed that we spend millions a year to maintain a proconsul in the West and keep a rein on the Turkestan states simply to hold Samarcand and Kuldja at a respectful distance ?   No ! all this labour has been to protect ourselves against the Hiung-nu, and now it seems that the work of a century is going to be undone in a single day ! May your Majesty think well of it before it is too late, and before we are plunged once more into the miseries of war !

Thus reasoned the philosopher. The Emperor at once perceived the significance of his arguments, and recalled the Hiung-nu envoy, who had already taken his leave and was just starting to go back. A written reply was sent to the Jenuye accepting his offer to visit the capital. But in the meantime the Jenuye had fallen sick, and was obliged to postpone his visit for a year. Hitherto the Jenuyes had brought with them a suite of about 200 individuals of all ranks. Otyuru now sent word that he should bring 500 the next time " so as to accentuate his appreciation of the Emperor's policy," —or, in plainer language, so as to get more presents.   In the year B.C. 1 he presented himself, and owing to something unusual in the aspect of the planet Jupiter, (which astronomers may perhaps be able to explain), quarters were assigned to him in the Zoological Gardens, with the explanation that this equivocal compliment was intended as a special mark of respect,—much as in modern times our European envoys were at first cajoled into paying their respects to the Manchu Emperor in some outside hall of the Peking palace.   Presents were given as on the last occasion in B.C. 27, with the addition of 30,000 rolls of silk, and more clothes, with 30,000 pounds of floss for wadding.   On each successive occasion the presents had been increased, or at any rate never diminished, so that the incidence of this regular tax was now becoming a serious consideration.   Otyuru on his return sent two or three princes and their wives to serve as pages at the Chinese court.   This new departure was probably owing to the fact that Ai Ti's stepbrother the boy-Emperor P'ing Ti (who officially commenced his reign A.D. 1) was in the hands of the Empress-Dowager, who again was more or less a puppet of the future usurper Wang Mang, nephew of the above-mentioned maternal uncle of Ch'êng Ti, and therefore a sort of " outer " cousin or *cognatus* of Ai Ti and P'ing Ti, who were both nephews of Ch'êng Ti. The Empress-Dowager was flattered at having these Tartar women amongst her ladies-in-waiting, and, in order to curry favour with her, Wang Mang hinted to the Jenuye that he might send one of Vughturoi's daughters by the Chinese wife (who had already served five Jenuyes with great satisfaction) : the girl was sent.

Now it so happened that one of the petty kings in the Karahodjo or Pidjan region, with a prince of the Lob-nor parts, had gone over to the side of the Hiung-nu, on account of some dispute they had had with the Chinese proconsular officials in the west. The Jenuye admitted in writing that he had harboured the refugees together with their followers, but offered no excuse beyond the bald statement of fact. Envoys (including the Chinese wife's cousin) were sent to call him to book, but Otyuru claimed the right to stand by the letter of Khughanja's solemn treaty, and the understandings with Divus Süan and Divus Yüan. His father had moreover left dying injunctions to the effect that no deserters from China must be received ; but, it was now argued, these people are not from China, but from foreign states, and there was consequently no irregularity in their being harboured. The envoys reminded the Jenuye that, when the five Hiung-nu rivals were cutting each other's throats, China had stepped in and secured peace for the Khughanja dynasty, which might well confer a small favour by way of requital. On this the Jenuye consented to give up the refugees. However, when all preparations had been made to receive them, he suddenly changed his mind, and sent them back each to his own country : he at the same time asked for forgiveness. This was refused, and several Turkestan kings, including the two offenders, were subsequently beheaded as a warning, at a grand Chinese durbar held somewhere in the West, to which as many as possible of the petty potentates were summoned. A new rule was now established to the effect that " in future no " Chinese, Tunguses, Kuldjans, or natives of states holding " seals of office issued by China shall be received by the " Hiung-nu." Special envoys were sent to deliver this new rule to the Jenuye, and to recover from him the treaty sent in a casket by a former Emperor.

At this time Wang Mang caused an innovation to be introduced into China by doing away with the practice of using two personal names, and invited Otyuru to conform to this rule of civilization. It is not very clear what were the rules governing either Chinese or Tartar names at this time, but the analogy of later history tends to show that no Tartar races made a fuss about names at all, or had any idea of the complimentary taboo (avoiding the private names of fathers and emperors) until the Chinese taught it to them. On this occasion Otyuru Jenuye, whose personal name was Nanchegas, readily complied by changing it to Chemantayüt ; though it is not by any means obvious how, by so doing, he conformed to the new rule, or what the rule really was. The Chinese characters selected to transliterate this Tartar name were apparently chosen so as to convey a sort of punning personal compliment to Wang Mang. The Jenuye's obsequiousness only made the usurper more exacting. He now openly extended China's protection to Tungusic envoys, and announced to the Tunguses that they need no longer pay taxes in skins and cloths to the Hiung-nu. This was altogether more than the Jenuye could tolerate, and he was backed up by the whole trading body of his nation, male and female. He therefore sent envoys to demand the usual taxes, which were refused on the ground that China had forbidden their payment. This led to violence, rapine, and murder on both sides, in which the Tunguses came off decidedly second best. In

A.D. 9 the ambitious Wang Mang threw aside all disguise, and sent envoys with magnificent presents to announce that he had received Heaven's commands to replace the House of Han : at the same time he sent a fresh seal with a new-fangled superscription upon it, and the envoys commanded the Jenuye to restore the old one. He was about to do so when one of his princes whispered :—" If I were you I would first " find out what superscription the new seal bears." The Jenuye held back his hand, requested the envoys to be seated in the tent for a few moments, and meanwhile ordered wassail liquor to be served. General Wang, the first envoy and a relative of the usurper, demanded the old seal at once, but the prince repeated his warning. The Jenuye, however, weakly surrendered the seal, saying that he saw no reason why the superscription should be changed. He fastened on the new seal, which he was unable to decipher, by the usual ribbon attached, and then the whole party set to work eating and drinking for the rest of the day. When the envoys retired, one of them suggested that it would be as well to break up the old seal at once before the fraud could be discovered. The question was who would take the responsibility, as imperial seals are sacred objects in China : but the proposer was a bold fellow ; taking his colleague's prudent silence for consent, he proceeded to smash it up with an axe. The next morning, sure enough, the Jenuye sent to demand the old seal on the grounds that the words " Seal of the Hiung-nu Jenuye " had been changed to " Signet of the New Hiung-nu Jenuye," and that mere signets were intended for persons below the status of ruling monarchs. When it was explained to him that a new dynasty was now reigning, and his messenger saw the fragments of the old seal, the Jenuye perceived that it was of no use insisting ; so he accepted the presents, and contented himself with sending the Right Dugi, one of his brothers, back with the envoys to take a letter begging for the old seal once more. On their way back, as they passed through the territory of another brother, the envoys came across a number of the Wu-hwan prisoners, held as security for the taxes due, and called the said brother's attention to the new rules. This brother was the elder of the junior pair borne by Chwangü's younger sister as previously described (pp. 46, 47). He asked and obtained permission to send a confidential message to the Jenuye, who replied evasively :—" Shall I send them by the inside or the " outside of the Wall ? " This uncanny question had to be referred to China, and the answer came :—" By the outside " route." The seal incident and Tungusic question had thoroughly irritated the Jenuye, who, under pretext of escorting back the Wu-hwan prisoners, sent over 10,000 troopers to the Wall near modern Ning-hia on the Yellow River. The next year there was again trouble with the petty Karahodjo rulers, and one of them went over to the Hiung-nu with 2,000 men and all the cattle and sheep he could collect in the country. The Jenuye not only received him, but joined him in a raid, wounding the imperial proconsular officers and killing one of the mediatized Chinese kinglets. Two Chinese clerks, foreseeing a general revolt in Turkestan, murdered their superior officer and deserted to the Jenuye, who conferred military titles upon them and received them at his private mess. Wang Mang, on hearing of this general break-up, did not by any means shrink from responsibility. His first act was to declare the Hiung-nu dominions divided into fifteen Jenuyeships, and he sent 20,000 horses to the Wall near Ta-t'ung Fu with a view of buying over with rich presents Khughanja's other sons. The Jenuye's brother, who had been in charge of the Tungusic prisoners when the Right Dugi had come about the old seal, received or had forced upon him the title of " Filial Jenuye," besides 1,000 pounds of gold, emblems of rank, and other handsome presents. His two sons were sent to the capital, where the younger was made " Obedient Jenuye," and received 500 pounds of gold. Otyuru's reply to this action was to inaugurate a wholesale massacre of every one he could get at in the region near the

Wall about North Shan Si, and to pass the word on to his eastern and western governors to do likewise : this was in A.D. 11. All the prudent work of the last half century was thus undone in an instant, and the whole line of frontier was set in a blaze, every living creature being driven off or killed. But Wang Mang, who was a sort of Charles the Twelfth of Sweden in reckless obstinacy, had no idea whatever of giving way. He had the accumulated treasure of several imperial generations in his power, and he poured it out like water. He appointed twelve generalissimos, who were to take 300 days' provisions and lead 300,000 men by ten different roads, sweep the whole Hiung-nu dominions, and drive the Tartars to the remotest fastnesses of the Kirghiz and Kankalis. The empire was ransacked for stores and supplies of all kinds to be carted to the frontiers. His best general protested against this impracticable scheme, and once more sketched out the whole history of China's relations with Tartary, which proves that even military men were then fairly well posted in the records of the past. [Sir Aurel Stein's haul of first century military documents illustrates this.] It was pointed out that it would take at least a year before 300 days' food for 300,000 men could be got to one place, and that the earlier arrivals would be demoralized long before the final drafts could reach the spot. He calculated that oxen, the only animals suited for the work, must be found to convey 200,000 tons of food for the men, and, as grass was only to be found here and there, rather over another 200,000 tons for themselves. Experience, he added, tends to show that before the first hundred days are out not an ox will be left alive, and the men cannot carry their own food in addition to their arms, pots, pans, charcoal, etc. [Precisely the same arguments were used in the Chinese campaign against Kashgar fifty years ago, when the armies had to sow and reap their own grain as they advanced.] Besides which, a diet of rice and water continued for a long time produces a distemper, for which reason one hundred days has always been the maximum

length for a campaign in such cold and windy regions. Moreover, with such a stupendous baggage train, open on all sides
to the attacks of the enemy, the fighting effectives will be
comparatively few, and in any case they cannot pursue the
enemy far, and leave the transport to take care of itself.
As, however, the first arrivals were already waiting, he proposed
that he should, if fighting must be done, do it at once, himself
march the men into the enemy's country, and at least strike
a vigorous blow to begin with.

But Wang Mang would not listen, and both troops
and grain were marched up from all parts of the distracted
empire without stint. Meanwhile the " Filial Jenuye "
seized the first opportunity to get back and explain to his
brother how the title had been thrust upon him. The
Jenuye was evidently ill satisfied with the explanation given,
for he changed his brother's original title to one of much
lower degree. The " Obedient Jenuye " dying of sickness,
his elder brother was appointed by Wang Mang to take his
place. Raiding went on, and prisoners captured made it
clear that a third son of the " Filial Jenuye " was amongst
the raiders. Wang Mang thereupon assembled all foreigners
in the great square of the metropolis and had the second
" Obedient Jenuye " executed in their presence. The result
of all this was that the frontier people, who had grown rich
and prosperous with fifty years of peace, lost their all, and were
most of them killed or carried off into captivity. The armies
accumulating without anything to do, got weary of camping
in idleness ; nothing effective was carried out, and the plains,
so lately covered with flocks and herds, were soon a howling
wilderness of bleaching bones.

Otyuru died in A.D. 13 after a reign of 21 years ; and now
the influence of the Chinese wife began to be felt once more.
One of her daughters was married to the Hiung-nu minister
then in power, and this daughter had not only frequently
spoken in favour of an alliance with the Empire, but had
noticed with satisfaction that Wang Mang's " Filial Jenuye,"

who was an intimate of hers, continued to receive complimentary advances from China. She therefore threw her weight into the scale, and secured his election in preference to that of the Right Dugi; that is, in preference to the brother who had come back with the Chinese envoys to negotiate about the seal. The new Jenuye assumed the title of Orei-yokte, and conferred suitable rank upon the brother thus passed over. It is not evident why the term " passed over " is used, for Orei was strictly the next brother, in point of age, of the six born of the two sisters (pp. 46, 47). The title of Left Dugi which had been borne by Otyuru's son seems to have been abandoned a few years before this for superstitious reasons ; but none the less the son was the proper heir, and Otyuru had, in fact, asked the son to pass on the succession to Orei. But Orei now paid off Otyuru for suspecting and degrading him by degrading his own nephew, Otyuru's son, to the now discredited title of Left Dugi. Orei seems to have allowed his patroness to conduct the diplomacy of the state, and accordingly she sent to the Wall to say that she would like to see her already mentioned (p. 53) cousin, the son of her mother's elder brother. Two cousins (brothers) were sent instead of the one asked for as envoys to congratulate the Jenuye. They tried, and apparently with success, to persuade him that his son, who had been so foolishly executed, was still alive. By heavy bribes, too, they succeeded in obtaining the surrender of the two clerks who had absconded from the proconsulate, together with the actual murderer of the superior officer. They were roasted alive with exquisite refinements of torture specially invented for their benefit by the vengeful Wang Mang.

Though the Jenuye took all he could get in the way of presents, he seized every opportunity offering to raid and kidnap. His return envoys, moreover, soon learned the truth about his son's execution, on hearing of which he obtained the assistance of the Tunguses and became more vicious than ever ; he always gave the most evasive answers when taken to task by the Chinese envoys. The remains of the young " Obedient Jenuye " and his retinue were carefully sent back to Tartarland under the escort of the Chinese Inchi's diplomatic cousin, and were received at the Great Wall by the son of the minister in power and his half-Chinese wife. It was announced to the Jenuye that the national designation must in future be not Hiung-nu but Kung-nu. The Chinese characters selected to represent the original Tartar word mean " Ferocious Slaves," and those chosen for the new designation (which 2,000 years ago probably differed in sound from the first much less than they do now) mean " Respectful Slaves." The long-headed Jenuye simply said :—" Good ! " He took his seal, presents, etc., and continued his raids. Wang Mang, who made dukes on as wholesale a scale as Napoleon the First did, liberally rewarded the diplomatic cousin and his colleagues.

Orei reigned five years and died in A.D. 18 : he was succeeded by his younger brother above mentioned, who took the appellation of Khutulz-daokao-yokte. It is not clear whose son he was on his mother's side, but he was not the sixth son of the two sisters (p. 47). He also developed a keen appetite for Chinese presents, and a son of each of the Chinese Inchi's daughters, two cousins, were sent to court. It seems that about now the minister in power and his wife also came to the Wall, where they were duly welcomed by the diplomatic cousin of their choice, and induced to visit the capital. One of the two young cousins, not liking the look of things, escaped back, and when the minister in power reached the metropolis he found that Wang Mang was bent on forcing him upon the Hiung-nu nation as their Jenuye. But these intrigues failed, and the unfortunate man died of sickness. Wang Mang gave a concubine-born daughter of his own to the late Tartar minister's son in marriage, and was about to make him Jenuye instead. But Wang Mang himself was shortly afterwards put to death (A.D. 23) by the soldiers of the old Han dynasty party, and both the young man and his mother perished in the general scrimmage which followed.

In A.D. 24 the last Emperor of the Early or Western Han dynasty sent a mission to the Hiung-nu with the old pattern of seal. The survivors of the Hiung-nu retinues were also sent safely back. The Jenuye put on great airs when this mission arrived, and claimed the credit of having got rid of the usurper, with the right to the same acknowledgment on the part of China as that which his father had rendered to China when the Hiung-nu usurpers were got rid of with her assistance. No arguments of the envoys could shake him, and the envoys returned rather crestfallen. Meanwhile the " Red Eyebrow " rebels then infesting China entered the Chinese capital, and the first Han dynasty came definitively to an end.

CHAPTER VI

DEPENDENCE, DISINTEGRATION, AND COLLAPSE

DURING the anarchy which preceded the re-establishment of order by the Emperor Kwang-wu Ti, founder of the second house of Han, Khutulz gave his assistance to a Chinese Perkin Warbeck near modern Peking. When things had settled down a little, the Emperor again sent a conciliatory message to the Jenuye, who was as insolent as on the previous occasion, and presumed to compare himself with the great conqueror Baghdur. Raiding went on actively, and the people of North Shan Si had to migrate for safety eastwards of the well-known Nan-k'ou Pass near Peking. The Hiung-nu even planted themselves on the Chinese side of the Wall; but the Wu-hwan Tunguses were now becoming a strong power, and soon thrust their rivals once more to the north of the Desert. Khutulz, coveting the heavy rewards offered by

China for the Pretender, sent that individual back under
escort. But the Pretender, as soon as he realized what was
taking place, was altogether too sharp for the Jenuye, and
told the Chinese he had repented and come to surrender
voluntarily. Thus Khutulz never got any reward at all,
and was ashamed to claim it. But he was the more incensed
in consequence, and for many years kept the whole north
frontier line in a state of misery and wretchedness.

It will be remembered (p. 46) that Khughanja had had one
son born to him by the Chinese handmaid, afterwards Inchi,
and that at first she had objected to marry her husband's son,
but that the Emperor sent her word to conform to the custom
of the country (p. 48).   Khutulz put this brother to death
in order to reserve the succession for his own son. When
Otyuru's son heard of this he was very dissatisfied, arguing
that, if brothers were to be exhausted in turn first, the murdered
man was the proper successor ; if sons were admitted, then
himself, as being the eldest son of Khutulz's elder brother
Otyuru. He therefore abstained from taking part in the
great assemblies, in consequence of which the Jenuye sent
two nobles to take command of the truant's troops. Khutulz
died in A.D. 46, and was succeeded by two sons in turn,
one of whom died almost at once. Otyuru's son, seeing the
prospects of his succession were becoming more remote than
ever, sent a secret envoy to present the Emperor with a map
of the Hiung-nu dominions (it is not said by whom made)
and offered to join the Empire. The two nobles reported
at the Dragon Sacrifice in the 5th moon (July) that treachery
was brewing, but their conversation was overheard by another
of Otyuru's sons, who happened to be sitting outside the
Jenuye's tent at that moment. He at once rode off to tell
his brother, who proceeded to assemble the 45,000 troopers
belonging to his appanage, (which seems to have included,
at least nominally the Wu-hwan territory,) and resolved to
kill the two uninvited nobles on their return. But they got
wind of what was intended as they were arriving, and at once

disappeared on fleet horses to inform the Jenuye, whose available force, however, was not strong enough to attempt anything.—The ensuing squabbles for the succession are too complicated and beset with strange personal names for us to make any attempt here to interest the general reader therein.

In A.D. 48 the chiefs of eight tribes ultimately agreed to elevate Otyuru's son to the dignity of Khughanja Jenuye, and to make that title hereditary, in view of the policy of peace inaugurated by the grandfather, the first of that name (p. 39). The new monarch, the first of what are called the Southern Jenuyes, proceeded to the Wall in the extreme north near where Shen Si and Shan Si join, and offered to be a " buffer " state for ever, charged with the duty of keeping off the Northerners. This offer was accepted, and the very next year his brother inflicted a serious defeat upon the Northern Jenuye's brother, who was taken prisoner. The Northern Jenuye was so panic-stricken that he abandoned 300 English miles of territory to the South. An old tradition of the Birnam Wood type was now raked up to the effect that " in the 9th " generation the nomads shall be driven back 300 miles." It is not apparent whether this means the ninth in succession counting from Khughanja, or the ninth generation from Baghdur ; but it comes about right both ways, and corresponds with the permanent appearance in the Sogdian region of the Hun nucleus afterwards destined to work their way into South Europe : as we shall see, forty years later the last of the Northern Hiung-nu disappeared for ever from the Chinese ken. It seems, however, at this earlier date, that the disaster stimulated several of the Northern princes to come over to the Southern Jenuye with 30,000 men. The Chinese Emperor also invented a kind of turret-cart, yoked to a number of oxen, and capable of being moved to any point of the Great Wall threatened by the enemy. The Southern Jenuye's headquarters were permanently established at a point 25 miles beyond the Great Wall in the Ordous Country at the

North-east corner of the Great Bend,—possibly at the modern Kwei-hwa Ch'êng or Polo's Tenduc. Envoys were sent to receive his formal submission, and the Jenuye came in person to meet them. They claimed that it was his duty to prostrate himself on receiving the imperial decree. The Jenuye after some hesitation did so, and formally declared himself a vassal. But after the obeisance had been performed he told the interpreter to say to the envoys that, newly elected as he was, he felt the indignity very keenly, and that he would be much obliged if the envoys would in future refrain from humiliating him in the presence of his own people. The nobles, including those who had deserted from the North, shed tears of mortification as they witnessed these proceedings, all which was reported to the Emperor ; who, however, let things stand.

The Northern Jenuye's brother who had been taken prisoner effected his escape together with five nobles and 30,000 men,—probably those who had come over for the superstitious reasons,—and the whole party encamped at a distance of 75 miles from the Northern headquarters, the exact position of which at that moment it is difficult to conjecture now. There they agreed to elect the brother as Jenuye, but they soon got to quarrelling amongst themselves, and the result was they all perished one way or another. That autumn the Southern Jenuye sent one of his sons to court as a page, and received under special decree a very large number of assorted presents of all kinds from the Emperor. A singular compliment was also paid to him by sending fifty armed criminals, under an officer, to settle his brawls for him, and to follow his movements. At the close of each year he made a point of sending a son with a submissive letter, and China always at once sent back the page who had already served a year under suitable escort. The duty of these sons was to present the Jenuye's respects at the new year, and to prostrate themselves at the deceased Emperors' tombs. Besides the annual presents to the Jenuye himself, his queens, sons, and those of his nobles who deserved it received various creature comforts, such as sauces, lichees, and oranges, [the last of which—those bitter ones from Wênchow—are still an annual speciality shipped by way of Tientsin for the Mongols]. At the three annual Dragon Festivals, in addition to the ancient sacrifices to Heaven, offerings were now regularly made to the tablets or possibly effigies of Chinese Emperors. Then followed camel races and public debates, trials of causes, and so on. It is again recorded at this date that the Hiung-nu administration was entirely carried on by word of mouth, and that there were no records or writings of any kind. We may therefore rest confident that Chinese were always employed in connection with the diplomatic correspondence with the empire, just as Cæsar was written to by the ignorant Britons in Greek. The Dugi, Rukle, and " Horn " system was still in force ; the three ancient clans that monopolized the judicial business and could intermarry with the Jenuye's clan had now become four, and the clan to which the Chwangü sisters belonged was " Left," which fact partly explains why, notwithstanding her inferior status (pp. 33, 34), that enterprising female was so noble. That winter the sons of the five above-mentioned nobles who had all perished in squabbling endeavoured to regain the Southern headquarters with their sadly diminished horde. They were captured by the Northerners, and the Southerners who came to the rescue were defeated. On this the Southern Jenuye was ordered by the Emperor to move farther south, and to establish his headquarters west of the range which separates the valleys of the Fên and Yellow Rivers, in a tract of Shan Si country where one or two small tributaries of the Yellow River run west into that great artery. It is well to specify this neighbourhood, now known as Lin Chou, because it gave birth three centuries later to a Hiung-nu dynasty of Emperors, who claimed the succession as " legitimists " of Liu dynastic family descended from Chinese princesses. Every winter 2,000 troopers and 500 criminals were sent to assist in protecting the Jenuye. The ground lost during Wang Mang's

harum-scarum administration was recovered, and the minor
Hiung-nu princes with their hordes were stationed at various
points along the line of the Wall to do scout duty, under
the orders in each case of the nearest Chinese city prefect.
These business-like dispositions seriously alarmed the Northern
Jenuye, who as a first step sent back a number of Chinese
captives, and whenever his men whilst raiding came upon
the Southern scouts they always said :—" We should never
" think of encroaching upon Chinese land : we are only after
" that traitor prince of ours " (i.e. the Southern Jenuye).
In A.D. 52 the Northern Jenuye tried another tack. He
sent envoys with amicable proposals. The council had
a difficulty in formulating a recommendation ; but the heir
to the throne was distinctly of opinion that if it was desired
to keep well with the Southerner, the Northerner's advances
should be rejected ; and the Emperor, accepting this view,
gave the prefect concerned orders not to admit the embassy.
In the following year the Northerner made another attempt,
this time with tribute of horses and furs. He also begged
for a band of musicians and for " permission to bring all his
" allies of Turkestan to submit their respects." Pan Piao,
(father of the two illustrious historians, the substance of whose
words we are now translating, and also father of the proconsul
under whose orders Parthia and Syria were discovered,) took
upon himself to deal with this embarrassing situation. In
his opinion the more anxious the Northerners were to curry
favour, the more it was evident that they dreaded our alliance
with the South. The more show they make, the poorer they
probably are, said he. Still, as no great advantage had as yet
been gained from the alliance with the South, it would be
just as well to keep a few eggs in the other basket, and send
the North a civil answer, with presents equal in value to those
received. So speaking, the wary old statesman took from
his sleeve a draft letter which he had prepared, and submitted
it to the Emperor. Its purport was as follows :—" The
"Jenuye does not forget the favours his ancestors have received,

" and naturally wishes to improve his position by making
" friendly advances,—a very proper condition of mind. In
" past times Khughanja and Chirche were involved in civil
" war, until Divus Süan extended his gracious protection to
" the pair, and received their sons as pages. After that Chirche
" broke with us in a huff, paying for his indiscretion with
" his head ; whilst Khughanja, wiser in his generation,
" secured the peaceful succession of his sons and grandsons.
" Of recent years the Southern Jenuye has turned his face
" south and submitted himself to our commands. As he
" is the oldest direct descendant of Khughanja, we have held
" that the succession is his due. But, when he goes beyond
" his duty and seeks our assistance in order to annihilate
" the Northern Horde, it becomes necessary for us to give
" due weight to the just expectations of the Northern Jenuye,
" who has so frequently made dutiful advances to us. We
" have, therefore, disapproved the suggestions of the South.
" China, as supreme director of the universe, upon whose
" dominion the sun never sets, cannot favour one barbarian
" over the other. Those who submit are rewarded ; those
" who resist, punished. Khughanja and Chirche are examples
" in point. There is no reason why the Jenuye should not
" give proof of his loyalty by showing the Turkestan chiefs
" the road to duty. At the same time, the fact of their
" forming part of the Hiung-nu dominions leaves them still
" what they were before,—part of the Chinese Empire ;
" and no innovation is necessary. The Jenuye's dominions
" must be exhausted with recent wars. Why then send
" valuable presents, which, after all, are only symbolical
" of an idea ? Presents according to the list in the margin
" are herewith made to the Jenuye and his envoys. The
" Jenuye says the musical instruments formerly presented
" to Khughanja are all worn out. Remembering that the
" Jenuye was fighting for bare existence and had something
" else to do than to fiddle and fife, we intentionally omitted
" to offer these trifling objects before : they now go by ordinary
" post-courier." The Emperor approved.

Khughanja the Second, whose personal name (p. 62) was Pi, died in the year A.D. 55, after a reign of nine years, and was succeeded by the younger brother who had defeated and taken prisoner the Northern Jenuye's younger brother. This brother only reigned a little over one year, and was succeeded by yet another brother. This last brother again reigned but two years, and was succeeded by the second Khughanja's son. There was another short reign of four years, when the son of the first younger brother succeeded, followed in a few months by his own younger brother (A.D. 63). All these Jenuyes assumed native reign names of portentous length, which, in the absence of any recorded deeds of derring-do on their part, are not alone sufficient to entitle them to further notice here. In A.D. 59 the Northern Jenuye, (a new man, as to whose origin and date of accession there is no information,) came in person to the Wall to offer submission, but three years later we find him raiding China and being driven back by the Southerners. In A.D. 63 the Northerner, after two years of harrying, applied for trading privileges, which were granted, in the hope that he would cease raiding ; and two years later a mission was sent to him. This aroused the suspicion of the Southerners, and the result was that certain discontented Southerners joined the Northerners. At last the Emperor was goaded into reprisals, and in A.D. 73 a great expedition was organized in several columns ; boats or rafts supported by horse-skins were made for crossing the rivers ; but the Hiung-nu, following their ancient tactics, made off across the desert. In A.D. 76 the loyal Southerners who were giving assistance against the Northerners suffered from a serious plague of locusts, and the Emperor had to feed 30,000 of them with grain. In A.D. 84 the Northern Jenuye was again granted trading facilities, in consequence of which the jealous Southerner carried off some of his rival's people and cattle. But the Northerners are now no longer described as Jenuyes ; their dominion was evidently in the hands of contesting chiefs. The great Empire of the later Wu-hwan, known as the Sien-pi Tunguses, was now rapidly forming, and the Sien-pi were assailing the luckless Northerners from the east, whilst the Southerners attacked them from the south, the Kankalis from the north, and the Turkestan tribes from the west, all which completed their destruction : they were totally unable to maintain their ground, and disappeared far away to the north, many of them no doubt finding their way (by the upper waters of the Selinga and the Irtysh to Issekul, the Aral, and the Caspian, struggling with the Bashkirs, the Alans, and the unknown tribes then occupying Russia) into Europe. Gibbon speaks as though Etzel or Attila boasted of his descent from the Jenuyes of Mongolia, but if there were any sound evidence of so important a fact it would doubtless have been forthcoming. Herodotus speaks of the Scythians sweeping over Asia Minor centuries before this ; and, indeed, the Shepherd Kings who introduced horses into Egypt many centuries before Herodotus may have been earlier " editions " of the Hiung-nu.

The Southern Jenuye, nephew of Khughanja the Second, died in A.D. 85, and was succeeded by the son of Khughanja's next brother. Straggling bodies of the Northern Horde were attacked whenever occasion offered, and so much a human head was paid by China to the Southerners who brought them in : this caused many Northerners to cast themselves upon the mercy of China. In A.D. 87 the Sien-pi struck them a final blow in the east, and secured what purported to be the Northern Jenuye's whole skin as a trophy. [Possibly the Persian king Sapor, who skinned and stuffed the Roman Emperor Valerian a century later, obtained the grim idea from bodies of Hiung-nu then passing near his dominions ; but Gibbon misquotes Vopiscus when he asserts that a Chinese ambassador assisted at Aurelian's triumph.] Finally a total of 200,000 souls and 8,000 able soldiers of the Northerners came in parties to the Wall at various points and surrendered to China. After this date the Northern Jenuyes are a mere shadow of their old selves, and quite a negligible quantity in the history of China. In fact in the year A.D. 88, when the Southern Jenuye died and was succeeded by a cousin, it was decided to annihilate the Northern Dominion politically, and to annex the remains of it to the South. Accordingly, next year a great army under the command of the Empress' nephew and assisted by the 30,000 troopers of the Southern Jenuye, inflicted a crushing defeat upon the Northerners at the same spot where the unfortunate conqueror of Kokand was beaten 180 years earlier, that is to say, somewhere in the elevated Hangai region, whence the Tula, Orkhon, and Kerulon rivers all take their rise. In this case the Chinese general recorded his exploits upon the face of a hill; and possibly, though in any case we find its text recorded, we may yet be fortunate enough to find it, as the Russians have recently (1888) found a number of Turkish tombstones with Chinese and Syriac inscriptions farther west: the most remarkable of the Orkhon R. Aramean-Turkish were explained by Radloff in his magnificent Atlas series of 1892. Two Chinese columns were sent in A.D. 91 in further pursuit of the Northern Jenuye, who barely escaped with his life, and lost the whole of his family and belongings, including his seal of jade-stone. His host was once more routed by a Chinese flying column in the same year, A.D. 91, after which he was never heard of again, and the Chinese, now in the neighbourhood of Barkul, set up a puppet of their own. It was intended that a Chinese Resident should take up his quarters at Hamil and keep the Northern Jenuye in a sort of tutelage like his Southern colleague; but the elusive Tartar soon tried to escape, and was therefore decapitated, whilst his horde was broken up.

In A.D. 93 another cousin succeeded as Southern Jenuye, and as he was not very popular, the Chinese Resident charged with his surveillance joined the chief Chinese general in an intrigue to supplant him. They intercepted his correspondence with the Emperor and charged him with conspiring to murder the popular and warlike prince who was their own candidate *in petto* for the Tartar throne. The intrigue

succeeded, and in the civil war which followed the Jenuye
was killed after a reign of one year. He was succeeded by
the more popular nephew, grandson of Khughanja the Second.
[It may be mentioned that most of this line of Jenuyes have the
Hiung-nu word *sedjugeute* attached to their titles; some of
them the word *urute*. In either case, like the word *yokte*,
some complimentary epithet is doubtless intended.] The
tribesmen were not yet satisfied : in fact, the addition of so
much new blood made it very difficult for Northern and
Southern factions to agree. A large body refused to recognize
the new Jenuye, elected a cousin, and endeavoured to reach
the north of the desert. Meanwhile the Emperor discovered
the intrigue which had led to all this confusion, and the authors
of it perished miserably in gaol. In A.D. 98 the Southern
Jenuye was succeeded by a cousin, whilst the revolters under
the seceding Jenuye struggled hopelessly with famine and
Tungusic enemies in the north. China turned a deaf ear to
all their advances and attempts to obtain recognition,
and in A.D. 117 the seceder surrendered unconditionally.
The Southern Jenuye enjoyed a long reign of 27 years,
diversified by war with his Northern rival, an attempt of his
own (which was crushed and pardoned) upon China, and war
with the Tunguses. He was succeeded in A.D. 124 by two
brothers, one of whom reigned four, and the other thirteen
years. The second one and still another brother committed
suicide together on account of the dissatisfaction with their
conduct expressed by China. From this date the genealogies
and even the names of the Southern Jenuyes become confused
and unintelligible. It is difficult to follow and wearisome
to recount the tangled web of frontier intrigue. In A.D. 177
the Southern Jenuye (whose personal name is stated to be
unknown) assisted the Chinese in a campaign against the
great Tungusic conqueror Dardjegwe, (of whom more anon),
but was defeated and died : his son and successor was executed
by a Chinese general, who set up in his place one Kiangü ;
he, again, in A.D. 188 was succeeded by his son Uvura. China

was then in quite as anarchical a condition as her protected Jenuye, who was shortly dethroned by a rival, having been really only a ruler in name, and a helpless exile. His brother Khudjuzen was detained at the Chinese court by the famous general Ts'ao Ts'ao, whose son founded the dynasty of Wei upon the ruins of the After Han house. The Hiung-nu power now broke up for ever, and China herself was for half a century split up into three rival empires, only one of which had any political relations with Tartary. The unofficial story of these three contending empires is told in a romantic work composed a thousand years later under the Mongol reign of Kublai Khan by one Lo Kwan-chung.

CHAPTER VII

HIUNG-NU ADVENTURERS BECOME EMPERORS OF NORTH CHINA

THOUGH, as we have said, the genealogies of the last few Jenuyes are not recorded, yet it will be observed that from first to last they were all, so long as the Chinese annals keep the run of them, direct descendants of the great conqueror Baghdur. Amid all the revolutions and civil wars, there is not the slightest hint of the succession having ever gone out of the royal clan. Thus, from Baghdur to Okyenküte all were sons, brothers, or nephews of their predecessors. Khughanja the First was Hülügwengü's son; and Khughanja's six sons succeeded in strict seniority of years. Khughanja the Second was undoubtedly the most legitimate heir, and his successors were, firstly, two brothers, and, secondly, six sons of himself and those brothers. Then come five grandsons, bringing us up to A.D. 141, or just 200 years for the three generations of men. It does not appear exactly who Kiangü was, but Uvura and Khudjuzen were his sons, and there is no reason to suppose that between 141 and 179 the regular order of things was broken. Of the Northern Jenuyes we have no record whatever. China, we see, was now split up into three empires, the northern one of which, that of Wei (not to be confused with the Tartar dynasty of Wei 150 years later), alone had dealings with the Hiung-nu. Their ancient dominions were now in the hands of the Tunguses, as will shortly be related in detail. Meanwhile general Ts'ao Ts'ao divided the remnants of the Southern Jenuye's horde into five tribes, and made Uvura's son chieftain of the Left Tribe. It appears that the descendants of Baghdur, (who, it will be remembered (p. 16) had a lady of the Chinese blood royal given to him in marriage,) considered themselves entitled to bear the clan name Liu, which was that of both divisions of the Han dynasty, and also of the Han dynasty ruling in West China whilst the Wei ruled in the North, and the Wu dynasty south of the Yangtze. It is not stated when these descendants actually began to use it, but most probably it was when Khughanja the Second became an un-mistakable Chinese vassal ; for he and his descendants all bore Chinese personal names of one syllable, such as would be quite inappropriate unless coupled with a monosyllabic Chinese clan name. However that may be, Uvura's son the Left Dugi was known by the purely Chinese name of Liu Pao, not having, like the Jenuyes, occasion to use a sesquipedalian Tartar title meaning *divus, pius,* and so on. The command of each of the other four tribes was also given to members of the Liu clan, and they all had their family residences in the land of their fathers (to which attention was called in Chapter VI, p. 65) between the valleys of the Fên and Yellow Rivers in Shan Si. Liu Pao had born to him by a lady of the noblest clan (that of the sisters Chwangü of old) a remarkable son named Liu Yüan, usually known to later history as Liu Yüan-hai, because his real name touched the taboo (Bk. IV, Ch. II) of the founder of the T'ang dynasty. This son was as well-read in history as he was well-exercised in the arts of war, and, having spent some years at the last Wei Emperor's court as a page, he had extended the horizon of his knowledge in various ways. On his father's death he inherited the post of chief ; and, when the Tsin dynasty had welded the three Chinese empires into one (A.D. 265), his honesty and disinterestedness of character soon secured him general confidence : he was created a Chinese Field-Marshal and Captain-General of the Five Hiung-nu tribes.

The second Emperor of the Tsin dynasty was a poor creature, and by his misgovernment soon brought about a civil war. Under these circumstances the leading chiefs of the Hiung-nu did not see why they should not strike out a line for themselves, instead of being passed on like so many cattle from one Chinese dynasty to the other. Liu Yüan was accordingly in A.D. 304 hailed by the ancient title of Great Jenuye, and in twenty days his host had already amounted to the respectable number of 50,000 men. He fixed his capital at first at Lin Chou, the old seat of Khughanja the Second, and styled himself Prince of Han, setting up to be worshipped the ancestral tablets of the Han Emperors ; that is, the Early Han, After Han, and Western Han, all of the Liu family, covering nearly six centuries of rule. He assumed the dignity of Emperor A.D. 308, and repeatedly moved his capital as he advanced south, until he at last attacked the Chinese metropolis—then at modern Ho-nan Fu. He died in the year 310, but his son Liu Ts'ung took both the modern and the ancient metropolis, murdered the third and fourth Tsin Emperors, and, having reigned nine years, was, after certain butcheries, finally succeeded by his kinsman and chief general Liu Yao, who was taken prisoner and killed by a competing Hiung-nu adventurer in the year 319. Liu Ts'ung had changed the dynastic title from that of Han to Chao, Chao being the ancient name of the feudal kingdom which had 700 years before offered so vigorous a resistance to the Hiung-nu, but whose Chinese king had at the same time adopted the Tartar mode of life, (see p. 7). One of the most distinguished generals of the three Liu monarchs was a " Wether " Hiung-nu named Pei, or, in Chinese, Shih Lêh, also descended from the Jenuye Kiangü. Upon the ruins of his patrons' dynasty he founded the powerful empire called Later Chao, which endured in North China for thirty years. Thus the Hiung-nu were, in all, *bonâ fide* Emperors of North China for nearly sixty years, which, when we consider the duration of many European dynasties,—that of the Bonapartes for instance,—is no inconsiderable period. In this way the Chinese were hoist with their own petard, and the marriages by which, centuries earlier, they had hoped to bring the Tartars under their thumb in the end placed Tartar Emperors upon the throne of China. It must be borne in mind, however, that the newly colonized countries south of the Yangtsze River were never even remotely ruled by any Tartar house (with one short exception, at the end of the 5th century, during the Toba dynasty, far away to the west) until the time of Kublai Khan, in the 13th century. Chinese dynasties always continued to rule at modern Nanking, Hangchow, or other places, when Tartars ruled in the north ; yet the centre of Chinese political and literary gravity crossed the Great River at about this time ; the true Chinese idioms likewise migrated to the south, and a corrupted form of speech popularly known to Europeans as the " mandarin language " began to grow up over the whole of the vast area north of the Yangtsze. It is clear from the language of novels written three hundred years ago that the present language of Peking is almost precisely what it was then, even to the smallest *minutiæ*, and that, just as French was formed out of Latin under the influence of the Normans and Franks, so was the modern mandarin formed out of Chinese under the influence of the Tartars ; with this difference, however, that in the case of Chinese the change of brogue has never been allowed to affect the purity of the original written language, which, always conforming itself to ancient canons of style, remains everywhere the same. Since the revolution of 1911, however, a new and easier literary style has been coming into vogue, and the dignified old " Latinity " will probably soon be the speciality of purists.

Like Liu Yüan, our hero succeeded his father as chief of one of the Hiung-nu tribes, quartered in this case farther south, in the modern Ts'in Chou of southern Shan Si. During the civil war and anarchy of 302–304, he was taken captive and sold as a slave ; but his Chinese master found he had literally " caught a Tartar," and before long the slave became a leader of bandits. After various vicissitudes, he became one of Liu Yüan's generals, fought some great battles with the Chinese, and also with certain Tungusic pretenders ; assisted Liu Ts'ung to sack the capital ; and ended by putting Liu Yao to death, himself assuming first the title of Prince of Chao, and then that of Emperor. He died in 334, after a reign of fifteen years. His son and heir was murdered by a younger brother Shih Hu, more commonly known as Shih Ki-lung, who also reigned fifteen years. Then there were quarrels about the succession, and finally the whole family were butchered in 379 by an adoptive heir.

Shih Lêh was no contemptible man : he was a kind of eastern Alaric, and the Chinese historians speak of him with great respect. He codified the laws, and showed great favour to Buddhism. A Hindoo quack named Buddhôchinga, who came to China in 328, and concerning whom a legion of anecdotes are told, had immense influence at his court, and also at that of Shih Ki-lung. Shih Lêh's dominion at quite an early stage embraced 24 (Chinese) prefectural divisions and 300,000 households, which, considering the devastating wars which had almost depopulated many parts of China, and the probability that only taxable heads of houses were then counted in the census, probably means a population of at least 3,000,000. After he and his successors had obtained the submission of the Tangut or Tibetan adventurers of Shen Si, his empire reached far away into the north-west ; and even independent Chinese kingdoms, as for instance that of Liang,—Marco Polo's Erguiul, the modern Liang-chou Fu in Kan Suh,—accepted his suzerainty. At this period, known as the Sixteen State Period, there was a general tussle for preëminence in the north between Tunguses, Hiung-nu, Tibetans, and Chinese. It resembled nothing so much as the period when Ostrogoths, Visigoths, Vandals, etc., precipitated themselves upon the Roman Empire, sacked her capital, and founded barbarian dynasties in Spain, Africa, and Gaul. The Roman centre of gravity oscillated between Constantinople in the east and Rome in the west, just as did the Chinese capital between Shen Si or Ho Nan—places in the north—and (what we now call) Nanking or Hangchow in the south. The same causes, intrigues, and mistakes produced the same effects in each case, and the similarity in the main outlines of each history is really startling.

Amongst the competitors for power at this time was one Tsugu Mêngsun, whose ancestors had held the post of Left Tsugu amongst the Hiung-nu of the modern Kan-chou Fu region. He adopted the word Tsugu (see p. 13) as a clan name, and succeeded in establishing himself as duke or ruler of the ancient Hephthalites or Yüeh-chĭ country,—or, roughly speaking, the modern province of Kan Suh. Here he had to defend himself against the onslaughts of various Tungusic tribes, and finally succumbed to the Toba dynasty of Wei in A.D. 433, after a ducal reign of 33 years. It is unnecessary to follow the thread of his comparatively obscure career here, but it is important to mention him and to keep him in mind, because he seems to be the only link that can be discovered in Chinese history positively to connect the ancient Hiung-nu with the later Turks by specific evidence.

Besides the three Hiung-nu dynasties above described, there was the Hia dynasty of Ghoren Borbor in the Ordous country. When Ts'ao Ts'ao put an end to the old Jenuyeship, Uvura's son, Liu Pao, was Left Dugi (p. 73). But there was also a Right Dugi, named Küpi, at the Chinese court when Khudjuzen was detained there (p. 72). Küpi was allowed to go back to his people, and during Liu Ts'ung's time an ancestor of our hero, as one of the royal blood, was made superintendent of the various Sien-pi armies. But the Toba Sien-pi were serving the royal Chinese house of Tsin against both the Hiung-nu and the so-called " White Tribe " of Sien-pi, and their victories over the latter caused the same or another ancestor of our hero to go beyond the Wall, where he collected the various tribes and developed considerable power. Shih Lêh's brother and successor Shih Ki-lung created him Jenuye of the Kankalis, and, when his father returned within the Wall, the Tanguts of the Ts'in " empire " conferred upon him the title of Western Jenuye. These Tanguts, who reigned as Emperors at Ch'ang-an for half a century, were broken up by the imperial Chinese house of Tsin. The Tobas defeated and killed the father after this, but the son took refuge with the second Tangut dynasty of After Ts'in, and obtained high position as one of the councillors of the kingdom. The world-renowned Chinese pilgrim Fa-Hien passed through Ch'ang-an in A.D. 400. Revolting against his benefactors, Borbor now set himself up as monarch of Hia, with the titles of " Heavenly King and Great Jenuye." The name Hia seems to derive its origin from Hia-hou, the founder of the Chinese Hia dynasty in B.C. 2205. It will be remembered (p. 2) that a royal personage supposed to have been connected by descent with this dynasty fled to the Tartars about the year B.C. 1200, and in one way or another this person as founder of the Hiung-nu was held to be a link between the semi-mythical Chinese Hia dynasty and Liu P'oh-p'oh, who now abandoned the Chinese clan name of Liu and took that of Gheren or Ghoren, which last appears to be a Tartar word of high-sounding meaning. It is out of all this that we derive the *supposed* Tartar name Gheren Borbor. Having defeated the Tufa state (an offshoot of the Toba), Borbor founded a capital city at or near the modern Ning-hia,—Marco Polo's Egrigaia—the solid ruins of which considered very remarkable several centuries later. After the destruction of the Latter Tangut dynasty by the new Chinese dynasty of Sung (capital at Nanking), Borbor resolved to compete with the latter for empire, and took the ancient capital of Ch'ang-an (Si-an Fu). He assumed the dignity of Emperor, and reigned for thirteen years. He died in the year 425, and his successors were soon overcome by the imperial Toba house of Wei, ruling in the northern half of China.

This somewhat involved story, which it is difficult to make at all intelligible without using many uncouth and strange names, is necessary to the completion of our work, the object of which is to show the progress of the struggle between Tartars and Chinese, and to trace the processes by which the barbarians of the north at last succeeded in setting themselves upon the throne of China. During the 6th century, when the Sien-pi Tartar dynasties were ruling in North China, there was a race of semi-civilized Tartars living in the old Liu Yüan domain between the Fên and the Yellow Rivers. It was doubtful if they were his descendants or were connected with the Kankalis. Anyhow, they had become settled, grew the silk mulberry, and could read Chinese, though they spoke their own language. Evidently they were undergoing the process of assimilation to which allusion has already been made.

Here we must close the first book, which runs rapidly through the whole history of the Hiung-nu so long as the name exists. The next Empire to be considered will be that of the Tunguses, known to the Chinese as the Wu-hwan or Sien-pi.

BOOK II
THE EMPIRE OF THE SIEN-PI

BOOK II

THE EMPIRE OF THE SIEN-PI

CHAPTER I

THE WU-HWAN AND SIEN-PI TUNGUSES

EAST of the Hiung-nu were what the Chinese in ancient times called the Tung-hu, or Eastern Hu, the word *hu* in its broadest sense including every species of what we call Tartars, besides Coreans, Kashgarians, Turkomans, Affghans, and to a certain extent Syrians, Hindoos, and Persians (cf. p. 5). It is never applied to the Japanese, Tibetans, Indo-Chinese, or any of the European races. In a narrower sense it frequently means those nations using Sanskrit or Syriac as distinct from the yellow-skinned races, or those using Chinese writing. The term " Eastern Hu " seems to be confined to the Coreans and progenitors of the Manchu races ; in fact, to what we call the Tungusic races, and all tribes speaking cognate languages with them. It hardly seems likely that the European word Tungusic can have immediate etymological connection with the Chinese words Tung-hu, but at any rate the signification of the two terms is conveniently coincident. The Turkish word *Tungus*, meaning " a pig," may possibly owe its origin, as applied by them to the Chinese, to an attempt on their ancestors' part to accommodate the Chinese syllables Tung-hu with a Hiung-nu word of similar sound but offensive meaning. If there is one thing remarkable about the ancient Tungusic races, it is the fact that they all reared and all ate swine, which the Hiung-nu apparently did not. Hence, just as the Chinese turned the Hiung-nu national designation into Chinese syllables meaning " fierce slaves," so would the Hiung-nu style their eastern neighbours (described to them as *Tung-hu* by the Chinese) " pig people " ; and, as North China has been, off and on, for many centuries, and continued from 1644 up to 1911 under the rule of Eastern Hu, the term " pig people " would be extended to the Chinese, who certainly are as a nation the most universal pig-eaters the world has ever seen. In Genghis Khan's time the Mongol-Turkish Zagatai states of Persia used to style the Emperor of China the " pig emperor." Genghis and his successors did in fact replace the " pig-tailed " emperors of the Nüchên or Kin Tartar dynasty, admitted by the pig-tailed Manchus to have been their kinsmen. The Chinese never wore the " pig-tail " or queue until forced thereto by the Manchus nearly three centuries ago. Even the Corean youths wear pig-tails until they are married, though possibly there have been changes since 1887, when I left. Thus there is a fairly sound basis for something more than mere coincidence between the ideas Tung-hu, Tungusic, and pig. Possibly, on the other hand, the Chinese may have called their eastern neighbours *Tung-hu* because the Hiung-nu called them *Tungus* ; and, in support of this view, it may be mentioned that the expression *Si-hu* or " Western Hu " is exceedingly rare, and never refers to a dominion.

Nothing definite is known of the Tunguses as a political power previous to our era ; but, as the great Hiung-nu conqueror Baghdur broke up their power as a state, it would seem that they had an organization, and had probably existed side by side with the Hiung-nu, Coreans, etc., for many hundred years ; if not as a monarchy, then at least as a republic or series of republics. When Baghdur broke them up, the remnants of them took refuge in the Wu-wan or Wu-hwan Hills in the modern Aru Korchin land of Eastern Mongolia ; whence their name. As to their manners, they much resembled those of the Hiung-nu : they were good horse-archers, and followed their herds wherever there was grass and water. They had no fixed residence, and lived in tents which always faced east (the modern Mongol tents face south-east). They used to hunt birds and beasts; their food was flesh, their drink kumiss, and they utilized feathers in the manufacture of clothes. One point is specially signalled in which they differed from the Hiung-nu : the mother was considered the fountain of kinship, and whilst, in a fit of rage, they thought nothing of killing a father or brother, they never under any circumstances injured a mother ; and no family feud was generated when members of one fountain womb murdered each other. Still, like the Hiung-nu, they married the widows of their fathers and elder brothers. From the not very clear Chinese account given, it appears that sons only took over the wives if there was no brother to do it ; and that, failing both, the paternal uncle married the vacant widow, who, after death, reverted to her first husband in the next world, thus solving a knotty point raised in our own Scriptures. Like the Hiung-nu, they despised the old and feeble. Their chiefs were not hereditary, but were chosen for their martial, judicial, and administrative qualities. [Here, again, is a point in which they differ from the Hiung-nu, and, as we shall see when we come to the history of the Cathayans, this quality gradually developed them into a pure republic, with a president, and perhaps a vice-president.] Each community of a few hundred or a thousand tents had its own chief, and, in the absence of writing, orders were transmitted by notched pieces of wood, which were so well understood as to command instant obedience. They had no continuous family names, but the personal names of valiant chiefs were used as such. [As will appear later on, the Mujung, Tukuhun, and Toba dynasties all took their names from valiant Tungusic chiefs.] From the chieftains downwards each man had his own flocks and herds, and managed his own property : no man served another. Their marriages always began with clandestine commerce and then capture of the woman. After from three to six months a go-between was sent with presents of horses, oxen, or sheep as marriage gifts. The son-in-law then returned to the wife's family, where everyone offered salutations to him ;

but none were offered by him to the parents. After serving in the family for one or two years, he was escorted back with liberal gifts. The house and outfit belonged to the wife, who had her own separate property, and was consulted on all points except matters of war : hence the custom of counting genealogies from the mother's side. Father and son, males and females, all squatted about without ceremony in each other's presence, and cut the hair short for convenience sake ; but when a marriageable age was attained the hair was allowed to grow, and was parted and done up into a top-knot, over which a gay bonnet with pendants was worn. " They watch " when the bird and beasts bring forth, in order to time them- " selves to the seasons, and to judge from the cry of certain " birds when it is time to plant the grain. The land grows " millet of various kinds, and also a kind of rank grass with " a fruit like the mallow, which ripens at the end of November. " They make a sort of small beer, but have to get Chinese " yeast for making fermented spirits. They manufacture " bows, arrows, saddles, and bridles ; fashion metals into " weapons, etc., whilst the women work patterns into leather, " weave cloths, and press felts. They have no knowledge " of acupuncture or drugs : sick people are treated with " the moxa, or by bleeding, the application of heated stones " or earth, invocations to the unseen powers, and so on. " It is considered noblest to die in battle. Corpses are " enshrouded and placed in coffins. After death, lamenta- " tions are made ; but singing and dancing take place at the " funeral, when the horse, clothes, and ornaments used by " the deceased are all burnt, together with fattened dogs " brought as presents and led along by gay cords, in order " that they may go with him : the dogs are considered of " special importance, as they are supposed to conduct the " soul back to the Red Mountain, which is several thousand " *li* north-west of Liao Tung " [say 1,000 miles by ordinary road, which would place it in Barin or Korchin Land]. " On " the day of the funeral the relatives and intimates assemble

" at night-time and sit in a circle. The dogs and horses are
" led past the seated people, whilst one or two of the weepers
" or singers throw food to them, and two men pronounce an
" incantation, so that the soul may pass, unmolested by
" ghouls, to the Red Mountain : then horses, dogs, and clothes
" are burnt. They have great awe of ghosts and spirits.
" They worship Heaven, Earth, the sun, moon, planets,
" mountains, valleys, and such deceased chieftains as have
" left a valiant name behind ; burnt sacrifices of oxen and
" sheep are made to them. A thank-offering is always made
" before eating or drinking. By their customary laws death
" is the penalty for disobeying a head chief's commands,
" or for persistent robbery. Tribes avenge their own murders,
" and if the feud goes on indefinitely the head chief is asked
" to arrange it. Oxen and sheep are accepted from the
" offender as composition for life taken. It is no crime to
" kill a father or elder brother. Deserters or rebels captured
" by the head chief are, if no tribe will receive them, relegated
" to a place of limbo in a sandy desert, full of snakes, north-
" east of the nomads of Kuldja and south-west of the Kankalis."

The hordes decreased in numbers and power after the
conquests of the conqueror Baghdur, and they had to pay
to the Hiung-nu a regular tribute in oxen, horses, and sheep ;
if this tribute was not ready by due date, their wives and
children were carried off. But after the great Chinese victories
over the Hiung-nu in B.C. 120 (pp. 27–28), the Wu-hwan
were removed to what is now the northern part of Chih Li
province between Kalgan, Dolonor, Jêhol, and Moukden,
where they served the Chinese as scouts and as a sort of
" buffer " state. The head chieftain or chieftains used to
come to the Chinese court once a year. A Chinese political
resident (cf. p. 41) was appointed with the double duty of
superintending their administration and preventing their
communicating with the Hiung-nu, very much as the Manchu
amban in Tibet in our own time used to keep an eye upon
the doings of that hierarchy. Between B.C. 86 and 73 the

Wu-hwan so gained in strength that, as has been related
(p. 34), they dug up the tombs of the Jenuyes in order to
avenge the wrongs done to their race by Baghdur. The result
was that they were worsted, and the Chinese, we have seen,
took the opportunity to administer a further kick when they
were down. Their raiding attempts met with little success,
and they gradually fell back upon the Wall and gave in their
adhesion to China. This is about all we know of their history
and doings up to the beginning of our era.

When the usurper Wang Mang (pp. 54, 57) was preparing his
gigantic expedition for the annihilation of the Hiung-nu,
he sent a general—the same one who remonstrated with him
on account of the impracticability of his scheme—to march
up the Wu-hwan fighting men too : their wives and families
were left in charge of the different prefectural governments
adjoining the tribes as hostages. The Wu-hwan soon got
tired of waiting, and moreover disliked the change of climate
and the prospect of a long campaign in an unknown country :
they broke into revolt and took to plundering, in consequence
of which all the hostages were butchered in cold blood. This
threw the majority of the tribal chiefs once more upon the
Hiung-nu, and naturally gave rise to an implacable feeling
of hostility against China, upon whose frontiers they made
raids in company with the other Tartar power. Growing
daily stronger, they drove their rivals away north of the
Desert ; and, when the founder of the Second or After Han
dynasty sent an expedition against them (A.D. 45), the Chinese
got distinctly the worst of it. However, by means of bribes of
high-sounding titles and presents of food and clothing, they
were gradually induced (A.D. 49) to settle quietly along
the line of the Wall from North Shan Si, past modern Peking,
to the frontiers of Corea : here they were employed on scout
duty as before, both against the Hiung-nu and against another
branch of their own race called the Sien-pi, as to whom more
anon. A political resident was once more appointed to reside
at a point not very far from Kalgan, and a scheme was drawn

up for their orderly administration by Pan Piao,—the old
statesman (p. 66) who composed such a cunning letter in order
to trim with the two rival Jenuyes. During the next hundred
years or so nothing very important occurred ; there were
raids, quarrels, civil wars, alliances, intrigues with and against
the Hiung-nu, rebellions, and migrations ; but nothing of
sufficient importance to make an era : no great man appeared
among them to bring their latent power into focus : in fact,
they never achieved a great position at all apart from their
kinsmen the Sien-pi, whom we shall now proceed to consider.

CHAPTER II

THE EMPIRE OF THE SIEN-PI CONQUEROR, DARDJEGWE

AFTER the breaking-up of the old Tung-hu commonwealth
by the great Baghdur, the Sien-pi, like the Wu-hwan,
took refuge amongst the mountains of Eastern Mongolia,
and also derive their name from the range of hills which they
occupied. They were north-east of and bordering upon
the Wu-hwan, and seem to have settled in the rolling steppes
west of the River Liao and south of the Sira Muren. The
language and their customs, with slight variations, were the
same as the language and customs of the Wu-hwan. A
speciality of theirs, however, was the shaving of the head
just before marriage. This operation, which seems to refer
to the youths only, took place at the great assembly held in
the third month of spring, about May, when there were feasting
and merry-making on the river-bank, and when marriage
matches were arranged. They also had a meeting in the
eighth moon, when they all rode thrice round a coppice, or
round a bunch of twigs symbolical thereof, and took stock
of the animals as they went past. They possessed certain

animals unknown to China, such as the wild horse, the horned sheep or argali, and the musk-ox, of the horns of which they made bows. [When Genghis Khan was marching upon India he came across one of these animals and abandoned his purpose on account of the evil omen : possibly he was startled or affected at seeing an animal known as he thought only to his native land.] The Sien-pi also possessed the beaver, the sable, and the marmot, the beautiful furs of which were famous the world over and made splendid coats,—as they do now. It is very distinctly stated that they never had any relations with China until A.D. 45. A little time before this they had accompanied the Hiung-nu and the Wu-hwan in their avenging raids upon the Empire; but the Chinese, who were then gaining influence in Kokorai or North Corea, inflicted a severe defeat upon them ; and after that they were occasionally employed to cut off the heads of their former allies, and used to proceed to the Liao Tung proconsulate to receive their rewards. [Here they would probably meet with the tribute-bearing Japanese, who were now heard of in China for the first time, and with whom, as we shall shortly see, the Sien-pi had interesting economical relations. In fact, we are distinctly told that the Japanese chiefs and petty kings of peninsular Corea came to offer their respects at the proconsular court of the identical general who severely defeated the Sien-pi as above related. Japan, whose pretensions to antiquity are utterly fictitious so far as any imperial history previous to our era is concerned, was then a congeries of minute semi-barbarous states, each under a petty chief. Corea was somewhat in the same condition, but distinctly in advance of Japan. The southernmost parts of Corea were still inhabited by a few Japanese, who, so far from having ever, as they pretend, conquered parts of Corea, seem to have been driven out of Corea in prehistorical times by Corean tribes emanating from what we now call South Manchuria. The ancestors of the Nüchên Tartars of the 11th century and of the present Manchus (mere tribes of the same race) were the lowest of all in the scale of civilization. They occupied the land north of Corea, east of the Sien-pi, south of the Amur River, and west of the ocean. They were a filthy race of pig-breeding savages, living in holes and feeding on raw meat : yet they were famous pirates and hunters, and used to make boat raids upon the Corean sea-board. The history of Manchuria, Corea, and Japan does not form part of our present scheme, and it is sufficient therefore parenthetically to mention their existence and dismiss them from further notice.]

After the crushing defeat inflicted by the Empress' nephew upon the Northern Hiung-nu and the consequent disappearance of their Jenuye, the Sien-pi entered into occupation of his abandoned land : there were still 100,000 Hiung-nu tents left behind, and these in order to secure peace styled themselves Sien-pi. This incident shows how easily the nomad races coalesced. In very remote times, if we are to judge by the construction of their languages, the Hiung-nu and Tunguses must have shot off from one main stock, and at the time of which we are treating there seems to have been much less difference between the habits and customs of the two than between the habits of the Sien-pi and the ancestors of the Nüchên-Manchus, the identity of whose language in its main features with that of the Sien-pi's descendants the Solons even the Emperors of the late Manchu dynasty were able to perceive. It may assist us to picture to ourselves less incorrectly the effect of a battle in those times when we reflect what was the condition of England and France, both as to ruling caste, basis of population, and language during the time of our Plantagenets, when provinces and even countries were bandied about indiscriminately from day to day, and where it was often difficult to say where an individual Englishman ended and a Frenchman began, though as a whole the two sets of people were always clearly distinct.

As the Southern Jenuyes grew weaker and the Northern Jenuyes disappeared, their place on the Chinese frontier as formidable enemies was gradually taken by the Sien-pi.

Notwithstanding this general result, there was continually a triangular duel going on, instigated by the Chinese, between the two rival nomad powers, between one subdivision and the other of the same power, or between this subdivision of one power and that of the other. It would be unprofitable to attempt to follow out the clue to these intrigues throughout a whole century. Each reader can picture the same general group of details for himself. Quarrels of rival chiefs, raidings of the frontier, murders, slavery, waste, destruction, bribes, titles, and patched-up peace. Such was the wearisome reiteration until the appearance of the great Dardjegwe. During the absence for three years of a certain Sien-pi chieftain amongst the Hiung-nu, his wife gave birth to a son. The chief naturally had (to use the language of Falstaff) his own opinion as well as the mother's word as to who the father was, and wished to kill the brat at once. But the mother managed to prevail upon her husband,—by concocting a miraculous story in explanation of her conception,—to allow a servant to rear the child, who as he grew up, displayed, in an extraordinary degree, alike bravery, strength, and intellectual capacity. At the age of 15 he distinguished himself by his courage and energy in recovering single-handed some cattle and sheep belonging to his maternal relatives which the chief of another tribe had lifted and driven to a distance. After this he drew up a system of prohibitory laws, and no one ventured to question the wisdom of his judicial decisions. The consequence was he was soon elected chief. He established his capital or headquarters in the extreme north of modern Shan Si, probably at or not far from the capital of the former Southern Jenuyes, who disappear from history at this time. Chiefs from all sides flocked to his banner, and his armies soon became very numerous. He drove back the Kankalis in the north, the northernmost Coreans in the east, attacked the nomads of Kuldja in the west, and soon possessed himself of the ancient Hiung-nu dominions in their entirety. His empire extended over 4,000 English miles from east to west, and rather more than half that from north to south.—Gibbon, in his 26th chapter, says that, after their defeat by the Sien-pi, the first of the Hun [by which he means Hiung-nu] colonies settled in Sogdiania, bearing the epithet of " Euthalites or Nephthalites," and being called the White Huns from the change in their complexion produced by intermarriages : Gorgo or Carizme was their capital. All this (which Gibbon himself must have copied from the French Jesuits Du Halde and others) has been of late years repeated by various writers not acquainted with their subject at first hand. We have already shown (p. 24) that the Hephthalites, largely through the instrumentality of whose king Kanishka and his successors Buddhism was introduced into China, were the ancient Yüeh-chï, whom the Hiung-nu drove west three centuries before Dardjegwe came into existence. The Huns are, according to Gibbon, first mentioned in Europe by Dionysius of Charax in the year 330 ; and as the Sien-pi empire endured until the year 200, and the Hiung-nu name practically disappeared (p. 72) after that date as a nomad power, it is reasonable to suppose that the Hiung-nu, who disappeared from China in or before the year 200, might have been the Huns who appeared in Europe in the year 300, and who, or some of whom, after a career of little over a century in Europe, presumably made the best of their way back to Asia, where we may afterwards be able to identify them with various sub-tribes of the Western Turks. Indeed, even in Manchu times, a horde of Eleuths made their way from the Tarbagatai region to the Volga without the Chinese knowing anything about it ; and when, in 1755, the Emperor K'ien-lung broke up the Eleuth empire, this same horde, known as the Turguts, secretly made its way back to the Manchu reconquered land, and was comfortably quartered in 1771 on the Yulduz River, where they still are.—But this is another story.

Dardjegwe now became an object of serious uneasiness to China, as he went on annexing mountains, valleys, marshes, and salt-flats with insatiable appetite. The Chinese Emperor who reigned from A.D. 146 to 167 sent a resident-general with the Hiung-nu Jenuye and a considerable force to march against him. (This is not the same event as that already mentioned under the heading of the Hiung-nu (p. 71) in which the Jenuye perished.) Seeing that force did not avail, the Chinese had recourse to other devices, and an envoy was sent to confer a seal and ribbon upon Dardjegwe, together with the rank of prince. But he was totally indifferent to Chinese titles of honour, and, preferring to rely upon his own strong right arm, set to work raiding more vigorously than ever. Following the old Hiung-nu precedent, he portioned out his empire into three divisions, but very unequal ones. The easternmost part embraced the greater part of modern Manchuria to the sea; but the northern Coreans, who held a great part of Liao Tung, seem to have always maintained their independence of his rule, though perhaps driven out of their old home on the Upper Liao. The central division seems to have been the ancient Tungusic land between the Liao, the Sira Muren, and the Great Wall. The western division extended to Kuldja. There were in all fifty settlements or tribal encampments in these three divisions, of which the central contained ten and the other two each twenty. One of the chiefs of the central division bore the name of Mujung, which, as will be explained in due course, was subsequently the clan name of a powerful semi-Chinese dynasty,—though its simple origin as a chief's name was forgotten in favour of other fanciful and far-fetched derivations, such as the name of the peculiar hat worn by the clan ; the reverence of the chief for Heaven, etc., etc. In the same way one of the western division chiefs whose son's name was Shamo Khan, seems not only to have been the ancestor of the famous Toba dynasty which afterwards ruled North China for several centuries, but to have first used the title " Khan," which, though later much used by the Turks in its form of " Khakhan," at any rate originated with the Tunguses in its earlier form, though perhaps not positively with Shamo Khan, the whole three syllables of which name may be a personal appellation.

Dardjegwe went on consolidating his rule, and the dozen or so of generalissimos who acted as his governors or viceroys were kept well under his thumb. He continued to raid China without mercy, not a year passing but what there was an attack of some sort. At last in A.D. 177 the Chinese and the Southern Hiung-nu organized a grand expedition and marched out 600 miles to fight with Dardjegwe ; but, as has already been stated (pp. 71, 94), with disastrous results, ninety per cent both of men and horses losing their lives, or at any rate never returning home. The Sien-pi population went on increasing at such a rapid rate that Dardjegwe began to find the proceeds of hunting, the increment of his flocks and herds, and his scant harvests insufficient wherewith to feed them. The Japanese had already obtained a high reputation in China proper for their expertness in fishing and diving. He therefore imported over a thousand families of Japanese, and set them to work as fishermen in one of the lakes of Eastern Mongolia, which was 100 miles in circuit and which was known to be full of fish, though the indigenous population were unable to take them. At this time the purely Chinese name " Japan " was totally unknown, and the people who four centuries later appropriated that name (meaning " Rise of the Sun ") were then called Wo, which seems to mean " crooked men " or " dwarfs " : one authority uses a character meaning " dirty " or " muddy." It is said that Dardjegwe attacked the country in order to obtain these people. The story seems a very strange one, but it is related very positively, and it is also added that the families in question remained with their descendants round the lake, if not in perpetuity, then at least for several centuries, that is up to the 5th century, when the After Han History was written. One remarkable feature in connection with the Sien-pi is alluded to by the Chinese statesmen of the time, and that is that, besides being able and vigorous, they were intelligent and possessed of " growing ideas." This feature seems to have characterized the Tungusic nations, in contrast with the Turks, from the beginning of history until now, and no more illustrious examples could be adduced than the first four Emperors of the recent Manchu dynasty. Even in warfare, in the efficacy of their weapons, and in the speed of their horses, it was conceded that the Sien-pi were ahead of the Hiung-nu.

Dardjegwe's successors were by no means up to his mark. He died at the early age of forty-five, somewhere about the year A.D. 190, and was succeeded by his son Ghoren, who, besides being a man of mediocre capacity, was avaricious, lewd, and unjust in his judicial decisions, in consequence of which the half of his people were soon in revolt against him. He was assassinated by some obscure enemy. Then followed family disputes ; a nephew named Buduken finally succeeded to the diminished horde, whilst a brother named Vuloghan separated from the main body and marched off with his own party to seek new pastures. A sub-chief of one of the tribal divisions now began to assert himself, and, before very many years had passed, this man, whose name was Kopinêng, had got rid of both brothers, and by his activity, bravery, disinterestedness, and just decisions had secured his own election. From first to last this elective feature, in contra-distinction to the hereditary claims of the Hiung-nu and Turks, has always been a characteristic of the Sien-pi and of the Cathayans their successors. Kopinêng amongst other attain-ments had acquired a fair knowledge of the Chinese written character, and thus he was able to conduct his administration much after the Chinese fashion. At this time the Second or After Han dynasty was tottering to its fall, and large numbers of Chinese, in order to escape the anarchy prevailing in the empire, and the tyranny and conscription of rival aspirants, deserted to Kopinêng ; they taught his people how to manufacture a new style of weapons, coats of mail, shields, and other useful things. Kopinêng erected his standard wherever he happened to go on his hunting expedi-tions, and manoeuvred his men in the field by the sound of the drum. The formality of election or confirmation under the standard and the drum is frequently mentioned in later times in connection with both Turks and Cathayans. Still, Kopinêng was nothing like the equal of Dardjegwe, after whose death the Sien-pi Empire may be said to have fallen to pieces. Kopinêng got to fighting with his brother Suli, and also with some of the eastern chiefs of his race, notably with Shamo Khan, the one whom we suppose (p. 94) to have been one of the progenitors of the celebrated Toba family. There was another chief named Tatur, who made a bid for supreme power at this time, and even presumed to compare himself with the great conqueror Baghdur. But Tatur, which seems also to have been a tribal name, was utterly defeated by the renowned Ts'ao Ts'ao (p. 72), virtual founder of the (Chinese) Wei dynasty; he would hardly deserve the distinction of bare mention did it not seem in some measure likely that he and his tribe are really the origin of the not much later word Tatar, which again seems, in some circuitous way (the connecting links of which are not all forthcoming), to refer to that tribe—or one of those tribes—which in after generations formed the nucleus of the great Mongol power. We find the "White Tartars" mentioned in the 12th century near Marco Polo's Tenduc, the same spot where in the 6th and 7th chapters of our first book (pp. 69 and 78) we have found the "White Tribe" of the Sien-pi. The popular name in North China for both Mongols and Manchus is Ta-tsz,—a diminutive of Ta-ta; and the History of the Ming Dynasty (1368–1644) roundly calls the Mongols T'a-t'a throughout.

Though the early Tunguses proved in the long run far superior in every lasting quality to their rivals the Hiung-nu, yet in the first stage of their history, with the short exception of Dardjegwe's brilliant but not very detailed reign, they were unable to make anything like the political show that the Hiung-nu had made. Like the Germans and the Saxons, their democratic principles were irreconcilable with unity and empire, until the operation of external circumstances and a blending of foreign blood and manners worked a change.

The Turks have had their chance as Chinese Emperors, but they are now discredited as rulers everywhere : they have done little political good to the world at any time ; but the Wei dynasty of Tobas (386–550) were really a very respectable semi-Chinese dynasty : the Cathayans and the Nüchêns at least knew how to assert themselves, whilst the once obscure and petty tribe of Manchus has given China the best dynasty she ever had.

CHAPTER III

Sien-pi Adventurers become King and Emperors in North China

WE have seen that the Sien-pi towards the end of the second century were in possession of the whole of the ancient Hiung-nu Empire. Consequently they occupied the valleys of the rivers Chui, Tula, Kerulon, Orkhon, and the elevated tract of Hangai,—a second roof of the world, whence the Tartar races have always been engendered, even as the Aryan races are supposed to have emerged in swarms from the heights of Bactria and the Pamir. Three wandering tribes of Sien-pi having made their way from the north of the Desert, the story goes that a foundling was picked up on the road by an old man of the Kivugh tribe, and, developing great qualities, was elected chief with the title of " Kivugh Khakhan tokdogh." The last word is said to mean " neither god nor man." They settled about A.D. 265 in the east of modern Kan Suh, and after several generations numbered quite 100,000 tents. At that time Shih Lêh had just extinguished the rival Hiung-nu power of Liu Ts'ung's successor Liu Yao, and was extending his empire westwards. The Kivugh tribe threw themselves under the protection of the Tangut house (pp. 76–8), which was then engaged in endeavouring to establish an empire in the west of China : the founder of this house

had been a general under Shih Lêh (p. 78). The Tangut
Emperor or " Heavenly Prince " conferred upon the Kivugh
chieftain the title of Southern Jenuye ; and, when the ruling
house of Tsin in China inflicted a tremendous and historical
defeat upon the Tangut monarch in the northern part of An
Hwei province, the Kivugh family established themselves
as kings of Western Ts'in and reigned for 46 years. The
world-renowned Chinese traveller Fah Hien (p. 78) on his
way to Affghanistan and India passed through the Kivugh
kingdom, having started from Ch'ang-an in A.D. 399 or 400.
It may be mentioned that, when at Peshawur, Fah Hien
discovered several relics of Kanishka (B.C. 15 to A.D. 45) and
the other Nephthalites. After passing through the Kivugh
country Fah Hien traversed another Sien-pi kingdom, that of
Tufa, which is almost certainly the same word etymologically
as Toba : in any case it is conclusively proved that the Tufa
kings of Southern Liang and the Toba Emperors of North
China descended from the same Sien-pi ancestor. The Tufas
settled in the west about A.D. 270, but it was not until 397
that they became a power. Their chief also assumed the
ancient title of Great Jenuye ; but, after some fighting with
the Tsugu family mentioned in a previous chapter (p. 77),
the Tufa were absorbed by the Kivugh, who again were crushed
by the Tanguts and by the Hiung-nu house of Kheren,
" Heaven," or Ghoren Borbor (p. 77). The words Tufa and
Toba have, like the word Mujung, various fanciful derivations,
such as "bald heads," "born in the sheets," etc., etc. But
they are probably an eponymous chief's name.

Far away to the east there was another tribe of Sien-pi
called Jumen, who had settled in Liao Tung in the year 317.
Their capital was near the modern Liao-yang. There seems
to be some doubt whether this tribe was of pure race ; for
their own history, when they became Emperors of North China
two centuries later, connects them with the Southern Jenuyes ;
and when, 700 years later, a branch of their family, called
Ghei, united with the Cathayans to form a great empire,

it was found that, though otherwise much the same as the
Cathayans, their language was different. However that may
be, when they were still a mere tribe, it was clearly stated of
them that their language differed considerably from that
of the other Sien-pi, and they were remarkable for cutting
off all their hair except a small tuft in the crown. [This,
it may be remarked, is not unlike the modern Corean practice,
at least as it existed in 1887.] The women, too, wore a long
gown reaching to the feet, but no other nether garments.
The second chief became so powerful that he dreamt of contesting power with the great Mujung family; but he and his
successors were defeated in battle after battle, and, after
flying to the north of the desert, at last took refuge in Corea.
The horde, numbering 50,000 tents, was settled by the
victorious Mujungs, near the modern Jêhol; but they soon
scattered and disappeared from history, except, as mentioned,
in the shape of one or two able individuals who, as generals,
carved out a high position for themselves. One of them
conducted an army of 300,000 men to Corea, and his son
murdered the foolish Sui dynasty Emperor who made the
vain attempt to conquer that country at the beginning of
the 7th century.

Another Sien-pi family which came into notice was that of
Twan. The first of the line was slave to a Wu-hwan chief.
At an assembly of leading men when each official—as was
and presumably is still the custom in Corea—carried his
spittoon with him, the master of our hero, who seems to have
forgotten his utensil, used his slave's mouth for that purpose.
This indignity (or this honour, for it is uncertain in which
sense it was taken) seems to have inspired the slave with
ambition to outshine his master. During a famine he was
sent on a mission in search of food, and took the opportunity
to swell his troop of men with all the discontented vagabonds
he could lay hold of. In time his nephew and successor had
50,000 horse-archers under him, and the Chinese house of
Tsin (265–420), on the look-out everywhere for allies, gave

him a seal as Great Jenuye and Duke of Liao Si. One of the family named Twan Pirte had a struggle with the Hiung-nu adventurer Shih Lêh (p. 76), and for some time held possession of modern Peking. In the long run this family, known as the Twans of the River T'u (in modern Kin-chou Fu), was broken up by the rival Sien-pi house of Mujung, and a large number of their adherents were butchered in a body. It is to be noted that during this troublous period a Tibetan named Lü Kwang, who finally set up a dynasty in Liang [Marco Polo's Eriguiul] for a short time, brought with him a large amount of property from Kuche, upon which state he had first had designs. Kuche was a settled and civilized semi-Indian kingdom, and a great Buddhist centre. Kumâradjîva and other notable bonzes came to China thence.

One of the most illustrious of the Sien-pi houses was that of Mujung, which settled in Liao Si about the year 220. There are all sorts of fanciful derivations for this word; but, as we have just seen, Mujung was during Dardjegwe's time the name of a chief; and, as the Chinese historians state, the only clan names used by this people were those derived from the personal names of valorous chiefs; so that we may reject fanciful traditions. The first of the family served the Ts'ao Ts'ao Wei dynasty (p. 73) with credit, and was made a prince. He fixed his headquarters in the modern Tumet Mongol country. His grandson was created Jenuye of the Sien-pi, and, removing to Liao Tung, gradually took to and became imbued with Chinese ideas. Owing to a quarrel about pasture, Tukuhun or Tuyühun, the elder son of this grandson, migrated westwards to the Koko-nor region, where he (p. 85) founded a powerful state. The younger, Mujung Hwei, who was a man of great talent, remained in charge of the ancestral horde, and in the year 289 moved to the neighbourhood of the River T'u. But he soon began to yearn after the old home in the Tumet country, to which accordingly he returned in 294. Here he instructed his people in the arts of agriculture and silk raising, encouraged Chinese to migrate to his dominions, and by the excellence of his administrative system soon attracted vast numbers of persons who had become disgusted with the misrule of the Chinese house of Tsin. He assumed the Hiung-nu title of Great Jenuye ; for, as has been related (p. 85), the Sien-pi in ancient times never had any supreme ruler, and never seem to have independently conceived the idea of one, or to have had a word of their own to express it. At the same time this Mujung Hwei faithfully paid tribute to the house of Tsin, whose learned men he used to invite to his court. His son Mujung Hwang was also a very able ruler and intrepid captain. In the year 317 the Second or Eastern Tsin dynasty, unable to make headway against the Tartars, removed its capital across the Yangtsze to the modern Nanking. Mujung Hwang now styled himself Prince of Yen (the country round Peking), and in the year 345 abandoned the Tsin calendar,—which means that he used independent reign-dates of his own. Accordingly he is considered the founder of the Yen dynasty, which lasted till the year 407, and for some time had its new capital at the Ting Chou of to-day in the province of Chih Li. It will be remembered (p. 76) that the reigning Hiung-nu family of Shih were all butchered by an adoptive heir,—this adoptive heir changed his dynastic style from Chao to Wei, but was defeated and put to death by the Mujungs, who now declared themselves Emperors. There were at this time three empires, the Chinese Tsin in the south, the Tangut Ts'in in the west (p. 78), and the Sien-pi Yen in the north. In 367 the latter occupied the second of the ancient Chinese capitals now known as Ho-nan Fu. After various vicissitudes, shiftings, subdivisions, and defeats, the last branch of the family called Southern Yen came to an end : its capital in modern Shan Tung province was taken by the founder of the new Chinese Sung dynasty (420–473), and the defeated monarch Mujung Ch'ao was executed at Nanking. There is one fact worthy of notice in connection with this Mujung dynasty : they are said to have compelled their kinsmen the Cathayans and the Ghei (p. 99) to take refuge between the Sungari River and the Desert, whence they emerged a few centuries later to form a dynasty of their own.

The most successful Sien-pi house was that of Toba, which in historical times found itself west of the Jumen tribe (p. 99) between Peking and Ta-t'ung Fu, and westwards of that again. In A.D. 315, Ilu, chief of that one of the three Toba tribes which was farthest west, was created by the Tsin house of China Prince of Tai (i.e. the country near Ta-t'ung Fu) for his services against the Hiung-nu and the White Tribe of Sien-pi : at the same time he was supplied with a proper staff of officials. His grandnephew Zibigen was the first to introduce a reign-period of his own : this prince had as many as 500,000 Tartars under his command. His grandson Shifkwi was the first actual Emperor of the distinguished dynasty of Northern Wei, which existed contemporaneously with the mushroom Chinese Empires of the south in an unbroken line of fifteen Emperors, mostly very capable men, from 386 to 535. The capital was at first at Ta-t'ung Fu and afterwards at Loh-yang (Ho-nan Fu). The first two Emperors had to share the north of China with the Mujung line of Sien-pi Emperors of Yen to the east, the Tangut lines of Ts'in and After Ts'in to the west, and the Hiung-nu or Ghoren line of Ordous, which last was extinguished in 428 by the Tukuhun Sien-pi of Koko-nor (p. 101). A singular custom is mentioned as being an invariable rule with the Tobas, that of murdering the Empress so soon as ever her son was officially declared heir-apparent. Doubtless this was part and parcel of the old Sien-pi custom of counting genealogies solely by the mother's venter. It was also the custom to cast a molten image of a proposed Empress or heir-apparent in order to see if, by a successful cast, the augury was good. The second Toba Emperor is described as having been yellow-bearded, which suggests an admixture of Corean blood, and militates against the supposition that the smooth-faced modern Mongols have Sien-pi blood in them.

In the year 423 the Tobas built another length of Great Wall, about 700 miles in extent, not marked upon the maps, but apparently running north and south almost along the line of the Kan Suh and Shen Si frontiers : their object was to protect themselves against a powerful tribe called the Jeujen (p. 112), then struggling for supremacy with the Kankalis. The third Toba Emperor Vuri (423–451) absorbed the Tsugu ruler's dominion of the Liang principality (439), and also the Mujung empire in the east : he was besides frequently at war with the Chinese Sung Empire in the south. It is to be noted that the principality of Liang had become about this time a highly civilized centre, having extensive relations with Turkestan. The Tobas themselves sent envoys to Tashkend. The same Emperor encouraged the study of the Confucian doctrine and persecuted the Buddhists, whose temples were becoming, under the cloak of religion, dens of lewd vagabonds. The Toba armies swept like a devastating avalanche over the modern province of An Hwei during this reign, and even reached the River Yangtsze opposite modern Chin Kiang. About 460 a new calendar was introduced with the assistance of learned men from the old principality of Liang. In 483 the Tobas, now rapidly becoming Chinese in sentiment, followed the Chinese practice, and publicly interdicted marriages between people possessing the same clan name. In 495 the Tartar costume was prohibited : also the use of the Tartar language, weights, standards, and measures. The old dynastic name of Toba had been replaced in 476 by the Chinese word Yüan,—the same as that adopted by Kublai Khan 780 years later. The Emperor was able to draft his own decrees in Chinese, and ordered a rigorous search for books of antiquity. The question of clan names for his own people received attention, and every Toba seems to have had now what we call in English a surname. Six surnames or clan names were set apart as being particularly aristocratic, probably in imitation of the four old Jenuye and Hiung-nu aristocracy clans. Some Toba Emperors patronized one form of religion and some another, but in 518 an envoy was sent to Gândhâra or Candahar to obtain Buddhist books. The custom of murdering Empresses on the recognition of one of their sons as heir was now relaxed or abandoned, and a Chinese-born Sien-pi Tartar named Gholughun began to intrigue for the succession against the Tobas. This was the famous Shên-wu Ti, who died in 549 : his son founded the Northern Ts'i dynasty in 550. It was apparently from his father's posthumous title that the imitative Japanese applied the name Zimmu to one of their mythical emperors : they would of course hear of Zimmu's, or *Shên-wu's*, fame through their countrymen engaged in fishing in Eastern Mongolia. In 543 the Eastern Tobas found themselves obliged to construct a second Great Wall in Shan Si, considerably farther south than the old Wall, to keep out the nomads, and in 545 they sent an embassy to the Turks, now first coming into notice as a powerful tribe, but still seated in the old Tsugu territory between Kan-chou and Lan Chou in Kan Suh province. The Wei dynasty had just (534–5) split up into two, i.e. the Western dynasty in the hands of one of the Jumens at Yung-p'ing Fu in modern Chih Li, and the Eastern dynasty in the hands of Gholughun at Loh-yang and Linchang Fu in Ho Nan. A few years later the sons of these two adventurers set themselves up as Emperors respectively of the Northern Chou and Northern Ts'i dynasties, the latter at Si-an Fu. Both were replaced by the brilliant but short-lived Chinese dynasty of Sui, which lasted from 581 to 618. Thus, it will be seen clearly, from what we have said above, the Sien-pi possessed the northern half of China as legitimate Emperors for 300 years, and previously to that had been already in practical possession, conjointly with the Hiung-nu and Tangut adventurers, for another hundred. In the year 555 the N. Ts'i dynasty employed 1,800,000 men to build a Great Wall from near modern Peking to Ta-t'ung Fu : this is the Wall which visitors to Peking usually see ; but it is 800 years less ancient than the true Great Wall of Mêng T'ien (p. 7). The last of the Toba Emperors got well across the Yangtsze River, in its upper parts, and Western Wei put an end to the Chinese dynasty of Liang in the year 555 ; the Liang capital was then at King Chou, between the treaty ports of Hankow and Ichang, [where the Manchus to the last (1911) still kept a Tartar garrison force]. Eleven years ago (1913) the Chinese Jesuit, the Rev. Mathias Tchang, published a most interesting work called *Tombeaux des Liang*, with beautiful illustrations showing the present ruins. For a short time the two rival Tartar dynasties had through their sub-emperors the whole of China in their nominal possession, each one having under it as vassal a puppet Chinese Emperor in the south. The N. Ts'i Emperor massacred the whole of the royal house of Toba (numbering 721 persons) except one, and it is perhaps from this barbarous example that the custom of rooting out the heirs of each dethroned dynasty took possession of the Chinese mind : the Manchus, however, not only spared, but generously kept up the Tombs of the Ming dynasty. In 577 the N. Chou Emperor captured his rival's capital, and in turn massacred the whole of his family stock. The founder of the Sui dynasty once more butchered the whole of the N. Chou ruling race, and thus ends what may be called the first act in the drama of Tungusic Tartar rule in China. The northern branch of the Sien-pi falls under the Turkish yoke, to reappear in the 10th century as a great power under the name of Cathayans, whose modern representatives, in the opinion of the Manchu Emperors, are the " Solon-Manchus," four *aimaks* of whom are permanently settled on the Khorgos River of Ili, and five banners of whom are still at Hurunpir in North Manchuria. The southern branch, as we shall now proceed to show, lived an entirely separated and isolated existence until it, so to speak, lost itself in the sands of the Desert, and dribbled under the Ouigour sovereignty ; but it never became imperial.

CHAPTER IV

The Tuyühun or Tukuhun Sien-pi of Koko-nor

MENTION has already been made (pp. 85, 101, 103) of the separation of Tukuhun from a younger brother who carried on the administration of the Mujung patrimony. This younger brother's name was Yoglogwe : the father's name was Shifkwi of the River T'u,—the same syllables, it will be noticed, as those employed in the name of the founder of the Toba dynasty (p. 103). Tukuhun said to his younger brother : — "If you get angry " with me because my horses happen to fight with " yours in the friskiness of spring, it is evident that we shall " not live together long without a quarrel, so I shall put a few " thousand miles between us." On this, in spite of his brother's repentant apologies, he moved west to North Shan Si, whence, during the troublous period accompanying the transition from the West (Loh-yang) to the East (Nanking) Tsin dynasty (p. 102), he again took his hordes further west to the region between the T'ao and the Yellow Rivers, just east of Koko-nor : here he founded a dominion which embraced the bleak region of Tsaidam (=depression) and even parts of North Sze Chuen. "Their land had always snow and ice at all four seasons of " the year, except in the 6th and 7th moons, when there were " terrific hail-storms. When it was fine, the wind blew " hurricanes of sand and small stones. There was wheat " [or barley] but no rice. There is a small island in Koko-nor " and every year when the lake is frozen a number of fine " mares are driven onto the island : the foals are collected " the following winter. A number of splendid Persian " mares were obtained by the Tukuhun for this purpose, " and their young obtained great repute for swiftness as

" Koko-nor colts ". The grandson of Tukuhun resolved to use his ancestor's personal name as a clan name for the nation, in accordance with what he termed ancient Sien-pi custom (cf. p. 99), and because he had been the first to migrate from the ancient seat of the race near Jêhol. The first five or six kings of the Tukuhun were men of education as well as administrative ability, which proves, once more, that the Sien-pi race was from the first susceptible to the better influence. All the ministers and commanders-in-chief were also men of reading. The sixth king annexed a very large extent of Tibetan territory, and took great pains to ascertain that one of the rivers in his dominions, after passing Pao-ning Fu and Chungking, entered the Yangtsze at the latter place, and then flowed through South China into the sea : accordingly he sent envoys to open a friendly correspondence with the Sung dynasty at Nanking. The seventh king attacked the Ghoren horde (pp. 77, 99) after the Tobas had driven them from the old Chinese metropolis, broke it up, and handed over the last of the dynasty to his victorious kinsman. The eighth king, however, was defeated by the third Toba Emperor, and, flying west, broke up the Khoten group of states, the tribes of Dabsun Nor, and others : for a time he even got as far as the Pamir, having the state of Cophene or Cabul to his south. This is a remarkable journey ; but, as we shall see, the Karakitai or Black Cathayans, also of the Sien-pi race, migrated as far as Kermané near Bokhara during the 12th century : buildings and other vestiges of this branch have of recent years been discovered in Persia by Sykes and other British specialists. Carpini visited them in 1245. The Tukuhun did not remain long as wanderers in the West ; after a few years they returned to their old settlements in the Koko-nor region. It would seem extremely probable that it was during this migration to Cabulistan that the Persian mares were obtained (p. 107). The customs of the Tukuhun are interesting :—" The ruler did up his hair in a knot, and " wore a cap of black set off with pearls. His wife wore a woven

" petticoat, over which an embroidered robe. On her head
" she wore golden flowers with a chignon behind. The men's
" dress was not unlike that of the Chinese, but most of them
" had a cap like a net : some had caps of silk. The women
" all bound the hair with strings of pearls, the number used
" being a mark of distinction. The weapons included bows,
" arrows, swords, spears, and bucklers. There were no
" regular taxes in the country, but when money was required
" the rich and the traders were called upon to furnish supplies.
" When fathers or elder brothers died, the sons or younger
" brothers married their stepmothers and sisters-in-law after
" the northern nomad fashion. The dead were buried with
" a funeral procession, but mourning clothes were removed
" when the ceremony was over. The national character was
" greedy and bloodthirsty."

About A.D. 500 the Tukuhun chief Kwaru assumed the
title of Khakhan, which, as has been stated, was first used
in the third century by the Kivugh family of Sien-pi (94, 99).
Kwaru reigned nearly a hundred years, and in his old age
received severe defeats at the hands of the Jumens of After or
N. Chou and the rising Chinese dynasty of Sui. His successors
abandoned the name of Tukuhun and resumed the ancestral
one of Mujung, which had become extinct a century ago so far
as political power went. The Sui Emperor induced the
Kankali Turks to surprise the Mujung hordes, who had to
take refuge somewhere in the south. For a short period
the whole Tukuhun realm (measuring, it is said, 1,300 miles
east and west and half that much north and south, embracing
the old Yüeh-chï country, Lob-nor, and Koko-nor) was in the
hands of the Sui house, who divided it up into administrative
districts, established posts, populated it with the criminal
classes, and endeavoured to assimilate it to regulation China.
But, after the fall of the short-lived Sui house, the Mujung
ruler, who had taken refuge with the Tibeto-Tartar tribes
west of Ordous, recovered his old dominions.

When the great Chinese T'ang dynasty was establishing

itself upon the ruins of Sui, the king of Ta-ning, as the Mujung
or Tukuhun ruler now styled himself, alternately assisted and
attacked the new empire; but in the year 635 the Chinese
generals inflicted a crushing defeat upon these nomads, whose
power now began to fall off in favour of the Tibetans. In
670 the Chinese, who were growing alarmed at the rapid
progress of the Tibetans (already a civilized power, versed
in Sanskrit literature), made an unsuccessful attempt to
re-establish the Tukuhun power, but the Tibetans conquered
the whole Tukuhun dominion and part of China's outlying
territory as well. The question was where to quarter the
broken up Tukuhun tribes, so as to keep them away from the
Turks on the one hand and not to let them get involved with
China's horse-breeding population in Kan Suh on the other. It
ended in their being quartered where they then were, in Kan-
chou, Suh-chou, and Sha-chou,—the old Yüeh-chï territory,
Polo's Campichu, Sachiu, Sukchur. But the Tibetans gave them
no peace, and the wretched remnants of them had to fight their
way across the Yellow River to Shan Si, whence their ancestors
had originally come, on their way far west, from Liao Tung.
Here the corrupted term T'ui-hun was applied to them, and,
indeed, they are often spoken of by Chinese historians as simply
Hwun or Hun. This syllable is the last one of Tukuhun's
personal name, and has nothing whatever to do with the old
word Hiung-nu; still less with the European word Hun.
The corruption T'ui-hun suggests that of the two original
pronunciations T'u-yü-hun is best justified, k or g being slurred
over in Turk-Mongol. In the year 798, one Mujung Fuh, in
Chinese employ, was appointed Prince of Koko-nor with the title
of Khakhan, and on his death the hereditary succession of the
family rulers ceased. From the commencement of their
kingdom at the close of the Western Tsin dynasty in A.D. 310,
to their dispossession by the Tibetans in 663, the Tukuhun
house of princes had endured for 350 years, and the tribe
was not entirely broken up for another 150 years. From this
time they disappear from Chinese history; but a Hwun or

Hun tribe is mentioned amongst the vassals of the Ouigours, so that we may well believe that this branch of the Sien-pi, having maintained its independence throughout the Turkish supremacy, at last became absorbed in the Kankali or Ouigour branch of the ancient Hiung-nu stock, and migrated to the north of the Desert.

BOOK III

THE EMPIRE OF THE JWEN-JWEN OR JEU-JEN

BOOK III

THE EMPIRE OF THE JWEN-JWEN OR JEU-JEN

CHAPTER I

THEIR OBSCURE RISE AND THEIR PRECIPITATE FALL

THE Jwen-jwen are described as having possessed the clan name of Ukuru Toba. When first heard of they were known as the Jeu-jen, which Gibbon, following the French writers upon China, writes Geougen : he identifies them with the Avars of Europe, which must be a complete mistake, for which, however, Gibbon himself is not responsible (pp. 125–6). They were a petty tribe vaguely described as being " of the northern wilderness," and there is nothing to show that they had any ethnological connection with the Tunguses except that, according to their semi-mythical traditions, they borrowed a Tungusic clan name : that was scarcely to be wondered at, seeing that the Hiung-nu power had long since given way to that of the Tunguses. The only positive statements about them are that they were a kind of Hiung-nu, and that their " astrological position "—that is, the latitude and longitude of their habitat—was coupled with that of the High Carts, Kankalis, or Ouigours, all of whom appear but very faintly in history, if they appear at all, previous to the establishment of Toba power, and all of whom certainly lived in the Baikal region north of the Desert. Tradition says that a young slave was captured during one of the Jeu-jen raids ; as he had forgotten his own name, he was given that of Mukkuru (Gibbon's Moko), which signifies " bald." This was on account of the peculiar way in which his hair grew, and *mukkuru* must have been a Jeu-jen word. During

the reign of the already mentioned (pp. 102–3) Toba Prince Ilu
of Ta-t'ung Fu, Mukkuru, who had on account of his valour
been made a free trooper, had rendered himself liable to
decapitation for not presenting himself in due time for military
service. He therefore fled with a number of others to the
Desert, where he managed to collect together a few hundred
vagabonds like himself. His son Cherugwei, being a warlike
individual, was the first to have under him anything deserving
the name of a horde, and this horde was styled Jeu-jen
(Gibbon's Geougen). It is only in the year 394 of our era
that we get any distinct information about this people ;
at least four generations having then elapsed since the word
Jeu-jen was first used, we may therefore safely assume that
the Mukkuru incident, like the Kivugh foundling incident
(p. 98), took place (so far as it took place at all) about the year
300, during that anarchical period when the Hiung-nu had
scattered, the Dardjegwe empire had fallen to pieces, and
Tanguts, Tunguses, and Hiung-nu were all alike disintegrated,
and endeavouring each to form a nucleus for a new growth.
In 394 the " sixth grandson," by which is probably meant
the seventh or eighth in descent from Mukkuru or Cherugwei,
crossed to the north of the Desert, and conquered many of
the Kankali tribes : hence, from the fact of his ancestors
having served Prince Ilu, who came forward prominently
in the year 315, we must suppose that the semi-mythical
tribe which picked up Mukkuru, and the Jeu-jen tribe, to
which Mukkuru's son first gave its name, were both settled
in the mountain hunting-ground which separates Shan Si
from the Desert, and that the " astrological position " was only
fixed after the migration north. This grandson, Shelun or
Zarun (whom Gibbon, misled by the French translators,
calls Toulun), soon organized a formidable military system ;
adopting the title of Khakhan, he put together an empire
which extended east and west from Corea to Harashar, and
south as far as the country of the Tukuhun and the modern
Kan Suh province. His courts were held at places north

of Kan-chou (probably near Marco Polo's Etzinai) and Tun-hwang (practically Polo's Sachiu) ; so that we may be sure all the roads but the main one to the west were in his hands. The Chinese say that this was the first occasion on which the title Khakhan was used, but it has been already shown that the Kivugh foundling had been so styled at least, even if he did not use the title, over a century earlier. Zarun's full title was " Kudovar Khakhan," meaning in the Toba Tungusic language "the governing and spreading Emperor." We are told that the word Mukkuru was changed to the very similar word Ukuru " later on," because Ukuru was the clan name of a Toba Empress who lived in the year 452. We are also told that the Toba Emperor who died in 451 changed their national appellation from Jeu-jen to Jwen-jwen, a Chinese word meaning " squirm," because they wriggled and squirmed about like so many vermin. Now, as Mukkuru was a fugitive from the Tobas in 315, and Zarun had carved out his own empire a century later, we may be sure that the clan name Ukuru Toba was given about the same time that Jeu-jen was changed to Jwen-jwen ; that is, when the imperial Tobas had made their power felt. Those writers who make the tribe one of the same family as the imperial Sien-pi have evidently been misled by the name Toba, which no more makes a Hiung-nu tribe Tungusic than the clan name of Liu (p. 65) makes it Chinese. North-west of Zarun's empire were the remains of the Hiung-nu, and they were all gradually annexed by him. This modest statement, which precedes the distinct limitation of his dominions in a westerly direction to the north of Harashar,—at the utmost Tarbagatai or Kuldja,—is evidently the ground for Gibbon's mistaken statement that he " vanquished the Huns to the north of the Caspian." We are also told that the Jwen-jwen custom was " for princes " and ministers to take titles or names corresponding to their " actions or abilities, like such as are given posthumously " in China, except that in the Jwen-jwen case the names " were used during life, and that no other names were given

" after death." This statement again tends to connect the Jwen-jwen with the Turks and Hiung-nu ; for, in addition to what has already been said about Hiung-nu names, we shall find that the Turks were all called after personal idiosyncrasies : thus the Western Turk, called by the Chinese Ta-lo-pien or " the fat," is, according to Schuyler's (doubtful) view, the Dalobian Khan or Dizabul to whom Justin the Second sent the envoy Zimarchus. Cervantes, in his *Don Quixote*, mentions this custom of *los Turcos*.

Zarun, having thus consolidated a sort of empire in the north, began to harry the frontiers of the Toba dynasty, now securely seated on the throne of North China. He was succeeded by his uncle or cousin Dadar, against whom in the summer of 429 the third Toba Emperor, whose Tartar name was Vuri, led an army of over 100,000 men. Dadar was taken completely by surprise, and, after setting fire to his own encampment or ordo, took to the Desert, leaving no trace behind : the various settlements of his people scattered in every direction, and vast flocks and herds were left to wander about uncared for all over the country. Dadar must have had his capital somewhere near Caracorum, for we are told that the Toba Emperor found himself 1,200 English miles from where the first Han Emperor (pp. 15–16) was surrounded by Baghdur, and that he passed the old camp of the Empress' nephew who nearly three centuries later (p. 70) defeated the Northern Jenuye : the Toba monarch then scoured the whole country for a distance of 1,500 miles east and west and 1,000 miles north and south, embracing all Mongolia between the Onon in the north-east and the Etzina in the south-west. The Kankalis took the opportunity to pay off old scores, which accumulation of worries in the end killed the fugitive Dadar. The total gains of the campaign to the Tobas were a million killed or captured in horses and men, and 300,000 voluntary surrenderers. The same Toba Emperor, after various feints with the son and successor, undertook a second campaign against Dadar's grandson Tughochir, and, in the usual vague language of

the Chinese, captured the whole of his tents and flocks to
the number of over a million. Tughochir's son continued
to trespass in 467–470, and it was then that the construction
of a fresh Great Wall over a distance of 300 miles in length
was proposed, the soldiers to be utilized, when they were not
fighting, as builders of it. The then Emperor conducted
a third expedition, cutting off 50,000 heads, taking 10,000
prisoners, besides innumerable horses and weapons, and
pursuing the enemy for nineteen days. It is not to be wondered
at that, after a series of such crushing defeats, the unfortunate
Jwen-jwen should try and effect an alliance with the southern
Chinese Empire, with a view to crushing the all-powerful
Tobas : advances were made in succession to the ephemeral
Nanking dynasties of Sung, Ts'i and Liang; but, it seems,
without any result. The Jwen-jwen were, however, not by
any means destroyed. In the year 516 Tughochir's grandson
Cheunu punished the rebellious Kankalis to the west, and again
raised his country to a considerable degree of power ; he
sent a s'ramana to offer a pearl image to the Toba Emperor.
Cheunu's younger brother Anakwe was unable to obtain the
succession without opposition, and had to seek refuge at the
Toba court, where he was well received, the Emperor admitting
a common ancestry, or at least a common place of origin.
A cousin bearing the Hindoo name of Brahman then took
charge of the horde, and punished Anakwe's enemies ; but
Brahman too had to surrender to the Toba Chinese governor
at Liang Chou (Polo's Erichew or Eriguiul), as he was hard
pressed by the Kankalis. The question was what to do with
them, and it is significant, as further evidence that they were
of Hiung-nu and not Sien-pi race, to find that the Emperor's
advisers warn him " not to have a repetition of the Liu Yüan
" and Shih Lêh events (pp. 65, 73), which led to those
" hospitably entertained settlers becoming rulers on their own
" account." The thinly populated lands around Tun-hwang,
Suh Chou, and Kan-chou (Marco Polo's Sachiu, Sukchur,
and Campichu) would be suitable (they said), only that the

Kankalis are too near. We must treat the rival nations as two dangerous beasts, encouraging them to damage each other as much as possible, and only stepping in when one or the other becomes immediately dangerous to ourselves. It was finally decided to quarter Brahman in the far west, at a spot which appears to be at or near the modern Hami or Hamil, and to supply him with a Chinese resident, nominally to assist in his government, but in reality to protect him and watch the Kankalis (whose capital of uncertain appellation in the Altaï Mountains was 300 miles distant), afterwards moving him to the north of the Desert when strong enough to protect himself. This was done ; but before long Brahman conspired to rebel, and was taken to China, where he subsequently died (520) ; he seems to have at first taken refuge with the Hephthalites, or with a nation which may well be the Avars. This is not unlikely, for the king of Ili had sent envoys to Dadar, and we have seen (pp. 43, 52) that even Hiung-nu princes took refuge in distant Samarcand. It is distinctly stated, however, that Brahman's three sisters married Hephthalite husbands.

Anakwe was settled somewhere " in the east " where he could not co-operate with Brahman. He assumed the title of Khakhan, and was made Duke of Shoh-fang (Polo's Tangut) and king of the Jwen-jwen by the Tobas, from which we may conclude that he was somewhere in or near the Ordous country. Here his family contracted marriage alliances with the Tobas and the Tartar dynasty of Ts'i. During the anarchy which accompanied the collapse of the Toba Wei dynasty, Anakwe was able to consolidate his power, and he discontinued the practice of calling himself vassal. He had Chinese literates in his employ, and a number of eunuch clerks : he established an official body, and presumed to claim an equality with the expiring Toba dynasty. In the year 546 his former vassals the Turks applied to Anakwe for a wife : his answer was to make war upon them : he was utterly defeated, and committed suicide : his heir Amrodjin fled to the new Ts'i empire founded by Ghologhun's son, and was quartered in North Shan Si, but, revolting soon afterwards, his horde was broken up. [The attempt of Hirth, approved by Chavannes, to connect this Anakwe with the Anagai of Valentine's mission to the Turks sent by Tiberius Cæsar in 576 can hardly be supported in point of date.] A cousin of Anakwe was now elected ruler, but after repeated defeats at the hands of the Turks he had to take refuge with the Jumen adventurer who was "running" the Emperor of Western Wei (p. 105). The Turkish Khakhan had now sufficient power to insist upon the butchery of the Jwen-jwen, who had with their king thus sought asylum, and this was done (555) either by or in the presence of the Turkish ambassador outside the gates of Si-an Fu, only the younger males being spared, to be passed into the princely and ducal families as slaves.

From this moment the Jwen-jwen are never so much as mentioned, even as a tribe under the Turks and Ouigours, and, as we have seen, their destruction was nearly complete before the remnants of them were massacred in the dastardly way recounted above. Hence it is impossible on this ground alone that they can be identical with the Avars who took the place in Hungary of the Huns, as Chavannes seems to believe. Gibbon's statement that Attila,—who died in 453, after his great defeat at Châlons,—vanquished the khan of the formidable Geougen and sent ambassadors to negotiate an equal alliance with the Emperor of China, is totally devoid of foundation. Zarun or Toulun certainly never got as far west as the Caspian, or even as far as Issekul, and his cousin Dadar (p. 118) had been routed by the Tobas four years before Attila and his brother Bleda succeeded to the Hun throne in Europe. There is not the faintest trace of any Jwen-jwen intercourse with any western people except the Hephthalites and people north-west of Ili, and even the "Jenuye king" of Ili, or Yüeh-p'an as it was called by the Chinese at that time, turned back when he saw what a filthy and barbarous people he was visiting at " this dog kingdom," and never reached Dadar's court. Gibbon says that " Attila, the son " of Mundzuk, deduced his descent from the ancient Huns " who had formerly contended with the monarchs of China." This specific piece of evidence, if warranted, would clinch all the arguments that we have advanced. Everything conspires to show that the ruling castes of the Hiung-nu who suddenly disappeared from China were the Huns who suddenly appeared in Europe, and there is nothing to show against that view ; but still, that does not improve the quality of specific statements of fact, which do no good to a sound case and no harm to a weak one unless based upon positive evidence. Friedrich Hirth once endeavoured to show (from a mis-translated *i* in a Chinese text) that Attila's son Hernak's or Ernas' name appeared in Chinese official documents ; but this supposition must be rejected, for no final *k* appears in any part of the final one of the three Chinese syllables ; nor a final *s* (cf. the same *i, ki, ssŭ*, in margin of p. 120) : it is *i*, " already," and belongs to the next sentence.

The Southern Chinese as distinct from the Tartar-Chinese dynastic records call the people we have just described by the name of Jwe-jwe, and, as we have shown, such evidence as there is, scant though it be, tends to show that they were a Hiung-nu race, and not—except perhaps by adoption for political purposes—a Sien-pi race as supposed by Rémusat, whose further suggestion that they may be the progenitors of the modern Mongols is worthy of being borne in mind, and is possible : but it is not supported by any direct evidence. Moreover they were as a ruling race exterminated by the Turks (p. 121).

CHAPTER II

Their Struggle with the Kankalis

WHEREVER we have hitherto used the word Kankalis we have meant that race of people known to the Chinese in Hiung-nu times as Ting-ling or Tik-lik, in Toba times as High Carts, in Turkish times as Ouigours, and in Mongol times as *Kankly*,—a Turkish word meaning " cart " ; but the term Ting-ling seems to have referred to two nations, one near Baikal, the other not far from Balkash, being near or included in the dominions of the Kirghiz, much farther west than the first. Nothing is known of the Ting-ling except that sometimes they formed part of the Hiung-nu Empire, and sometimes fought for or against this or that side during the period of struggle between the various Tartar-Chinese dynasties. The traditions of the High Carts, however vague, connect their origin with the Hiung-nu, and they are first known under that name (High Carts) in the 5th century. There is some reason to suppose that the Chinese form *Kao-ch'ê* is really the origin of our European words *Kutsche, coche,* and " coach " ; but against this it must be admitted that *ch'ê* was not the literary form, but *kü* or *chü* (p. 115). Their history may be related in a line. They were constantly at war with the Jwen-jwen, and, when the first Toba Emperor set out on his great expedition against the latter (p. 116), he took the opportunity of breaking up the High Carts too. He returned with 50,000 captives of both sexes, 200,000 of their very high-wheeled carts, and over a million horses, cattle, and sheep. The third Toba Emperor also obtained the submission of several hundred thousand High Carts whilst he was engaged in punishing the Jwen-jwen : he quartered them south of the Desert, but they soon revolted and went back north. It will be noticed that the Toba dynasty of North China was much more successful than any purely Chinese dynasty had ever been in crushing the nomads of the north ; but that, so soon as they adopted Chinese manners and customs, they themselves fell into decrepitude. It appears to have been the policy of the Tobas to prevent the Jwen-jwen and the Hephthalites from communicating with the Tukuhun (p. 107), and from the way in which this is related it would seem that the Hephthalites (at this period called Yetta or Ept'a in Chinese, pronounced *yip-tat* in Canton, *yöp-tal* in Corea) were not those of the Pamir, but the smaller body, at first called by the Chinese "Lesser Yüeh-chï," who remained in the Koko-nor region at the time of the exodus, and seem to have gradually worked their way west towards Kuldja (see pp. 21, 42). On this assumption we need not suppose that the Jwen-jwen who took refuge with the Hephthalites ever crossed the mountains east of Issekul. During the times of the Sien-pi dynasties in North China, the High Carts usually got the worst of it in their struggles with the Jwen-jwen : at any rate they never seem, under the name High Carts, to have founded an empire of their own of any description, and would appear to have finally settled somewhere near modern Urumtsi as petty kings enjoying Chinese recognition.

The character and manners of the High Carts are thus described. Every race or clan had its own tribal chief, and they never had any supreme ruler over all. Their disposition was rough and impetuous, but in times of general danger they could take harmonious action together. In battle they had no military array, but each individual rushed on and off the attack as he chose, and they were incapable of sustained fighting. It was their practice to squat and sprawl about in the most unreserved way without any respect of persons. In marriages, cattle and horses were the usual betrothal gifts ; the more, the finer the display. They had no grain, and made no spirituous liquors. On the day when the bride was fetched, men and women went together carrying with them kumiss and cooked meat, and the host made no distinctions of degree in his treatment of the guests. They all sat down promiscuously in front of the tent and feasted the whole day, remaining for the night too. The next day the girl was carried off, after which the husband's party was conducted back to the family corral of horses to select the handsomest

animals. Their habits were decidedly dirty. They were
fond of attracting thunder-claps, and whenever a clap came
they shouted aloud, shot arrows up into the sky, abandoned
the place, and migrated, coming back to the same spot the
next year when the horses were fat.   There they buried a ram,
lit a fire, and drew their swords, whilst witches uttered
exorcising incantations.   Then the whole body galloped their
horses round it a hundred times, when some one, taking a
bundle of willow branches, bent them, and stuck them in the
ground, anointing them with kumiss.   The women wear
as part of their head-gear the shin-bone of a sheep wrapped
up in the skin, twisting their hair round it so as to form a sort
of head-piece, which they bedizen to look something like
a crown.   When deaths take place, a funeral procession is
formed, a grave dug, and the body set in it in a sitting posture.
A drawn bow is placed in the hands of the deceased, upon
whom a sword is girt and to whom a spear is attached, just
as with a living person : but the hole is left unfilled, and they
ride round it several hundred times : every one goes to this
function, young or old, of either sex.   They keep migrating
to wherever there is pasturage.   They wear skins, eat flesh,
and rear flocks and herds exactly as do the Jwen-jwen,
except that the wheels of their carts are very large, with an
enormous number of spokes.   Thus the Chinese historians.
The rest of their history is merged in that of the Turks and
Ouigours, of whom we shall soon proceed to treat.

   The Yüeh-p'an of A.D. 400 are distinctly stated by the
Chinese historians to be the weaker body of the Hiung-nu
who fled west after the great *debâcle* of A.D. 89–91 (p. 91) :
at the time they settled on the Yulduz River north of Kuche,
and later shifted farther west.   I must here add a word to
state more at length why I suppose these Yüeh-p'an to be
the Avars.   In the first place, the Chinese syllable *Yüeh*
often does duty as the foreign initial *E*, as, for instance, in
the word Ephthalite ; whilst *pan* or *ban* occurs in the Chinese
Sanskrit *Pan-lo* for *Vara*.   In the second place, when the great
Chinese T'ang dynasty, after (as we shall see) breaking

up Turkish power about A.D. 658, established sixteen "governments" in the West, all under the political direction of the Proconsul at Kuche (Kwei-tsz), one of the sixteen still bore the name of *Yüeh-p'an*, and its new site on the Upper Oxus would naturally have historical reference to the Avars' or Evars' old position in A.D. 450 between the Turks and the Ephthalites, then known as *Ye-t'a*. The Avars passed into Europe with the help of Constantinople's foe the Alans or Azes, both of which names occur in Chinese history with reference to Caspian tribes through which the Yüeh-p'an must have passed when they fled from the rising Turks (under the *Jenuye* Tumen and his brother Istämi), and utterly disappeared from Chinese history ; (compare Carpini's Alani *sive* Assi, and Rubruquis' Alani *sive* Aas). The Turks, at the date when that name first occurs, never had any relations with the Yüeh-p'an, whose only eastern neighbours had been and were the Jwen-jwen. After destroying the latter, the Turkish Khakhan Istämi (the western Dizabul), uncle of Mukan, broke up the Ephthalites ; and, according to Menander, the Turkish Khan "Silzibul" said in 562 that he intended to attack the Avars as soon as he had finished with the Ephthalites ; so that the Yüeh-p'an or Avars must have already gone far westwards before Mukan's death in A.D. 572, leaving nothing behind them near China but the memory of the site their ancestors had occupied in A.D. 88 when the Northern Hiung-nu were broken up (p. 70) ; the name survived until the Turks drove them from the Oxus region and the T'ang dynasty perpetuated that Oxus site as a government. Finally, it is recorded in the Chinese official history of the Toba Emperors of North China that the Liang Chou people were in the habit of calling the Yüeh-p'an ruler "the *Jenuye* King," and there was even a Yüeh-pah city in that region. M. Henri Cordier pointed out in 1903 that the Ghuz Turks in A.D. 1000 still made use of the term *Jenuye* for their ruler, and it is on this account that in the present edition I have throughout changed the word *Zenghi* to *Jenuye*. In Russia the Avars and Lesghians, both ardent Mussulmans, still occupy Daghestan, west of the Caspian Sea.

BOOK IV

THE EMPIRE OF THE TURKS

BOOK IV

THE EMPIRE OF THE TURKS

CHAPTER I

EARLIEST NOTICES OF THE TURKS: PERIOD OF PEACE WITH CHINA

THE ancestors of the Turks were a group of Hiung-nu families bearing the clan name of Assena. It has been recorded (p. 104) how the third Toba Emperor absorbed the Tsugu dominions in the year 433 ; and we are told that, when that event took place, 500 families of the Assena clan fled to the dominions of the Jwen-jwen, and for several generations occupied the southern slopes of the Golden Mountains not far from the city of Shan-tan in modern Kan Suh. In the Tsugu times this city was itself called Kin-shan (meaning " Golden Mountain "), and we know (p. 118) that Zarun and Dadar held one of their courts near this place. What really happened therefore was this. Tsugu, a Hiung-nu Prince of the Liang principality reigning at Kan-chou Fu, had to succumb to the Sien-pi Empire of Wei, and some of his people, to wit the Assena group, preferring the rule of Hiung-nu to that of Sien-pi, moved away a short distance to that part of the Tsugu dominion nearest to the Jwen-jwen, or that part of the Jwen-jwen empire nearest to Liang. Here, on account of the helmet-like shape of a certain hill, they took from it the national designation of *Türk* or " Turks," a word still meaning " helmet " in at least some of the Turkish dialects.

This similarity in name between an insignificant range of hills in the Etzinai region and the Kin Shan or Altai Mountains of Western Mongolia has caused the French writers, (and perhaps to a certain extent even the Chinese), to place the original Turks north of the Desert, and to give undue weight to certain fabulous incidents handed down by tradition. We may allude to one,—their supposed descent from a she-wolf,—because that myth is repeated in connection with other Turkish tribes, and has something to do with the symbolic use by them of a wolf's head at particular functions. But, in this as all other cases connected with our subject, we brush away the cobwebs of myth and fable, and confine ourselves to such plain matters of fact as can be adduced from the Chinese records.

The Turks served the Jwen-jwen as workers in iron, an art in which they are as likely as not to have improved themselves at the highly civilized centre of Liang. Towards the end of the 5th century the tribe became strong, and for the first time appeared on the Chinese frontiers in order to trade, and purchase silk and floss for wadding. Here, again, it is plain the Turks must have been near the frontier : it is absurd to suppose that their then masters the Jwen-jwen would have allowed them to come a thousand miles from the Altai Mountains in order to make friends with China. Here also we have once more the ancient Hiung-nu barter of horses for silk. [In his 1912 edition of Gibbon, vol. iii, Professor Bury has recognized these and other points concerning the Turks and Hephthalites ; and it was he also who explained to me Vopiscus' actual words, misquoted by Gibbon (p. 69), in connection with Aurelian's triumph. The demand of the Turkish chief Tumen for a Jwen-jwen princess ended, as (p. 120) we have seen, in the defeat of Anakwe by what he called his " blacksmith slaves."] Tumen thereupon (551) appropriated the khanish title, and styled himself Ili Khakhan [possibly " Ilkhan," but in any case the Bumin Kagan of the Turkish inscriptions]. He only reigned one year after that.

[We do not know what *ili* means in Turkish; it occurs very often; but here it certainly has nothing to do with the well-known town of Ili near Kuldja, though both words have, not improbably, the same origin and meaning ; the works of Thomsen and Radloff must be carefully studied.] He styled his wife Khatun or *Khaghatun*, a word which we are told is equivalent to the ancient Inchi of the Hiung-nu. All this is very reasonable. When the Hiung-nu fell, the Sien-pi borrowed their title of Jenuye until they themselves invented or introduced the new one of khan or khakhan. On the Hiung-nu,—that is the Jwen-jwen and Turks,—once more obtaining supremacy from the Tunguses, they not unnaturally appropriated the title then in fashion.

The description given of the Turks is pretty full. Princes of the blood were called *teghin*, which was thought to be probably the Mongol word *dere* suggested by Palladius, and each separate tribal command was called a *shad*. However, it is now certain that the Chinese characters *k'in* and *lêh* (so much alike) are misprinted in 90 per cent of cases, and that *teghin* is here the genuine Turkish word. Their highest official rank was that of *külüchür* ; then came *apo*, *gherefa*, *tudun*, and *djigin*—so far as we can guess at the sounds intended by the light of the transition-staged Chinese pronunciation of that date. We are also told that personal peculiarities were habitually seized upon as appellations for individuals (cf. p. 118), who were also named after animals or articles of food. The words *sheporo* and *bagatur* were applied to " valiant " personages, and we find these, or closely similar words, recurring throughout Turkish and Ouigour history. To the fat and ungainly was applied the term *sandalo*, because *dalobien* signified a squat drinking-horn. [This remark is interesting, for we have already (p. 118) made allusion to Dalobian Khan, a personage according to Schuyler visited by Zimarchus.] The above offices were high in dignity, and could only be held by the agnates of the blood,—a system which at once recalls the " ten horns " of the Hiung-nu, (p. 13). *Koli* or *kari* meant " old " ; hence the *kari tarkhan*,—

tarkhan being a word we often come across in allusion to ambassadors or counsellors. " Horse " was called *ghoran*, hence the qualifications of *Ghoran-suni* and *köl-suni* in allusion to military commandants. " Black " is *karapien*, hence the *Kara-chur*, an officer of very high rank and always an old man. [The syllable *pien* or *bien* thus appears superfluous in two words, and must be some agglutinative Turkish particle.] " Hair " is called *soko* ; hence the term *soko-tudun*, a sort of provincial governor. *Peni-jekhan* is the name for " fermented spirits," and thus the *jekhan* does general supervising duty, and keeps a control over the ranks of the executive. [One is inclined to suspect an accidental synechdoche here, and to connect this officer's duties with " serving " out the grog."] " Meat " is called *andjan* ; hence we have the *andjan-kuni*, who manages the family matters of the royal house. Sometimes they appoint in addition a *lin-khakhan*, *lin* being the name for " wolf," the idea conveyed being that of greed and murder. There were also khakhans whose degree was below that of *jabgu*, a word meaning " young " bloods of the royal house." There are also members of great families living quietly at home, called *i-khakhan*, from the Turkish word *i*, " a house," the idea being " stay-at-home " khakhan."—It is not very easy to follow the train of Turkish thought in all the above, but doubtless competent antiquaries and philologists, with help of Radloff and Thomsen—the discoverers of Old Turkish,—will be able to discover a significant identification or two.

Tumen's successor was his son Kara (552), and then came Kara's brother Djigin, also called Yenin, the Mukan Khakhan (552–573), and the father of Dalobian. [Mukan was nephew and Tumen was elder brother to the Istämi Kagan of the Turkish stone inscriptions : in Chinese this last figures as Shih-tien-mi and Sê-ti-mi— probably the Stembis of the Greeks, the Dizabul of Zimarchus, the Silzibul of Menander. Schuyler perhaps got the word Dalobian from old French sources, for there is no European or Persian authority for the identification of the Turkish khan Dizabalus (p. 118), to whom Zimarchus was sent by Justin, with the Chinese *Ta-lo-pien*; the old translators say that Dalobian was the son of Muyui, the two Chinese characters *kan* and *yü* being almost indistinguishable when typed. But at present we have nothing to do with the schism which led Dalobian to go westwards : we shall discuss that later on.] Mukan's personal appearance must have been more striking than prepossessing : his face was very red, and over a foot in breadth : his eyes were like glass, and his disposition tyrannical but sagacious. [So Attila was described, by Jornandes the Goth, as having had a large head, swarthy, small deep eyes, flat nose, few hairs ; broad, short body.] He broke up the remaining Jwen-jwen, and (assisted from afar by Istämi) the Hephthalites ; drove back the Cathayans to the east, annexed tribes in the north, and exercised paramount dominion beyond the Great Wall. His empire extended east and west over 3,000 miles, from the western side of the Liao Tung Gulf to the Western Sea (which here must mean either Lake Balkash or Issekul), and 2,000 miles from the desert in the south to the North Sea (which must mean Lake Baikal). The Chinese give many vague descriptions of the moose-deer, snow-shoe hunting, dog-sledging, " fish-skin " and other Tartars in the north, forming part of the Turkish and Cathayan Empires at different times ; but the populations were (and still are) so scant, the influence they exercised so very slight, and their power so insignificant, that they may from this moment be dismissed from our further consideration, except where this or that tribe needs mention for some specific reason. There is nothing to show that the Chinese ever crossed far into what we call Siberia, or that they ever conceived the faintest notion of the real North Sea, apart from the fact that they may have observed the rivers to flow north, or been told so.

To return to the as yet undivided Turks. Their manners were as those of the ancient Hiung-nu. They differed in this, that, when their lord first succeeded, the highest officers in immediate attendance carried him round nine times a day in a carpet, his officers performing obeisance at each turn. [Perhaps this is historically connected with the piece of felt upon which Genghis Khan and his successors were crowned.] When this was over, he was set upon a horse's back with a silk cord or handkerchief twisted round his neck, so tightly that he was all but strangled; after which it was loosened, and he was hurriedly asked how many years he was likely to reign. His wits being naturally in a state of confusion, he would probably fail to consider his answer; but, whatever it was, his officers took him at his word. Their weapons included horn bows, singing-arrows (see p. 9) coats of mail, spears, swords, and knives. As to their bedizenments, they had amongst other things a *vugh-dugh*, being a golden wolf's-head fixed at the end of the standard pole; and their guards were called *vuri*, which in the language of Hia also means " wolf," for thus they always kept their wolfish origin in mind. [This probably refers to the extinct Ghoren dynasty of Hiung-nu (p. 78), and not to the Toba dynasty growing out of it which, as we shall find, set up in Hia or Ordous in the 9th century : but it will be remembered (p. 118) the personal name of the third Toba Emperor was Vuri, and *hu-li* is still the Chinese word for " fox "; this powerful 9th century Hia or Tangut dynasty existed until Genghis Khan destroyed it just before his death in 1227.] In making levies of troops and cavalry, or collecting taxes in cattle and such like, they always carved the number required upon a piece of wood, adding an arrow with a golden barb sealed with wax as a mark of genuineness. [The " broad " arrow," or as some call it " broad A," of the Druids was a mark of authority : it is still, or was under the late Empire, the " warrant " to take life in China.] They used to wait for the end of the moon to commence their raids [the old Hiung-nu practice of attacking on a waxing moon]. As to their punishments, rebellion and homicide were visited with death; lewdness with castration, or cutting the body in twain. For wounding a man's eye in the course of a brawl a daughter was given as compensation : if no daughter, then a wife had to go until there should be one. For maiming a limb, horses were paid. For robbery, ten-fold compensation for what was taken. In cases of death, the corpse was laid out in the tent; the sons, grandsons, and other relatives of both sexes each killed a sheep or a horse, and set it in front of the tent, wounding their own faces with a knife [as was done at Attila's death], and wailing so that the blood and tears rolled down together; ["blood-weeping" is still the Chinese expression for the lamentations of the chief mourner]. This operation was repeated seven times. Those who died in spring or summer were not put into the grave until the fall of the leaf, nor those who died in autumn or winter until the spring vegetation was in full bloom again. Stones were erected at the place of sepulture, with an obituary mark or sign, the number of stones varying with the number of men killed by the deceased during his lifetime. On this day every one, male and female, put on the best clothes and ornaments available, and assembled at the grave [as with the High Carts]. If any man felt a liking for any girl present, on his return home he sent proposals of marriage [as with the Sien-pi], and as a rule the parents accepted him. Although the Turks moved about without fixed abode, yet all had their share of land [as with the Hiung-nu]. The khakhan's residence was in the Tukin Hills [exact whereabouts unfortunately unknown, but somewhere north of the desert], and every year he went there to sacrifice to his ancestors' manes [as did the Hiung-nu Jenuye]. In the middle of the 5th moon [exactly as with the Hiung-nu] he assembled other persons to sacrifice to the spirits and Heaven. There was another lofty and prominent mountain, about 150 miles west of Tukin, called *putengiri*, which in the Hia language means "spirit of the earth" [possibly the word *tengri*, "heaven," is part of it] and was destitute of all vegetation. Their written language is like that of the Hu [shortly after these words were written in 1894, Professor V. Thomsen and Dr. W. W. Radloff both communicated to me their wonderful discoveries of a Turkish script, leading to a practical reconstruction of the old Turkish language] ; but they have no knowledge of the calendar, simply guiding themselves by the greenness of the verdure. The men are fond of playing at dice and the women at football [possibly shuttle-cock with the feet]. They drink kumiss [? Attila's *kamos*] until they get drunk, and sing songs in repartee. They entertain awe of the good and evil spirits.

This is the first mention of any written character except Chinese that we come upon in the chapters relating to Tartars. But the Chinese pilgrim Hüan Chwang, who visited the Western Turks about A.D. 630, found a modified form of Hindoo character in use in the state of Kuche, which, as we have seen (p. 101), became the Chinese proconsular centre 20 years later. The History of the Sui dynasty speaks of the Hu books obtained from Western Asia by the After Han dynasty. I believe the Persians generally used the Greek alphabet during the interval between the abandonment of the old cuneiform writing and the adoption of the Arabic. The Chinese usually call Sanskrit and Pali *fam*, or *vam*, by which they mean " Brahm " ; or sometimes *balamên*, by which they mean "Brahman" (cf. p. 119). Very soon after the events here recorded, the Chinese and Tibetans drew up bilingual treaties in Chinese and a sort of Sanskrit ; [our expedition of 1904 to Lhassa found the identical treaty stone still *in sitû*] ; and at about the same time (A.D. 635) the Nestorians came with their Syriac, [I have given a full account in the *Dublin Review* for October, 1902, since which time numerous other versions have been published]. The truth probably is that then, as now, the Chinese knew next to nothing about the subject, and that the historian's vagueness is in each case the measure of his ignorance.

It will be remembered that, when Djigin or Mukan became sufficiently powerful, he insisted on the Western Wei Toba dynasty, then in the hands of the Jumen family, handing over the Jwen-jwen refugees to the Turkish envoy to be butchered in cold blood (p. 121). The After or Northern

Chou Emperor Wu Ti, who was the son of the Jumen intriguer in question, married Mukan's daughter. Mukan was succeeded in 572 or 573 by his brother Tapor, who was originally a minor khakhan in the east, as Chief Khakhan. He had several hundred thousand troopers at his disposal, and the two Sien-pi Emperors of the Chou and Ts'i dynasties of North-China were so afraid of him that they were only too glad to ally themselves with him by arranging marriages, and spared no expense to conciliate his good will. Every year they sent him 100,000 pieces of silk. The Turks at the western metropolis were treated in the handsomest way, there being frequently as many as a thousand there at a time " clothed in silk and " feasting on flesh." Tapor showed little gratitude for this, simply remarking :—" So long as my two sonnies in the south " are dutiful, I shall never want for anything."

The ferocious Turk proved amenable to the softening influences of religion. Amongst his captives of war was a Chinese Buddhist s'ramaṇa who expounded to Tapor the doctrines of predestination and eternal causes [just as 650 years later the Taoist hermit from China softened the heart of Genghis Khan in the wilds of Transoxiania ; see also p. 119 for Buddhist influence]. He also persuaded Tapor that the Empire of Ts'i owed its wealth and power to its being so Buddhistic in sentiment. Tapor lent an ear to these representations, founded a monastery, and sent an envoy to the Ts'i capital in modern Ho Nan Province in order to obtain Buddhist books. [It was just at this time too that Buddhism was introduced, viâ Corea, into Japan.] Tapor submitted himself to a certain amount of austere discipline, built pagodas, and practised the rites of the religion, only expressing a regret that he had not had the advantage of being born in China. When a fugitive prince of the expiring Ts'i dynasty took refuge with him, Tapor made a raid upon modern Peking, and gave out that he was about to avenge the exile's cause ; but, on the rival Chou dynasty offering him a princess in marriage, Tapor surrendered the pretender.

Tapor was succeeded by Shipdu the son of Irski (581 A.D.), who took the title of Shaporo Khakhan [cf. *Sheporo*, p. 131] with his seat of government at Mount Tukin : he had previously had conferred upon him one of the local khanships above described. Tapor's son Amro occupied the valley of the Tula River as Second Khakhan. Dalobian (see pp. 118, 131), the son of Mukan by a less noble wife, was discontented with this arrangement, but was quieted for the moment with the status of Apo Khakhan, and sent back to his own horde. Shaporo was a brave and popular prince, in consequence of which all the tribes in the far north readily submitted to him. The marriage of Mukan's daughter to the Chou Emperor Wu Ti had brought an inroad of as many as ten thousand greedy Turks to the western metropolis, and naturally these silk-clad flesh-feasters were annoyed when the Sui house (581 A.D.) took over the succession and dispensed with their unprofitable services. The Chou princess, too, who had married Tapor, at once commenced to revenge her family's wrongs at the hands of the Sui dynasty by raiding the western line of frontier and carrying off every living thing. The new Sui Emperor immediately issued a manifesto announcing his determination not to pander to barbarian insolence any longer, and he sent out an army which put Shaporo to flight. Matters were made worse for the Turks by the fact that there was a dearth in their land, and they were reduced to grinding down bones for sustenance. Yet in spite of all this Shaporo, through his brother the *jabgu* Chulagu, declared war upon Apo, who had to fly west and seek protection from Shaporo's uncle Dardö [the Greek Tardu] the self-nominated Bukha Khakhan of the Western Turks, who now became a quite separate nation instead of a mere province, and kept up continual war with the Northern Turks, or mother country. During this fighting the Apar branch of a Kankali tribe called Tölös had taken the opportunity to carry off Shaporo's family; but the Emperor of China recovered the captives and returned them to Shaporo, who was so pleased that he entered into a treaty recognizing the Desert as the boundary between China and Turkey. [Incidentally it may be mentioned that Julien seemed to think these Apar (who appear in the Turkish inscriptions) might be the Avars ; Chavannes rightly disapproves.] It is interesting to note what titles the Turkish monarch confers upon himself :—" Shipdu, " the *Sheporo Baga* Khakhan of the Ili-külu horde of Great " Turkey." It will be noticed that he uses in modified form the previously explained word *sheporo*, and not the word Shaporo or Shaporio given to him as a name by the Chinese. We cannot help thinking that the two last syllables of Dizabul must be in some way connected either with *Jabgu* or (less likely) with Shaporo, especially as the Roman embassy is said to have visited the Khan in the Altai Mountains in the year 568, which is twelve years previous to the extinction of the Chou dynasty and the schism of Dalobian ; but a close study of the Greek authors is necessary before we can presume to dogmatize. Persian or European history makes it quite clear that, in as many words, " The Turks had been approaching the confines of the " new (Sassanidæ) empire, having extended their dominion " over the Great Ephthalite kingdom, by force of arms and by " the treachery of the Ephthalite chieftain Katulphus, while " they had also received the submission of the Sogdians " and of the other tribes of the Transoxianian region previously " held in subjection by the Ephthalites." Whilst asserting the divine right of Turkey and its equality with China, Shaporo admits that there can no more be two Emperors than two suns, and loyally styles himself a vassal. One account says that he shed tears of shame when the Chinese envoy insisted on humiliating forms. On his death in 587 the Emperor paid him the compliment of suspending all court functions for three days.

Shaporo was succeeded, after various family rivalries and dissensions, by his nephew the Duli Khakhan, to whom the Emperor sent a princess in marriage. The Emperor's idea was to sow dissension amongst the nomads by exciting jealousies, and about the year 590 frequent envoys were exchanged. Duli now moved from the northern parts, where he was originally encamped, to the " old town of Dukin." If this is another way of saying " Tukin Hills," we must assume that the latter were not very far from North Shan Si, where the central tribe of the Hiung-nu under Baghdur seem to have been stationed as well as the Southern Horde under the second Khughanja (p. 63). Shaporo's son was angry at this exhibition of favour, got Bukha in the west to join him in an attack upon the Great Khakhan, and massacred a large number of his relatives. This caused Duli to seek Chinese protection : a city was built for him in North Shan Si, and on his wife's death a second princess was sent to him. As his enemies would not let him alone, he was ordered to move within the Wall, and was given the Ordous country with a considerable tract south of it ; a large canal was excavated for his benefit by forced labour, apparently with the object of defining his possessions, or perhaps for purposes of irrigation. Meanwhile a Chinese army marched against Shaporo's son, who was killed by his own people. Others of Duli's enemies, one a grandson of Tumen, and the other a brother of Shaporo, were defeated by the Kankalis, but at last the latter, together with certain of the old Sien-pi tribes, decided to migrate into China and join Duli's standard.

Duli now bore a new title, given to him by the first Sui Emperor, and when his imperial successor the celebrated madman Yang Ti came to the throne (A.D. 604), the two monarchs met at the Great Wall in North Shen Si. [It must be noted that Duli's real title was K'i-min ; but, after the T'ang dynasty replaced that of Sui, the word *min* (people) was replaced in all literature by *jên* (mankind), out of *tabu* respect for Li Shih-*min*, the effective founder.] Following the precedent of Khughanja, the second Sui Emperor gave the Turk rank above all the grandees of the Empire, granted him audience free from the usual degrading ceremonies, with his shoes on, his sword girt, and exempt from the necessity of pronouncing his private personal name (Jan-kan) : 200,000 pieces of silk were distributed amongst the tribal chiefs, of whom there were present two thousand five hundred. The Emperor then proceeded by boat to the Turk's encampment or ordo in North Shan Si, where Duli pledged Yang Ti in a goblet of wine upon his knees. The following year another audience was granted, and the Emperor's treatment of his Turkish brother was on this occasion still more magnificent.

Duli was succeeded in 599 by his son Tukir, usually known as the Sibir Khakhan. The Turks were now becoming so powerful that recourse was had to the old policy of exciting jealousies, so a princess and separate title were accordingly offered to one of his brothers commanding a separate *shad*. Sibir was so indignant that he made a sudden rush at the Emperor whilst the latter was enjoying the cool weather at his summer residence (not so very far south from where Baghdur surrounded the first Han Emperor 800 years before), and would have taken him prisoner had not the frontier battalions marched up in time to prevent it. This was in the autumn of the year 616. During the anarchy and misery which prevailed towards the close of the Sui dynasty, innumerable Chinese took refuge with Sibir, whose power now began to threaten the very existence of China. He gave asylum to the fugitive Sui Empress, and every one of the numerous aspirants for the imperial throne " faced north and declared themselves his vassals." It appears that the rising power of the Cathayans had not yet been broken by the Turks, whose empire extended from the land of the Ghei and the Cathayans in the east to those of their Sien-pi kinsmen the Tukuhun or Tuyühun in the west : the whole of the Karahodjo and Pidjan group of states recognized Sibir's suzerainty, and he had over a million bows at his disposal ; but it would not seem that his power extended to Persia, where at this time the Western branch of the Turks only had any influence.

CHAPTER II

PERIOD OF WAR WITH CHINA, AND COLLAPSE OF GHERI'S
EMPIRE

AMONGST the aspirants for imperial power in China was
one Li Yüan, whose father had married a Turkish lady
of the Duku family. It is somewhere stated by a European
writer that she was a Christian, which, even if untrue, is not
at all improbable, as the Nestorian Olopen arrived in 635
during the reign of her grandson, Li Shih-min, who issued an
edict in favour of Christianity. Envoys were sent by Li Yüan
(see p. 73) to bespeak Sibir's assistance, and the Turkish
Khakhan sent his Kankali *teghin* with a present of horses and
also a body of 3,000 troopers to assist the founder of the
T'ang dynasty, then fighting in East Kan Suh. After the
Sui dynasty had definitely ceased to exist, innumerable gifts
were made to Sibir, who sent the Kutluk *teghin* as his envoy
to the metropolis [*kutluk* is a Turkish word meaning " happy,"
which, as already pointed out on page 13, seems in the
form *kuttu* to have been in use in ancient Hiung-nu times].
But a year afterwards we find Sibir conspiring with two rival
pretenders to the Chinese throne, and raiding in the good old
time-honoured way. On Sibir's death his son was considered
too young for the chief khanship, so a brother was elected with
the title of Chula Khakhan, and the son was given the sub-
khanship of the east. Chula took over as one of his wives the
second Sui princess given to his uncle Duli : it is presumed
the lady had also served Sibir in that same capacity ; in fact,
the Sui Emperor said to her " Follow the custom of the
" country," when asked about it (cf. p. 48). On receiving the
notification of Sibir's death, the T'ang Emperor honoured his
memory by setting up a wail for him, and by closing the court for

three days ; he also ordered the whole official body to proceed
to the Turkish envoy's hotel and offer condolences. A special
ambassador was sent to express sympathy with Chula, and to
present a funeral contribution of 30,000 pieces of silk-stuffs.

It appears that the fugitive Sui Empress and one of the
young princes had fallen into the clutches of a Chinese
pretender, who had set up a state in or near Ordous called
" Great Hia." He was defeated and executed by Li Shih-min
in 621. Chula gave the fugitives a welcome reception at his ordo,
and conferred rank upon the young Sui prince. All the Chinese
who had joined the Turks were placed under the jurisdiction
of this scion of royalty, who had his abode somewhere near
modern Kwei-hwa Ch'êng : there were as many as 10,000
Chinese subject to him : he was provided with an official
staff, and continued to date by the reigns of the Sui Emperors.
Chula sent 2,000 men to assist Li Yüan's above-mentioned
son, the celebrated T'ang T'ai-tsung, then only known as
the Prince of Ts'in, who had been commanded by his father
the Emperor to march against the numerous rival aspirants
to empire. Chula himself came later on to one of the Chinese
cities on the (modern) Shan Si and Chih Li frontier : he received
a hearty welcome, which he and his men returned by seizing
all the pretty women in the streets,—whether for temporary
or permanent service is not stated. Chula died suddenly,
and his Chinese wife managed to secure the election of his
brother Tupi as Gheri Khakhan, the son being " too weak and
ugly." It is presumed that she was thinking of her own
conjugal comfort and position rather than the welfare of
the Turkish state when she delivered this opinion, for she lost
no time in marrying the new Gheri khakhan. Sibir's son was
created Duli Khakhan, and must not be confused with his
grandfather who bore the same title (p. 140). The Chinese
court expressed its sympathy in the usual deferential way.
Gheri at first showed a disposition to coquet with one of the
Chinese pretenders, but the Emperor by prompt and judicious
bribery managed to disengage the khakhan from his objection-

able ally. The envoy sent to conduct this delicate negotiation also successfully applied for the rendition of a certain ex-Sui general who was threatening to give trouble. Gheri had in his employ the usual crowd of Chinese renegades, ready then, as now, to flock wherever profit and power were and are to be attained : finding himself thus courted, he put on insufferable airs, and even conceived pretensions to the conquest of China. As the Emperor was not yet securely seated on the throne, and the time was unsuitable for external complications, he put up with Gheri's insolence as best he could, and endeavoured to keep him in good humour by heaping presents upon him. The ungrateful Gheri, at the head of 10,000 horsemen, joined a certain Chinese rebel who had 6,000 troops at his disposal in a raid upon North Shan Si. The force sent out against him inflicted such a severe defeat upon him that he made proposals for peace on his own initiative, and sent a present of a piece of glue as a symbol of the " firm cementing of the new alliance." During the year 622 the Chinese made a treacherous attempt, whilst the Turks were suffering from dearth, to take Horse City in North Shan Si, the identical town where (it will be remembered, p. 22) the Jenuye Kyundjin nearly fell into a somewhat similar trap. The attempt failed, as it deserved, and it is not to be wondered at therefore that Gheri forgot all about the glue, and, assisted by Duli, mercilessly raided the frontier for several years in succession. On one occasion the Prince of Ts'in (who was the Black Prince of Chinese history, and probably owed his unusual courage to his quartering of Turkish blood) rode with only a hundred cavaliers right up to the Turkish lines, and, reproaching Gheri with having broken the treaty, challenged him to either personal combat or a pitched battle. Gheri smiled, but made no remark, not quite understanding what was at the bottom of it all. The Prince then sent a knight to offer a similar challenge to Duli, who was silent also. The Prince then had recourse to those arts so dear to the true Chinese character and tried to work upon Duli's jealousy. The result was that

Duli was flattered, and, the other members of Gheri's clan being also somewhat disaffected, Gheri was constrained to make the first advances to the Emperor. But during the next two years he repeatedly invaded China, and even threatened the metropolis, which was now definitely in the same place (Si-an Fu) that it used to be in the time of the earlier Jenuyes. Gheri sent an envoy to boast of his master's power, and to say that a million soldiers were now on the march. The Prince of Ts'in was equal to the occasion. After having reproached the envoy with his master's ingratitude for all the favours lavished upon him and his father Sibir, he said :—" I shall probably have to kill you first any way!" This threat caused the blatant Turk to assume a humbler demeanour, and he willingly left the conduct of the further negotiations to the discretion of the Prince, who again rode up, almost unattended, to the Turkish lines, and addressed Gheri, having only a shallow stretch of the River Wei (near the capital) between himself and the Turk. The Turkish generals were so abashed that they dismounted and performed an obeisance. Meanwhile the Chinese troops had marched up, and Gheri, observing their strength, and aware that his envoy was in prison, was greatly alarmed. In spite of the remonstrances of his suite, the Prince advanced to hold a colloquy with Gheri, the two armies looking on. The Prince seems to have sailed very close to the wind, but, being a passed-master in the game of bluff, he carried the day, and Gheri sued for peace. This event would appear to have been in the year 626, when the Prince had really become Emperor, although the first year of his reign, according to Chinese custom, is the first complete year, that is 627. The Emperor argued :—
" The reason the Turks have advanced with their whole forces
" up to the banks of the Wei is that they know what internal
" difficulties our dynasty has had to contend with, and that
" I have only just succeeded to the crown. The question
" of who is to be master hangs upon the events of to-day.
" My advancing alone will take them by surprise, and they

" will be the more uneasy in that they are far away from their
" base. And, if fight we must, we ought to win ; whereas,
" if our bluff succeeds, our position will be enormously
" stronger." In imitation evidently of the old agreement
with Khughanja, the Emperor went a few days later to a bridge
on the west side of the city, where a white horse was killed,
Gheri and himself swearing fidelity (cf. p. 41) to a solemn treaty.
Gheri's army then withdrew. T'ai Tsung's chief minister
did not even yet quite follow the reasoning or the policy of
the Emperor, who explained :—" There is no order or discipline
" in the Turkish army : when the khakhan was alone on one
" side of the stream and his generals paying their respects to
" me on the other, I believe we could easily have broken up the
" host if I had but given the order ; but peace is necessarily
" the first care of a statesmanlike ruler, and in any case there
" would have been great bloodshed on both sides. Besides,
" if we had defeated them, they would have set to at once to
" improve their army, and the future consequences to us of
" this might have been serious ; whereas, by laying aside our
" arms and baiting them with presents, we cause the intract-
" able robbers to become more overweening, and we thus
" secure their ultimate ruin." Gheri a few weeks afterwards
sent up a large present of horses and sheep; but the Emperor
declined it, and " ordered " him by decree to return instead
the people he had carried off. It is not stated if Gheri carried
out this order.

In the year 627 a very important event took place. Three
tribes of what, for want of a better word, we shall still call the
Kankalis, to wit, the Seyenda, Baikals, and Ouigours, revolted
against Gheri's tyranny and turned out his officers. After
the breaking up of the Hiung-nu Empire these tribes, together
with many others, occupied the line of mountain valleys,
almost without a break, from the Caspian past Balkash,
eastwards to Baikal and beyond. The Ouigours and Baikals
were north of the River Tula ; the Seyenda were south of Lake
Hurun and the River Kerulon. [The more easterly of these

which were not under High Cart rule, including many which it is unnecessary to enumerate here, had formed part first of the Jwen-jwen Empire, and then of the Turkish. After the final fall of the Turks two or three centuries later, the petty tribe of Ouigour took the lead, gave its name to the state, and by reason of its having once formed part of the Turkish Empire was often spoken of as Ouigour-Turk. In speaking of " Turkish " races, therefore, we must not forget that both Turk and Ouigour were originally petty tribe names adopted by fragmentary remains of the Hiung-nu, just as the Angles and Saxons, petty tribes of the Teutons, subsequently gave their names to kingdoms of whose mixed populations the pure Angles and pure Saxons only formed a small part.] When these three tribes rebelled, Gheri sent his sub-khakhan Duli to crush the revolt ; but Duli's army was utterly defeated, and he himself, riding on a fleet horse, only just escaped with his life. Gheri was so annoyed at Duli's defeat that he put him under arrest. This irritated Duli, who at once proceeded to send treasonable messages to the Emperor of China, and troops were accordingly sent out to assist Duli against Gheri wherever practicable. Meanwhile the Seyenda set up a khakhan of their own north of the Desert : he styled himself the Bilga or " Wise " Khakhan, and with his son and nephew, who succeeded him, gave considerable trouble for some years. The Baikals, Ouigours, Kirghiz and the other eight tribes of the Kankalis east of Lake Balkash disapproved of Seyenda's independent action, gave in their submission to the Chinese Emperor in the year 648, and were made governors or proconsuls of their own tribal domains, which were now erected by China into what the Romans would have called proconsular provinces (cf. p. 126 for *West* Turks).

All this sadly clipped the wings of Gheri, who moreover was incurring great unpopularity with his own people on account of his predilection for " miscellaneous Tartars," by which probably Syrians, Persians, and other of the more sagacious Asiatics are meant : as these ministers and governors of strange blood were both arbitrary and rapacious, the result was general disaffection throughout the nomad empire. Besides this, the Western Turkish Empire was now in its prime, as is evident from the descriptions of Jabgu Khakhan's (cf. p. 139) court near Issekul, which was visited by the world-renowned Chinese pilgrim, Hüan-chwang, about this time (p. 136). To make matters worse, Gheri's dominions suffered during successive years from unusually heavy falls of snow, the result of which was a dearth of food. Gheri, falling short of funds, simply doubled or trebled the taxes, now so difficult to collect at all, and his dominions were consequently soon simmering in a general revolt. As, after suing for peace under these desperate circumstances, he rashly gave assistance once more to a Chinese pretender (whom he offered to surrender in exchange for a free hand with the Cathayans), the Emperor decided that the moment had now arrived to crush him once for all. The great and successful general, Li Tsing, was ordered to take supreme command of a grand expedition, which was to march out in four separate columns, whilst Duli and the other friendly *teghin* took refuge with the Chinese. Gheri was taken by surprise at night somewhere near Kuku-hoton or Kwei-hwa Ch'êng, and had to move his encampment somewhat hurriedly to what is called the " Mouth of the Desert " (cf. p. 30), a place about two days' journey north-east of that city, and perhaps the true original site of Tenduc. Thence he sent envoys to deliver up the Sui Empress and prince, apparently in order to gain time. Being now at his wit's end what to do, he took flight with the 30,000 or 40,000 soldiers still under his command to the Iron Mountains in the Kerulon Valley, and sent what is called in Turkish (approximately) a *chifshirslik* to offer his whole dominions to the Emperor. The wily monarch, whilst sending envoys to calm Gheri's mind, ordered Li Tsing to take twenty days' provisions and make a rush for him. The result was that Gheri, who fled almost absolutely alone on a very fleet horse to the horde of his nephew, Shaporo Sunishir, was followed up, taken alive, pardoned, and given quarters in the Imperial Mews. The historians triumphantly add that all the territory conquered 800 years ago from the Hiung-nu now belonged to T'ang. This was about the year 628. Gheri soon began to pine away in the irksome confinement of his new quarters, where he passed his time in singing melancholy refrains with his own people ; so the Emperor appointed him governor of a certain department in China where there was plenty of hunting to be had. But Gheri refused to be comforted. He was then given a more suitable post as General of the Guards, with free quarters, and died in the year 634 : he was honoured with the posthumous title of " the Wild." His people were allowed to deal with the body according to national custom, and he was accordingly cremated by them on the banks of a river near the metropolis. One of his *tarkhan* (cf. the Greek Turkhanthos), a man who had been given along with the marriage portion of Gheri's mother, cut his own throat so that he might accompany his dead master, an act of fidelity which so touched the Emperor that orders were given for his burial alongside of Gheri ; and a literary personage was commanded to compose a suitable memorial epitaph for the pair, to be carved in stone and placed by the graves.

Gheri was succeeded after his defeat by his nephew, Duli, whose government had originally been in the east, that is, north of the Upper Liao River or Sira Muren, for the Cathayans or Kitans had always succeeded in maintaining their independence of the Turks south of that river. Duli was in charge of two tribes of Sien-pi extraction called the Kumok-Ghei and the Sib. The former were the descendants of the eastern branch of the Jumens, and the latter, who never cut any figure at all in Chinese history, seem to have been as much Hiung-nu as Sien-pi : [possibly the Sibê Manchu-Mongols of to-day are their descendants ; they were, like the Solons, transferred to Ili in 1736, but they are inferior in caste, and do not inter-marry with the Solons]. The Mujung dynasty had driven the Kumok-Ghei along with their congeners the

Cathayans to the region between the Sungari and the Desert. The first Toba Emperor had occasion to punish them in the year 388 : he seems to have reached the River Amur, and amongst the 100,000 head of various animals he looted are mentioned pigs. During the next two hundred years the Kumok-Ghei seem to have brought tribute to the Toba court along with the Shirvi, Fish-skin Tartars, the ancestors of the Nüchêns, Manchus, etc., all of whom were then dirty, pig-breeding, hunting savages, infinitely below the standard of the Turks and Cathayans ; the Mungwa or Mungu were a sub-tribe of the Shirvi at this time; = Mongols. After the 5th century the Kumok-Ghei dropped the first part of their name and were ever afterwards known simply as Ghei. Their habits were like those of the Turks, but they had, like the Cathayans, the peculiar custom of wrapping up the dead like mummies and hanging them upon trees. These two peoples, then, had been part of Duli's appanage before he became Great Khakhan. But the Chinese Emperor did not recognize him as Great Khakhan : he only had the rank of Military Governor given to him, and was granted quarters near modern Peking, and ordered to conform his administrative system to Chinese ways : " Your namesake and grandfather," said the Emperor, " never made any return to the Sui dynasty " for the kindness received at their hands, whilst your father " Sibir was a positive curse to them : your bad government " has lost you the greater part of your horde, and you must " distinctly understand that you are now only taken on " trial." But Duli died in the year 631, on his way to the Chinese court, at the early age of 29. The Emperor, who was really fond of him and had " sworn a brotherhood " with him, uttered the regulation wails in his memory, and had an epitaph composed for his tomb also. The Sib and the Ghei now seem to have joined the Cathayans and paid regular tribute to China.

Duli's son Ghologhur succeeded to his father's honours, but in the year 639 he conspired with Duli's younger brother and other Turks in the Emperor's guard to attack the imperial camp and to set himself up once more as khakhan. They very nearly succeeded; but fortunately a Chinese general with a small force came up just in time, and they fled across the River Wei, hoping to reach the rest of their horde. They were all caught and decapitated, except Ghologhur, who was banished. After Gheri's great defeat, some of his men fled to Turkestan, others to the Seyenda, and many again took refuge in China. Previous to this, the question had been what to do with the Turks,—a hundred thousand at least,—who had already submitted. One idea was to make political prisoners of them all, teach them agriculture and weaving, and gradually turn them into good Chinamen. The most influential of the statesmen of the time thought that, if not exterminated (which, they said, would be the shortest and best process), they ought to be sent back to the north of the Yellow River Loop, being of an untamable, treacherous, alternately cringing and bullying disposition, such as it was impossible ever to rely upon : it was for this reason that Mêng T'ien (p. 8) and the Han dynasty (p. 26) had annexed Ordous, so as to keep the venue of diplomatic relations well at arm's length. If allowed to settle in or near China, the 100,000 will become 200,000 in a very few years, and be like a canker-worm in the very pith of China. The Tsin dynasty (p. 78) was foolish enough to employ the Hiung-nu for the conquest of their rivals, and the result was the Tartar dynasties of Liu Yüan and Shih Lêh, with the general turning upside down of all China (pp. 73, 75). This view was supported by the distinguished philologist and critic Yen Shï-ku, and by a number of other staunch and good men, who thought that the tribes should be split up and made as independent of each other as possible. The Emperor, however, who with all his faults seems to have been the fairest and most magnanimous monarch China ever had (unless it be the earlier emperors of the Manchu dynasty), decided to accept the advice of a comparatively subordinate officer who took quite a moral view, and argued that principles of human right and truth were universal, and irrespective of race or colour. " These poor " wretches, the remnants of their defeated race, appeal to us " in their extremity. If we give them asylum and endeavour " to educate them into a proper and useful frame of mind, " they can never be a danger to us. No harm came of our " quartering the Hiung-nu (p. 63) on the frontiers of China " in A.D. 50, and of our allowing them to preserve their own " customs, and utilizing them as a defensive outwork. On " the other hand, it would be a mistake to try and turn the " Turks into real Chinamen, and to arouse their suspicions " by importing them into regulation provinces." It was decided out of Duli's eastern appanage to create a single proconsulate, having under it four provinces, including the Ordous Country and North Shan Si. Gheri's dominions were formed into a second proconsulate, having under it six provinces. All this was previous to Ghologhur's attempt. But now, having himself had such a narrow escape from the treachery of Duli's son and brother, the Emperor regretted his mild decision, and resolved to move the Turks once more to the north of the Yellow River. One of the native governors of the four eastern provinces was selected for the post of khakhan, with his ordo north of the River Loop. Although this man was really one of Gheri's blood, his complexion was so dark that Chula and Gheri had always declined to believe him to be a true Assena, and had suspected him of being a Hu [which must here mean Sart, Syrian, Persian, or Hindoo] : for this reason, though allowed to hold *teghin* rank, he was never permitted to have a *shad* command of his own. But he was the only one who clung to Gheri to the very last and was taken prisoner with him. It was for this fidelity that the Emperor now appointed him. His new dominions extended from the North Bend of the Yellow River to the Desert : he was presented with a drum and a standard, and the Khakhan Bilga (p. 147) of the Seyenda (north of the Desert and south of the Kerulon) was ordered to live in amity with him on peril of

being punished. The old Hiung-nu titles of Left and Right
Virtuous Prince were revived in favour of two other members
of the Assena family, and all were ordered to move northwards
into their old haunts, clear of the Chinese frontiers. The new
khakhan, whose horde consisted of 100,000 souls all told,
40,000 able soldiers included, proved totally unable to govern
his people, who revolted and came in driblets to North Shen
Si, asking for permission to settle there. The khakhan himself at last came flying in on a fleet horse. He was given
a general's command, and in the end met with his death in
the great campaign against Corea, which was now conquered
for the first time and parcelled out into semi-independent
provinces under native rulers, subject to the control of a Chinese
proconsul. As an instance of T'ai Tsung's generosity of
character, it may be mentioned that, when the khakhan
was struck by a stray arrow, the Emperor himself sucked the
wound, and thus managed to keep him alive for a few days
until he could reach the metropolis. He was buried alongside
of the Emperor's father, and a mausoleum was erected to his
memory on the Pêh-tao River in his former dominions:
this is a stream much mentioned in history, and seems to be in
the modern Mao Mingan Mongol reserve to the north of Kuku-
hoton. Thus ends what may be called the first act of the
Northern Turkish Empire drama.

CHAPTER III

THE RISE AND FALL OF MERCHÖ'S EMPIRE

AMONGST the Assena princes was one Chebi, a petty
local khakhan somewhere in the Irtysh region, who on
Gheri's collapse set up as a rival to Seyenda (p. 147). He
had the three clans or " surnames " of the Karluks to the west,
and the Kirghiz to the north, both of which tribes acknowledged

his suzerainty. He sent his son the *teghin* Shaporo to court, and added a promise to come himself : but, as he never did so, in the year 649 the Emperor decided to send a body of Ouigours to chastise him : this force was under the command of a Chinese general. It must be here mentioned that, after the twelve Kankali, High Cart, or Ouigour tribes (for the national name was not yet fixed) had revolted from Gheri, the Emperor received them in state, and gave a " big drink," at which several thousand Ouigours drank their fill and swore maudlin allegiance to the Emperor in their cups. Though nominally parcelled out into provinces (p. 147) under a Chinese High Commissioner residing at or near Kuku-hoton, they were really under their own khakhan Tumed, who broke up the Seyenda, annexed their dominions, and ruled after good old Turkish fashion, subject, it is evident, to Chinese demands for military assistance. The expedition just mentioned was successful, and Chebi was brought in triumph to the capital. The three tribes of Karluks, who had for some time occupied the Tarbagatai region and trimmed, as suited their interest for the moment, alternately with the Northern and Western Turks, now submitted to China, and their territory was turned into three semi-independent native proconsulates. The Kirghiz also came with tribute, and continued to do so until the Ouigour Empire cut both them and the Karluks off from further intercourse with China. But that belongs to the future. T'ai Tsung died in 649, and was succeeded by his son Kao Tsung, who took over his father's concubine,—that Chinese Catherine the Great, the future able and voluptuous Empress Wu. T'ai Tsung himself had married a younger brother's widow, and it is therefore difficult not to discern Tartar influence in conjugal arrangements (cf. p. 142) so repugnant to the Chinese ritualistic mind. All the Turks now being subdued, the new Emperor went in state to report the matter to Heaven on the summit of the famous T'ai Shan Mountain in the province of Shan Tung. Over twenty Turkish chiefs, including one of the Karluk proconsuls at least, swelled the imperial train, and were honoured by having their names carved on the tablet (probably still there). For over twenty years after this there was no trouble whatever in the north. In 679 a general revolt took place,—it is not stated why,—but this was quelled with the assistance of one or two faithful Turkish generals. The Kitans or Cathayans had also now been organized into a native proconsulate, and in the year 640 Karahodjo had been annexed; so that the Chinese Empire was almost as great then as it was under the Manchus, the only T'ang exceptions being the settled or Sart kingdoms (from Kuche round by Kashgar to Khoten) and Tibet. In the year 683 Assena Kutluk, a distant relative of Gheri, took the field, induced a number of the clans to join him, made several successful raids, and set himself up as khakhan. This is the Elteres Kagan of the Kosho-Tsaidam Turkish inscriptions as identified by Radloff, etc. He gave to one of his brothers named Merchö the rank or command of a *shad*, and to another that of *Jabgu*. It seems that another of the Assena family had been allowed to remain within the bend of the Yellow River at the time T'ai Tsung changed his mind and turned all the Turks out of China. This man, being dissatisfied with the treatment he had received at the hands of a Chinese Political Officer, now offered his services to Kutluk. The famous Empress Wu was at this moment in undisguised possession of the throne, and she sent a famous Corean general named Black-tooth against the revolters. He would have been successful, had it not been for the rash jealousy of a Chinese colleague, whose pursuing force of 13,000 men was totally annihilated. The Empress in her fury, with silly feminine spite, changed Kutluk's name to Putsuluk, a purely Chinese combination of words meaning " useless fellow." Kutluk now carried his arms west against the Turgäsh, a branch of the Western Turks then occupying Ili, Sujâb, and Issekul (Sujâb, meaning the *âb* or " River " Suj, was the name of the Western Turk capital on what the maps mark as the River Chu or Chui of Issekul) ; but he died in the course of one of his battles in the year 691. Though Kutluk had left a son, the succession was usurped by his famous brother Merchö, perhaps the greatest conqueror of all the Turks. Dr. Radloff has identified him with the Kapagan Kagan of the Turkish inscriptions found on the above-mentioned branch of the Orkhon. In 693 the new khakhan made a great raid upon Shen Si, and the Empress (who was herself an ex-nun) sent one of her lovers, a Buddhist priest, to march against the offender, with eighteen sub-generals under his orders. The priest was of course totally unsuccessful, and never even came across the enemy : he was flogged to death the next year, nominally for arson. But to everyone's surprise Merchö voluntarily came to court, much to the delight of the Empress, who created him a duke, and presented him with 5,000 pieces of silk. Merchö after this sent an envoy with proposals for an alliance. In 696 the Cathayan proconsul broke out into rebellion, and styled himself the " Khakhan without Superior." Several imperial armies sent against him were severely beaten, and at last it was decided to accept Merchö's offer of assistance, made on the condition that all Turks in China should be returned to him. He completely broke the power of the Cathayans, and annexed them to his dominions, which were now becoming of dangerously large dimensions. Most of the Ouigour land fell into his power, but three or four tribes, including the true Ouigours and the tribe of Hun [as previously explained (p. 110), probably the remains of the Tukuhun], moved south across the Desert in order to avoid him, and settled in the old Turkish fatherland between Kan Chou and Liang Chou. Merchö does not appear to have interfered with the Kirghiz, but he broke up the power of the Western Turks proper, and the envoys of his successor disputed for precedence at the Chinese court with the envoys of the Turgäsh previously mentioned, who had now replaced the Western Turks of Assena family. The Empress in recognition of his services conferred upon him, in addition to his other titles, those of " Great Jenuye and Meritorious Khakhan."

In the year 698 Merchö sent up a dutiful application to be adopted by the Empress as her son; he also said he had a daughter, and would be glad to arrange for a marriage with her: he renewed his demand that all Turks settled in China should be restored to him, and asked for a stock of seed, with agricultural implements. When the Empress hesitated about granting all these demands he got very insolent, and even threatened to murder the Chinese envoy. Making a virtue of necessity, the Empress, on the advice of one of her ministers, drove out several thousand tents of surrendered Turkish families, and sent him 4,000 tons of grain for seed with 3,000 sets of agricultural implements, all which vastly increased Merchö's power and resources. As regards the marriage, she ordered a young prince, son of a half-nephew of hers, to go and marry the Turk's daughter. A military officer of exalted rank, with a brilliant suite and a vast quantity of valuable material for presents, was sent to escort the young man to the nomad court. When the mission reached the southern ordo at Black Sands (a doubtful place; perhaps between Kuku-hoton and Peking), the khakhan said to the Field-Marshal:—" I proposed to marry my daughter to " a scion of the imperial T'ang house of Li, and you now bring " me a stripling of the Wu family! We Turks have for " generations past recognized the supremacy of the house of " Li, and I understand that there are still some of the Li " Emperor's sons alive. I shall therefore march out an army " to assist in seating them upon their rightful throne." He forthwith placed the young Wu prince under arrest, made the Field-Marshal one of his subordinate khakhans, and proceeded to invade the region between Kalgan and Peking. Notwithstanding that two armies of 450,000 men were hurriedly raised to oppose him, Merchö took some towns on the (modern) Shan Si-Chih Li frontier line, burning and slaying every object and every living soul in his way without mercy. The foolish Empress again indulged her harmless spite by changing his name to a somewhat analagous Chinese dissyllable signifying

" Butcher-Sucker," to which Merchö replied by taking more towns and murdering more officials. The Empress now made her imbecile stepson, the dethroned Emperor (whom she had degraded to the rank of prince), take the field in person ; but before the new commander-in-chief could commence his royal march, Merchö had massacred every single one of the 90,000 persons, old and young, of both sexes forming the populations of two great cities which he had captured, and got clear away through the Great Wall at a point thirty miles west of the modern Yih Chou (west of Peking), brutally massacring the whole population as he went along. One of China's most celebrated generals pursued him with a force of 100,000 men ; but in vain. The next year Merchö appointed two of his own and one of his predecessor's sons to high military rank, with 80,000 men between them, and gave them orders to keep up a regular series of raids : he also carried off 10,000 horses from the (still existing) breeding grounds of Eastern Kan Suh, and extended his rule in the West at the expense of the Turgäsh, who were obliged to seek assistance from China.

In the year 703 Merchö sent an envoy with a demand for the hand of one of the Emperor's sons for his daughter. The Empress had to swallow her pride as best she could whilst the Emperor's two sons were paraded for inspection before the Turkish ambassador, and after this several friendly embassies were exchanged. In the year 705, in consequence of a military conspiracy against the Empress, the Emperor resumed the throne, and Merchö signalized the occasion by raiding near the modern Ning-hia, defeating a Chinese army, and lifting another ten thousand horses from the corrals. In the year 711 advantage was taken of Merchö's absence on an expedition against the Turgäsh to rebuild the Surrender Cities (p. 39) north of the Yellow River, which water-course had hitherto formed the Turkish frontier. On the north bank, sixteen miles from the river, the Turks had erected a monastery to which they used to repair in the autumn to pray for good luck : they then turned their animals loose, called a roster, and waited for the ice to settle in order to cross. Opportunity was now taken to recover the whole strip of land south of the Desert, and to build three citadels, each covering the other, at a distance of 125 miles. The central of these three cities, where the Turkish monastery was, was the modern Urad, which town since the fall of the Mongol dynasty 600 years ago has been in possession of the Urad or Orat league of Mongols : a high road to Ouigour Land in later times ran through this. As it is described as being south-east of Tenduc, it is plain either that the Tenduc of the T'ang dynasty must have been much farther west than the Tenduc of Cathay (the one clearly identified by Palladius) or that the province of Tenduc must have extended over a considerable area, and that the military centre must have shifted from time to time. The eastern city was not far from Kuku-hoton, the Tenduc of the Cathayan Empire, the Kwei-hwa Ch'êng of to-day (p. 30). The western was at a place where the Yellow River runs between steep banks, well known in the old Hiung-nu times. A space of over 100 miles to the north of these again, up to what in modern Mongol times are called the Kiran Torohai or Kiran Hills, was taken in, and 180 smoke-signal stations were established, so as to bring the whole territory under a watchful eye. All this had an excellent effect ; Ordous was safe from raids, and great reductions in military expenditure were rendered possible.

After having defeated and killed the Turgäsh khakhan Soka, Merchö's dominions extended over an area of 3,000 miles east and west : the Cathayans and Ghei had to pay him tribute, just as their ancestors the Sien-pi had to pay the Hiung-nu, and he had a standing army of 400,000 horse-archers always ready. His great power, however, made him grow tyrannical, and, as he waxed old, many of his vassal tribes became disaffected. In the year 714 Merchö sent an army to attack Urumtsi, the new residence of a Chinese High Commissioner, and then known as the Northern Ordo : it is interesting to learn the various distances from this place.

Sujâb, the Turgäsh capital (p. 155), was 700 miles to the west. The Kirghiz ordo was 1,200 miles to the north. The Ouigour ordo was 1,000 miles to the north-east, and 40 days by camel from the last. Hamil was 300 miles to the south-east, and Harashar 400 miles to the south-west.—All this tends to show that our available maps are mostly very incorrect. We had (1894) hoped to have been able to consult a new map published by Mr. Charles Waeber, the Russian Minister to Corea, but that gentleman had not yet completed his arrangements for its sale in China. [Mr. Waeber sent me a copy in 1895, but it only deals with Mongolia.]—The attack was a failure : one *teghin* had his head cut off, and Merchö's brother-in-law, afraid to go back to the tyrant, deserted to China together with his wife : they were well received, given titles, and richly rewarded. This led to the surrender of others, 10,000 tents in all : they were once more quartered in the Ordous country or Loop. Among them was Merchö's son-in-law. In the year 715 Merchö fought a tremendous battle north of the Desert, and utterly routed what were called the *Tokuz-Ügüz* or " Nine Clans " of the Kankalis settled there. In 716 he again went north to attack the Baikals, and completely defeated them on the banks of the Tula. Merchö was riding carelessly back, flushed with victory, when suddenly a small party of Baikals rushed out of a thicket, attacked him, and cut off his head : this valuable trophy was at once forwarded to the Chinese metropolis. [The late Professor Thomsen identified with this tribe the *Yér Bayirku* of the Kül *teghin* inscription.] On hearing this news, Kutluk's son Kül *teghin* assembled the tribe, killed Merchö's son and all his brothers, besides most of his relatives and intimates, and set up as Bilga Khakhan the Left Dugi Mercrin, usually known as the " Little Shad." This prince was of a benign character, and at once offered to resign in favour of his patron (a younger brother), who, however, firmly declined the honour, and contented himself with the titles of Left Dugi and Commander-in-chief. Sulu Khakhan of the Turgäsh now thought it a fiittng time to declare his independence, whilst the Cathayans and Ghei in the east also began to come in once more to China with tribute. It was Sulu's envoy who distinguished himself in the year 730 by contesting precedence with the (Northern) Turkish ambassador. Marriage alliances were now formed by China with the Cathayans, and the Turks were never afterwards able to assert a mastery over them.

There was one old Turk named Tunyukuk who had escaped the general massacre. His sarcophagus and two pillars, with 64 lines of "wail" inscription in pure Turkish, were discovered by Frau Klemenz 30 miles east of Urga in 1897. His "lament" confirms almost absolutely the Turkish history of the times as narrated by the Chinese. Although he had been a counsellor of Merchö, he had married his own daughter to the Little Shad, and thus he saved his life; but he had to go back to his tribe. He was now seventy years of age, yet he was so respected that before long the popular voice demanded his return; but a number of tribes, such as the Arslan, were still dissatisfied with the new arrangements, and came over to China. Now, when the last batch of surrenderers had been quartered in Ordous as above narrated (p. 152), the Chinese High Commissioner had deprived them of their arms, and soon afterwards sent them back across the River. As the absence of weapons made it impossible for them either to hunt or to defend themselves against their enemies, they naturally objected strongly, and this led to several fights, in which they of course at last got the worst of it : they had to take refuge in the Little Shad's dominions. Mercrin now thought of making a raid, but Tunyukuk dissuaded him on the ground that the harvests were good and the power of China formidable; chiefly, however, because there was no real ground for war; not to mention that the newly re-assembled horde required rest. The Little Shad next thought he would build a number of citadels and monasteries; but the wise Tunyukuk said :—
" No! The Turkish population is small, not one hundredth
" part of China's, and the only reason we have ever been

"able to cope with her is that we are all nomads, carrying
"our supplies with us on their own legs, and all of us versed
"in the arts of war. When we can, we plunder ; when we
"cannot, we hide away where no Chinese army can get at us.
"If we begin to build towns and change our old habits of
"life, we shall some fine day find ourselves annexed altogether.
"Moreover, the very essence of monasteries and temples is
"the inculcation of mildness of character, but it is only the
"fierce and the warlike who dominate mankind." These
rugged sentiments were highly applauded by the assembly
of councillors and the Little Shad. Compare them with those
of the eunuch renegade 850 years earlier (p. 19).

CHAPTER IV

RESUSCITATION AND FINAL COLLAPSE

IN the year 720 the High Commissioner for Ordous recommended that a great expedition should endeavour to
take the Turkish ordo on the Kera River (apparently Irtish
region) by surprise, invoking the assistance of the Ghei and
the Cathayans on the east and the Basmyls in the west. The
Little Shad was much alarmed when he heard of these preparations, but Tunyukuk calmly said :—"There is no occasion
"for panic. The Basmyls are at present at Urumtsi, which
"is very far west of the Cathayans. I do not believe they
"can ever unite, or that the Chinese army can ever get here ;
"and, even if it does, all we have to do is to move off a few
"days' journey farther north until their supplies begin to
"give out. Moreover the Basmyls are a rash and greedy
"people : when they receive their marching orders, they are
"certain to arrive too soon. Besides, I hear the High Com-
"missioner is on bad terms with the Chinese premier, who
"will probably put a spoke or two in his wheel. We shall

" then catch the Basmyls in a trap." From this speech, and from what follows, we must conclude that the Turkish ordo on the Kera River was, for the moment at least, somewhere near Hamil. Sure enough, the Basmyls did approach first, but, finding no allies, they retired in alarm. The Turks were only too eager to attack them, but the sagacious Tunyukuk said :—" No ! They are now 300 miles from their " home, and will therefore fight desperately. Let us dog " their steps." When they got to within 75 miles of Urumtsi, Tunyukuk divided his forces into two bodies, one going round by an unfrequented route and taking the town by surprise, whilst the other fell upon the Basmyls, the whole horde then on the march, male and female, being carried back into captivity. Tunyukuk took Liang Chou (p. 156) on his return, and carried off a number of horses and sheep. The Chinese governor offered the best resistance he could, but, owing to the very severe cold, his ill-clad men were unable to use their bows. It is not clear why such a petty tribe as the Basmyls (evidently the Bisermans of Carpini in 1246), who are mentioned in one place as being part of Chebi's Tarbagatai horde (p. 153), should have been honoured with a Chinese alliance : in any case they paid a heavy penalty for their temporary prominence. Nor is it clear how Tunyukuk in returning east *to* Hamil could find it convenient to pass to the south-east *of* Hamil. The result of it all was that Mercrin recovered nearly the whole of Merchö's ancient dominions. As unexpectedly as Merchö, he suddenly sent envoys to China, in this instance applying to be considered as the Emperor's son, which favour was granted : but, when he went on to ask for the more tangible favour of a princess, the Emperor " advised himself," and simply dismissed the envoys with gifts. In the year 725 Chang Yüeh [the distinguished statesman and scholar who wrote the preface of Hüan Chwang's book of travels] recommended an increase of soldiers as a precaution against the Turks. He argued that [Elteres Khakhan or] Kutluk's disinterested and warlike second son, with the sagacious Tunyukuk, and the benevolent Shad formed a very formidable combination or triumvirate, and that it was not safe for the Emperor and his guards to make a proposed journey eastwards to sacrifice on the summit of T'ai Shan [in Shan Tung], with such a power in the rear to threaten the provinces thus denuded of troops. Another councillor suggested that the leading Turks should be invited to take part in the procession, and be thus kept out of harm's way. This was agreed to, and an envoy was accordingly sent to try his luck. The Little Shad, his wife, his father-in-law, and Kutluk's other son the *teghin* Kül all sat round in the tent to receive the envoy, and the general picture of Turkish diplomacy is otherwise very graphic. They commenced as follows :—" China enters into marriage alliance with those " curs of Tibetans. The Ghei and the Cathayans were once " the obedient servants of the Turks, and even they are allowed " to marry Chinese princesses. How is it that our repeated " applications for a marriage alliance have never been granted?" The envoy was driven to Chinese shifts to answer this question : he said :—" As the khakhan has expressed a wish to be the " Emperor's son, how can father and son intermarry into " each other's families ? " The clever rejoinder was :-- " You have bestowed the imperial clan name upon the Ghei " and the Cathayans, and yet they can marry your princesses ! " Why should not we ? Moreover we have a shrewd idea " that these so-called princesses are none of them the Emperor's " real daughters. Still, we have never stipulated so curiously " upon this last point that the question of consanguinity of " blood should now be made an objection. Your refusal " makes us look foolish in the eyes of other states." [It must be here explained that the settled Tibetans of Lassa, as distinct from the various tribes that had given ephemeral dynasties to parts of China, had only come into notice as a powerful state within the past sixty years : they were soon able to treat with China on equal terms : their original treaty in Chinese and a modified form of Sanskrit is still in existence, and was found standing in its old place by our expedition of

CHINESE TEXT OF THE KÜL *TEGHIN* MONUMENT,
BEING NO. XVI. OF DR. RADLOFF'S ATLAS OF 1892.
This is the Emperor's eulogy and lament, as recorded in the
T'ang Dynasty's History.

1904.] In the year 710 the Emperor gave an adopted daughter to the gialbo of Tibet, and in 718 his successor gave girls related to the imperial family to the Ghei and Cathayan chieftains. The envoy could only promise to refer the question to the Emperor, and the Little Shad sent an ambassador back with the Chinese mission. The ambassador was " ordered " to form part of the Emperor's escort to T'ai Shan, and was otherwise very well treated ; but still no consent was ever given to the marriage proposal.

The Tibetans now sent written proposals to the Turks suggesting a joint raid upon China : but Mercrin declined, and sent the Tibetan letter up under seal to the Emperor. The Emperor was so pleased with this friendly action that he sanctioned mutual trade at the westernmost of the three Surrender Cities, and presented the khakhan with a large annual sum of money. Tea is now first mentioned as one of the staples given in exchange for horses. [As to the written communication between the Turks and Tibetans, it was probably in some form of Sanskrit or Sogdian, for we are told that some books sent in the year 648 from the king of the Tocharoi (p. 21, but now subject to the Turks) were written in a language " akin to the Buddha language."]

After the Little Shad's death the Turkish Empire rapidly fell to pieces. First his son, then his brother, then another son succeeded, if not two ; then followed a number of murders ; and finally, the Ouigours, Karluks, and Basmyls rose in a body and murdered the reigning khakhan. After a bloody struggle between the Basmyls (who supplied one khakhan for a short time) and the Ouigours on the one hand, and the old king-maker Kutluk's son Kül *teghin* on the other, the Ouigours succeeded at last in gaining the upper hand, and Mercrin's wife, the Khatun, was granted an asylum in China with a handsome allowance as " paint or face-powder money." All this took place about the year 743. Thus disappeared the original Northern or Eastern Empire of the Turks after a stormy career of two hundred years : its partial resuscitation under the name of the Ouigour Empire seems really to be rather a change of dynasty than of people ; but, before we discuss the Ouigours, let us go back and examine the position of the Western Turks after Dalobian's schism (p. 180).

Professor Vilh. Thomsen, of the Copenhagen University, was kind enough to send me (after I had left the original edition of this book to be printed in China), on my arrival in England in 1894-5, a copy of his *Inscriptions de l'Orkhon, déchiffrées par Vilh. Thomsen*, Helsingfors, 1894, in which Bilga Khan gives us in his own language (conveyed in a sort of Aramaean script adapted to Turkish uses) an account of his own doings and those of his brother Kül *teghin* : this stone inscription was set up in the year A.D. 732 under the direction of the Chinese Emperor, and has remained *in situ* ever since.

Shortly afterwards Dr. W. W. Radloff, of the Imperial Academy of the Sciences in St. Petersburg, was also obliging enough to present me with copies of his magnificent Atlases, giving large-sized photographic reproductions of the various Chinese and the Turkish inscriptions on stone monuments. The explanations are in German, and the title is *Arbeiten der Orchon-Expedition*, St. Petersburg, 1892.

Since then F. Hirth, Ed. Chavannes, Paul Pelliot, and others have contributed much to the solution of old Turkish questions from the Chinese side ; but, so far as I am aware, British savants have not been to the fore, the solid, serious, and (so far as possible) trustworthy work having been done by the gentlemen named ; they, again, borrowing from Bang, Marquart, Barthold, and others, translators of the Persian, Arab, Armenian, and Greek authors. Their labours have enabled me to amend various attempts to give the proper Tartar names. Thus the Bumin (p. 130) and Istämi Khakhans of the various inscriptions have been identified with the brothers Tumen and Shih-tie-mi (p. 132), whilst Kapagan Khakhan is our Merchö, uncle of Bilga.

TURKISH TEXT ON THE OTHER SIDE OF THE
KÜL *TEGHIN* MONUMENT, DISCOVERED 35 YEARS
AGO, BEING NO. XVII. OF DR. W. W. RADLOFF'S
ATLAS.

This is simply given here as a specimen, and may perhaps
be discussed in a further work on the nomad invasions of
the West during the past 3,000 years.

BOOK V

THE EMPIRE OF THE WESTERN TURKS

BOOK V

THE EMPIRE OF THE WESTERN TURKS

CHAPTER 1

TEMPORARY BRILLIANCE AND FINAL DISAPPEARANCE OF THE ASSENA FAMILY

ON Tapor's death, the Turks had elected Amro his son to be the Great Khakhan, because Dalobian the son of Mukan was born of an inferior quality of mother (p. 138). This led to a friendly contest between Amro and Shipdu the son of Irski as to which should give way to the other. Finally Shipdu succeeded as Shaporo Khakhan, and Amro settled on the Tula as " Number Two Khakhan." Dalobian went off in a huff to what was in the old Hiung-nu times the land of the Wu-sun nomads of Kuldja. He had Lake Balkash on the west; his dominions included Kashgar to the south, and reached to the desert beyond the Altaï in the north. His southern ordo was seven days' journey north-west of Harashar, which would be about the modern Kuldja : his northern ordo was eight days' journey north of this again, probably at or near the later Emil, founded by the Gurkhan about 1120 (p. 108). He had under him the Kankalis; the Kuche and other Sart states ; the Karluks, the Turruk [i.e. apparently Turkomans, not the same as Turgäsh], the Desert Turks north-west of Hamil, Hamil itself, and perhaps Tashkurgan to the east of Tashkend, " in all which states the manners " were much as those of the Turks, except that the languages " had trifling differences." As with the Turks proper, all the *jabgu, teghin,* and *shad* were Assena agnates of the khakhan ; and the other titles, all hereditary, were exactly as with the Easterners.

Dalobian was taken prisoner by the *jabgu* Chulagu, Shaporo's brother, father of Duli the First (p. 138), also known as the Jabgu Khakhan : [this was the man who received the Chinese pilgrim Hüan Chwang at a place called Thousand Springs, near Merke, west of Issekul (p. 148)]. [It must be noticed that the Chinese, rightly or wrongly, often use such titles as *jabgu* and *djigin* as personal names ; e.g. Mukan Djigin, which probably really is the *Djigin* Mukan ; but Mukan *alias* Djigin, according to the Chinese.] The succession was then given to the son of a certain *teghin* named Angsu, grandson of Tumen, and this son bore the title of Neri Khakhan. Neri married a Chinese woman who bore him a son called Darman. Darman succeeded as Nikül Chula Khakhan—a personage we are specially warned not to confuse with the eastern monarch of that name. His widowed mother, in accordance with the old Hiung-nu custom, now married her Turkish brother-in-law, the *teghin* Boshir, and the happy pair took up their residence in the Chinese metropolis. This was about the year 600. Chula usually resided in his Kuldjan dominions, but he had a number of subsidiary khakhans. One was stationed north of Chash, or Tashkend, and his duty was to keep the various Hu (in its narrow sense, p. 135) in order. Another was stationed north of Kuche (cf. p. 125). At the time when the Sui Emperor induced the Kankalis to co-operate in attacking the Tukuhun (as already mentioned, p. 109), he also endeavoured to persuade Chula to meet him ; but Chula's people objected to the risk. The Emperor therefore resolved to set the Western Turks by the ears, so as to prevent their growing too independent. It will be remembered (p. 138) that Dalobian had taken refuge with Dardö, Shaporo's uncle, when the great schism took place, and Dardö, till then a mere viceroy, had declared himself Bukha Khakhan. Now, the succession had passed through Dardö's son Turruk to his grandson Shifkwi, and Shifkwi had just sent an envoy to apply for a wife. The Emperor accordingly promised Shifkwi a wife if he would give Chula a thrashing, which he did. Chula

Sketch map largely based upon Professor E. Chavannes' "Turcs Occidentaux" of 1903.

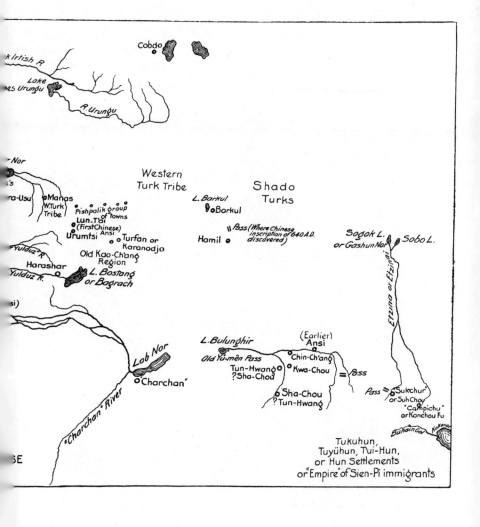

k Irtish R.

Lake
es Urungu

R. Urungu

Cobdo

Western
Turk Tribe

Shado
Turks

r Nor

's

a-Usu   Manas
        W.Turk
        Tribe   Pishpalik group
                of Towns
            Lun-Tai
            (First Chinese)
        Urumtsi   Ansi
            Turfan or
            Karanodja
        Old Kao-Ch'ang
            Region
'Yulduz'
    Harashar
'Yulduz R.   L. Bostang
            or Bagrach

L. Barkul
    Barkul

Pass (Where Chinese
inscription of 640 A.D.
discovered)

Hamil

Sogok L.
or Gashun Nor   Sobo L.

si)

Lob Nor

"Charchan" River

"Charchan"

L. Bulunghir
Old Yu-mên Pass
Tun-Hwang
?Sha-Chou

(Earlier)
Ansi
Chin-Ch'ang
Kwa-Chou

Sha-Chou
?Tun-Hwang

= Pass

Pass =   Sukchur
        or SuhChou
        "Campichu"
        or Konchou Fu

Buhain Gai   Kokonor

SE

Tukuhun,
Tuyühun, T'ui-Hun,
or Hun Settlements
or "Empire" of Sien-Pi immigrants

was taken by surprise, lost his family, and had to fly east to Karahodjo (p. 32),—a place not yet taken by the Chinese, who only appropriated it in 640. The Emperor now sent Chula's mother to try and persuade him to come in : her efforts were successful, and Chula subsequently did good service in Corea under that General Jumen who is already mentioned (p. 100) as having lost 300,000 men there. Ultimately Chula perished at the hands of an assassin sent by the Northern Khakhan Sibir (brother of the other Chula) to murder him.

Now, when Chula of the West came to court, there also came a *teghin* named Danö, along with Hassan Khakhan. [In his excellent work on the *Turcs Occidentaux*, 1903, Ed. Chavannes endeavours to clear up the mystery of these Turkish names, which differ in each dynastic history : he makes out that Nikül-Chula, Darman, and Hassan are one and the same person.] Danö did splendid service for the Sui dynasty in Corea, and subsequently contributed largely to raise the T'ang dynasty to the throne. He died full of honours in the year 638. Hassan was detained by the madman Yang Ti (p. 100), and thereupon the Western Turks elevated his uncle Shifkwi to the khakhan-ship. This was the first of the Western Turks to create a really great empire. His east frontier was the Altan Tagh or Altaï Range, and his west the Caspian Sea. From the celebrated pass at the west end of the Great Wall, westwards, all the nations submitted to his supremacy. He disputed power with the Eastern Turks (or " Northern " as the Chinese generally call them), and fixed his ordo " north of Kuche " (which probably means at or near Kuldja). But he did not reign long, and he was succeeded by his brother, known as the Jabgu-Superior or Chief Jabgu, whose duties had hitherto been, as above stated, to reside north of Tashkend and keep the various Turkomans in order. The new khakhan was known by his old name as the " T'ung Shê-hu or Jabgu-Superior Khakhan," and must not be confused with the Jabgu Chulagu (brother of Shaporo and father of Duli) who ultimately captured Apo (p. 138). The former was a great military captain, and, besides being remarkably brave, was very long-headed. He annexed the Kankali to the north, drove back the Persians to the west, and conquered all the old Hephthalite dominions up to the frontiers of Cophene or Cabul, which also during the third century of our era had belonged to the Yüeh-chï. Persia was one of the 16 governments in the west, described on page 126, after the Chinese had finally broken up the Turkish power : here, again, is confirmation of the fact that the Yüeh-pan must be the Avars, who cannot be the Jwen-jwen, for their very name disappeared a century before this. We know from European sources that Chosröes the Second of Persia, aided by the Khan of the Avars, was now making a gallant stand to save the tottering empire of the Sassanidæ, and that the Græco-Roman Emperor Heraclius was intriguing with the powerful Khan of the Khazars (which probably means the Khazars of the Caspian, and not either the Great Jabgu or one of his subordinate khakhans, whose Ouigour sub-tribe the Chinese call *Ko-sa* without the aspirate), to do as much injury as possible to Persia. The Turks had taken Balkh and Herat as early as the year 589, and in 599 " were assisting their vassals the " Koushans and Ephthalites against the Armenians and " Persians." The last of the Sassanides took refuge in China, and his son Firuz was sent back with the title of king in the year 684. The Arabs now threatened the Turks.

The khakhan, we are distinctly told in Chinese history, dominated the West from his seat in the territory of the ancient Wu-sun (which we have always translated " nomads of Kuldja ") : but he moved his ordo to a spot 300 miles north of Tashkend, which probably means some place on the River Taras. All the kings of Turkestan were made his *gherefa*, and supplied with a *tudun* [this last word appears in the Turkish inscriptions], or civilian administrator, charged with the collection of his tribute : the " Western Tartars " had never before seen so flourishing a power. On the accession of the house of T'ang, the khakhan sent tribute of ostrich-eggs from Mesopotamia [as the Parthian nomads had done

800 years previously when in possession of the same territory].
The Emperor engaged his services against Gheri, and Jabgu
promised that an army would be ready to leave in the winter
of 622 : this so alarmed Gheri that he hastened to assure
Jabgu of his peaceful intentions, and to secure his neutrality.
Jabgu then applied for a wife, and it was decided that the
best policy would be to promise him a wife in order to frighten
Gheri (p. 144), keeping the promise or not as subsequent events
should dictate. A personage of exalted rank was meanwhile sent
to keep him in good humour ; but the marriage never came
off, as the war with Gheri for some time completely severed
the communications between Jabgu and China, and, *a fortiori*,
between the mysterious Fu-lin (*Fereng*, or Franks) and China.
However, after the accession of T'ai Tsung in 626, the envoy was
escorted back by an officer holding the rank of Djigin-Superior,
who brought 5,000 horses and a girdle fashioned out of 10,000
gold nails as presents for the Emperor : yet Gheri would not
hear of a marriage with his rival, and threatened to cut off any
embassies passing with such negotiations in hand. The Jabgu-
Superior Khakhan became tyrannical, as was usually the case
in those regions, with the possession of unlimited power ;
the Karluks rebelled, and at last the chief khakhan was
murdered by a lesser one, his uncle Bagatur. But the Western
Turks would have none of him, nor would the man of their
choice accept the post. There was nothing for it, therefore,
but to set up Jabgu's son, who had taken refuge in the state
of Samarcand : he took the title of " Ilvi Shaporo Fourth
Jabgu Khakhan." Civil war followed, the Kankalis and the
Turkestan states revolted, and Fourth Jabgu received a severe
defeat at the hands of the Seyenda and Kankalis. Being
a violent, cruel, and obstinate man, he soon brought matters
to such a pitch of discontent that he had to take refuge in
Samarcand once more. One of his competitors who had
retired to Harashar was now elected : he was usually known—
apparently by a pun—as the Broad-minded Khakhan, and
the Chinese Emperor (who had himself accepted the title of

Heavenly Khan from the surrendered Turks) conferred upon him the additional purely Turkish title of Kutluk or " Happy " Khakhan. He died a year after this, and was succeeded by a brother, under whom the Western Turks underwent an entirely new organization into Ten Tribes, or " Ten Arrows " as they were also called, from the arrow of authority presented to each. Five were west of Sujâb, and five east, each under a *djigin* or a *chur*. A confusing civil war now took place, which ended in a division into Western and Eastern Empires. One khakhan, who seems to have originally held the viceroyalty of the Kirghiz, Khârism, Hephthalites, and Caspian tribes, took the tract to the west of the Ili River, with his ordo west of the (now) Alexander Mountains, having under him the tribes already named, and the Spotted Horses, a large nomad tribe bordering on and resembling but speaking a quite different language from the Kirghiz, living largely on cheese and kumiss, and so called from the fact that their horses were mostly piebald. The Turks are said to call a piebald horse *ghora* ; hence this people are also called Ghora. Whoever they were, they lived in a colder climate than the Kirghiz, possessed less iron, and had north of them a shy people who used the elk or moose-deer. It seems likely,—in fact it is distinctly stated in one place,—that they were practically the same people as the Basmyls, who used to hunt the deer on long snow-shoes, made of timber with horseskin covers bearing the hair, so as to facilitate their gliding rapidly along. In the struggle already alluded to (p. 163) between the Ouigours and the Basmyls, which followed the fall of Mercrin, one of the Basmyl chiefs, of Turkish or Assena blood, did indeed reign for a short time as the Ghora or " Horse " Khakhan. The other of the two western monarchs, who had his ordo north of the Syr Daria [at a place visited by the Chinese traveller Sung Yün about 520 and Hüan Chwang a century later], had under him Kuche, Tarim, Sherchen (Marco Polo's Charchan), Tochara, Harashar, Tashkend, and the Samarcand group of states. This khakhan was succeeded about the year 640 by another brother, the " Ilvirio Shaporo Jabgu Khakhan," also (much to the confusion of the subject) shortly known as Jabgu. He received every encouragement from the Emperor, who presented him with a drum and a standard in the year 641, and impressed upon him and his rival Turug in the north-west the advantages of peace. Turug, however, was bent on war, attacked his southerly rival through the *tudun* of Taskhend, killed him, and annexed his dominions. In the year 644 the Chinese High Commissioner transferred his seat after the conquest of Harashar from Barkul to Sujâb, where thirty-five years later a walled and well fortified city was run up in a couple of months : previous to this the Chinese had had several skirmishes with Turug ; his people were now getting tired of him, and sent envoys to ask the Emperor to appoint a new khakhan. The Emperor, nothing loth, therefore appointed the great Jabgu Superior's cousin, son of Bagatur, the uncle who had murdered him. This cousin took the title of " Ilvi Shifkwi," and at once proceeded to drive out Turug, who took refuge in Tochara. The new khakhan sent back all Chinese who had been kept in detention by his predecessor, and, in exchange for a wife, or, rather, as her dowry, arranged to cede to China Kuche, Khoten, Kashgar, Kargarik, and another small Pamir state,—or perhaps the control of the Belur Tagh passes is meant.

On the Emperor T'ai Tsung's death, in 649, a Jabgu of the Assena family, named Ghoru (descendant in the 5th generation of Mukan [i.e. Istämi's nephew], and who had been in charge of Emil and the Taras (Black Irtish) valley ever since the original incumbent had joined the Turug faction, and who, finding himself unsafe from the attacks of Ilvi Shifkwi, had sought the protection of the Chinese Commissioner at Urumtsi), turned his back upon his benefactors, occupied Turug's old dominions, and established his dominion, far westward at the Thousand Springs, as Shaporo Khakhan, having under him the Ten Arrows, five of which were called by a name which looks a little like Nushirvar, and are considered the westernmost of the Western Turks, just east of the Jaxartes River (Chinese *Yoh-sha*). Besides carrying war into all the tribes of the West, he made raids upon Urumtsi, in consequence of which a force of 50,000 Ouigour horse, commanded by a Chinese general, was ordered to chastise him, which they did most effectually. In 657 another army, accompanied by two high dignitaries of the Assena family as special envoys, inflicted a series of very disastrous defeats upon Ghoru ; first on the Chinese side of the Ili River, over which he was driven pell-mell ; and then, after taking possession of his ordo, once more upon the Syr Daria (also Jaxartes). His people and horses being now utterly exhausted, Ghoru and his staff sought refuge in one of the small cities of Tashkend state called Shoturkath, whose governor, after pretending to take them under his hospitable protection, surrendered the party to the Chinese. He was sent to the metropolis, where, after having been offered up as a living sacrifice on the tomb of the founder, he was graciously granted his life, together with those of his followers. The whole of the Western Turk dominions right up to the frontiers of Persia were now divided up into clans under the control of two Turko-Chinese presidencies (one of which is mentioned on page 126), subject to the supreme authority of the Chinese High Commissioner at Kuche. China at no period, before or after, ever extended her authority further west than at this time. Ghoru died in the year 659, and was buried alongside of Gheri (p. 149), his achievements being similarly recorded on stone.

Of the two presidencies, the seat of one of which was near Sujâb and of the other near Kuche, one was entrusted to a member of the Assena family named Mizif, who had once been a minor khakhan in the Far West, and who had since served with credit in the Chinese armies, and the other to the viceroy or president of Emil, one Assena Buchin, the man above-mentioned, who had joined the Turug faction ; in other words, the eastern and western divisions of the Western Turk Empire were continued under two Turko-Chinese presidents of Assena blood, who had the right to appoint many, if not all, of the subordinate governors, generals, and other functionaries attached to their presidencies. Both these men had assisted China to get rid of Ghoru. Buchin's ambition was to annex Mizif's dominion too ; so, when called upon to assist the Chinese in punishing the refractory Kuche people, he took the opportunity of poisoning the Chinese general's mind with whispered suspicions concerning Mizif's fidelity. The credulous general, fearing he was about to be entrapped, resolved to be the first in the field of treachery, and, having cajoled Mizif and his chief captains into his lines under pretext of distributing imperial rewards, had them all summarily decapitated. The tribes of the West were naturally full of wrath at this stupid and unjust act. In the year 684, when the Empress Wu began her reign, she thought it a mistake to leave the Ten Arrows without a properly recognized leader, and therefore appointed Mizif's son to the command of the Five Turug tribes proper, and Buchin's son Khusera to that of the Five Nushirvar in place of his father, deceased. In the year 692 the former was falsely accused of some offence by a corrupt statesman bearing the suitable clan name of Lai, who may be described as the Judge Jeffreys of Chinese history ; the khakhan himself was put to death, and his son was banished to the remote island of Hainan. " Judge Jeffreys " was killed in the year 697, and positively eaten by those he had wronged,—a by no means isolated circumstance in Chinese history. The innocent son was recalled in 703, but the Northern Turk Merchö had so accroached his rights that this son durst not return to his nominal dominons, and subsequently died at the metropolis. Meanwhile Buchin's son and Ochir's son Soka in turn continued in charge of the Five Nushirvar Arrows, until finally Merchö's incessant attacks so reduced the whole of the Ten Arrows that the shattered remnants of them, numbering barely 70,000 souls, migrated for protection into Chinese territory. And thus comes to an end the rule of the Assena house in the West, which, in spite of its temporary brilliancy, did not endure so long as that of the original northern dynasty. Harashar, Kashgar, Khoten, and Kuche became Tibetan for a few years; i.e., from 670 to 692 : then the Ansi Proconsulate was re-established at Kuche (cf. p. 126).

CHAPTER II

THE TURGÄSH KHAKHANS OF SUJÂB

THE Turgäsh chief Ochir belonged to one of the two tribal groups of Five Arrows which had been in occupation of the western parts of modern Ili : they were a branch of the Western Turks, and after the events just described the Nushirvar group fell under the rule of Buchin's son Khusera, until the cruelty and oppression of his rule caused them to abandon him in a body. Meanwhile he lived at the Chinese court, whilst the Turgäsh and Ochir managed to get along very well with another Assena chief, holding the Turkish rank of *Kül-chur*, whose name is only given in its Chinese form *Chung Tsieh*, meaning " Loyal " : they had the Northern Turks on their north-east, and the various Turkestan states to the west. It is presumed that the Kirghiz, who were at this time under the Chinese Commissioner at Urumtsi, bounded their dominion to the north ; as to their south, as we have seen, Kashgaria had already been ceded to China for some years. Ochir's son Soga received a high Chinese title on succeeding to his kingdom : he was presented besides with four maidens from the imperial seraglio, and given various ranks and privileges. But the *Kül-chur* above mentioned had conceived a great jealousy of Soga, and sent a bribe of 700 ounces of gold to the Chinese Minister of War with the object of getting rid of him. The Minister sent a confidential agent to discuss the matter with the *Kül-chur*, besides placing certain compromising suggestions of his own in writing. The agent was intercepted by Soga's scouts, and summarily decapitated. Meanwhile Soga assumed a very threatening attitude, and sent an envoy to demand the Minister's head. In the year 709 Soga was defeated and put to death, through the instrumentality of a treacherous younger brother, by the Eastern Turkish conqueror Merchö ; but he himself was killed by Merchö too, on the ground that a man who could betray a brother might also betray an ally. The remains of the horde were rallied by one Sulu, a man of pure Turgäsh stock, who, by his conciliatory manners and general ability, soon succeeded in securing the adhesion of the whole Ten Arrows : his military power was estimated at 200,000 men. In the year 715 he made friendly overtures to the Chinese court, and the Emperor sent him as wife the great-granddaughter of Assena Buchin. This princess, who had sent an officer of her ordo to the Kuche fair with a thousand horses to exchange for other goods, aroused the resentment of the Chinese High Commissioner there by " the airs which," as he said, " the woman Assena gave herself in addressing him " : the incensed satrap was indiscreet enough to flog the officer in charge, and to allow the princess's horses to starve. This led to a war with Sulu, who carried off all the people and stores he could lay his hands on from the " four market-towns " previously ceded to the Chinese, to wit, Kashgar, Khoten, Kuche, and Sujâb (or perhaps now once more Harashar). It was in the year 730 that his envoys struggled for precedence at the Chinese court with those of Mercrin, who claimed that after all the Turgäsh were only offshoots of the Turks proper : the difficulty was settled by the Turks being ranged on the east and the Turgäsh on the west side of the reception tent or pavilion.

Sulu was remarkably indifferent to gain and ostentation, and always made a fair division of the spoil after each battle. He slyly negotiated marriages with the Tibetans and Turks as well as with the Chinese court [Bilga.'s (p. 160) inscription says

" I have given my daughter in marriage to the khakhan of
" the Turgäsh "] ; but this triple seraglio cost money, which
circumstance led to his becoming less generous and more
penurious than before. Besides this, one of his arms became
palsied, which more or less incapacitated him for battle ;
and, as it will be remembered, the old Hiung-nu (p. 4) had no
mercy on weaklings. In the year 738 Sulu met his death
in a struggle between what were called the Yellow and the
Black Clans, and in 742 both Turgäsh and Kirghiz are
mentioned as being subordinate to the Chinese Commissioner
at Urumtsi. After this the Yellow and Black Clans got
fighting together again ; but China just then had her hands
too full with the Shans (early Siamese) and Tibetans to spare
much time for Turkestan. About the year 780 the Karluks
became dominant, and the remains of the two clans became
their vassals, whilst the Ouigours absorbed the rest of Buchin's
old horde. When the Ouigour power was broken up in 847,
these last occupied Harashar. From this time onwards little
is heard of them, but they occasionally came with tribute to
the very end of the T'ang dynasty in 907. After that a branch
of the Western Turks themselves became Emperors of China
in a way we shall now proceed to describe.

CHAPTER III

TURKISH EMPERORS OF NORTH CHINA

AT the time of the great Turkish schism (pp. 133, 139),
when Dalobian went off in a huff, there were living
in the Kur-kara-usu and Manas regions of to-day (i.e. north of
the T'ien Shan, Tengri Tagh, or Celestial Mountains) a small
tribe of Western Turks known as the Shado or " Desert "
Turks, having the clan name of Chuja or Chuzia. The early

history of the family is easily traceable during several centuries, but is not sufficiently remarkable or interesting to be given in detail here. When the Turks, etc., were divided up into two Chinese presidencies (pp. 126 and 177) the Shado tribe were located a little east of Barkul. Their chiefs did good service in the Chinese armies, and the horde usually hung about the environs of Urumtsi in order to avoid the menacing power of the Tibetans. During the period 756–62 both the imperial Chinese capitals had fallen into the hands of rebels, and besides this the Tibetans were very menacing in their demands : communication with the West was entirely cut off, and the only way for Shado envoys to reach China was by begging the favour of a passage through the Ouigour dominions. Under these circumstances the Shado Turks had no alternative but to throw themselves under Tibetan protection, and 7,000 tents of them were in consequence moved to the cradle of the old Assena Turkish race in the neighbourhood of Kan-chou Fu, where the Tibetans found them a useful advance-guard in their raids upon China. For generations their chiefs had been granted the imperial T'ang clan name of Li, but the present lineal representative, Li Tsin-chung, or " Li the Loyal," also enjoyed the Tibetan military title of *blon*. But, when the Ouigours took Liang-chou Fu, the Tibetans thought that it would be dangerous to leave a kindred race like the Shado in their proximity, and resolved to move them " beyond the river." Whatever direction this may have been,— evidently the Yellow River is meant,—it did not suit the ideas of the Shado, who said :—" After being dutiful subjects of " China for several generations, we have unhappily fallen " into the dirt. Surely it would be better to cut our way " east to China than to allow ourselves to be isolated in the " manner proposed ? " Accordingly in the year 808 the whole horde, by this time numbering 30,000 tents, fought their way step by step to that tributary of the Yellow River (the T'ao) which joins it near Lan-chou Fu : here the Tibetans hemmed them in and nearly exterminated them : " the

Loyal " was killed, and when the miserable remains of the horde, led by Chuzia " the Loyal's " counsellor Chuzia " the Just," reached the Wall at Ling Chou (south of Polo's Calachan), it was found that there were barely 2,000 horsemen, —and those mostly wounded—with 1,000 camels, and 700 other animals. A special prefecture was created for their benefit somewhere in the mountains of North Shan Si, and " the Just " was entrusted with the government of his own people. They were liberally supplied with sheep and cattle, and by degrees other driblets of their nation found their way by various roads to the parent stock. The Shado did excellent service in the wars, both under "the Just" and under his son " Loyal Heart," who is regarded as the progenitor of the Turkish dynasty of After T'ang (923–36). The Tibetan power suffered correspondingly, for they were no match as horse-archers for the Shado, whose assistance as bold raiders they now seriously missed. In 870 Chuzia " Loyal Heart " was formally presented with the imperial T'ang dynasty's surname of Li, and the personal designation " Illustrious to the State," whence he is usually known to history as Li Kwoh-ch'ang. At this time China was in an anarchical condition, and had a great deal of trouble with her military satraps, many of whom (like the so-called *tuchüns* of the Republic of 1911–23) aimed at making their commands hereditary and semi-independent ; add to which the celebrated rebel Hwang Ch'ao,—a sort of Chinese " Jack Cade,"—was devastating the southern provinces with his revolutionary mobs ; so that the services of the Illustrious and his able son Li K'êh-yung " the Useful One " were of especial value at this juncture ; but they had to fly before the victorious " Jack Cade " to the *Tatan* tribe in order to reinforce. [This solitary mention of " Tartars " at so early a date is very interesting.] Unfortunately, the tyranny and peculation of one of the Chinese border generals, who was summarily decapitated by the " Useful One," led to an estrangement, and finally to rebellion. At a great assembly of notables, the Useful One, after galloping about

and displaying his wonderful skill as an archer, suddenly
said :—" Why should we spend our lives in the Desert and
" leave the plains of China to the mercies of a miserable rebel
" like Hwang Ch'ao ?   Why not conquer China for ourselves ?"
Meanwhile the rebel mob was in possession of the metropolis
of Si-an Fu, and the various generals in charge of the imperial
forces were making arrangements to invite Li Kwoh-ch'ang
and his son to conduct the campaign, no other captains having
so much influence with the heterogeneous bodies of soldiers
employed.   It took some little time to arrange for their
pardon, and for the change of their status from that of rebels
to that of imperial generals :   however in due time this was
done, and they recovered the capital :   they were both rewarded
with the highest cabinet rank, the son being made a duke
in addition.   The father died in the year 887, and the son
was advanced by the next Emperor to the rank of Prince of
Tsin (i.e. Shan Si).   This rank was inherited by his son
Li Ts'un-hüh.   The T'ang empire fell to pieces in the year
907, and a usurping Chinese general established the Liang
dynasty upon its ruins :   but the Prince of Tsin remained as
loyal as ever to the name of T'ang, and, after destroying
the Liang dynasty, himself established a new ruling house
called After or Later T'ang.   His son Chuzia Maokire, *alias*
Li Sz-ch'êng is best known under his posthumous name of
the Emperor Ming Tsung :   it was under his auspices that
printing was invented, and applied to the cheap reproduction
of the " Stone Classics " first of all.   The Cathayans were now
first coming forward as a really formidable power ;   but two
other Turkish Shado dynasties, those of After Tsin and After
Han, ruled in the northern half of China under Cathayan
auspices until the year 950.   As was the case when the
Hiung-nu and Sien-pi dynasties ruled North China, so now
with their descendants the Turks and the Cathayans ;   they
never established their power beyond the Yangtsze River.
Then followed a Chinese dynasty called After Chou, the last of
the so-called *Wu Tai* or Five Dynasty Period.   Ephemeral

Chinese dynasties sprang up at the same time at Foochow, Canton, Hangchow, Nanking, and in the south-western province of Sze Chuen, until at last the soldiers, sick of strife, forced their general, who had fought for three successive dynasties, to " accept the purple " (in this case yellow) on the field, in Roman fashion; and at last the Empire was reunited in the year 960 under the sway of the illustrious Chinese house of Sung; reunited, that is to say, with the exception of very north China, where a Cathayan dynasty ruled for 200 years (906–1120) on equal terms with the Sung dynasty in central and south China. In 980 this Kitan or Cathayan dynasty assumed the official style of *Ta K'i-tan* or " Great Cathay," and as the Russians first heard of China through the Tartars, and knew nothing of the south, they to this day call China by the sole name of Kitai.

There do not seem to have been any exceptional peculiarities in the manners of the Shado Turks. Unlike the Northern and earlier Western ruling houses, they were not of the house of Assena, but belonged to one of the obscurest and smallest tribes, originally under one of the sub-khakhans, subject first to the viceroys of the west, and afterwards to Dalobian and his successors (pp. 133, 180). They seem to have been distinguished for their unusual courage, loyalty, bravery, and skill in fighting, while the whole of their history, so far as we know it, is bound up with Chinese interests. It is singular that the weakest of the Turkish tribes should have been the only one to attain to the dignity of Chinese Emperors. Maokire, especially, is spoken of by the official historians with extreme respect. The Shado were still in the old quarters—those last assigned to them near Kuku-hoton—in Marco Polo's time. The Nüchên dynasty, a century later than Maokire, moved the Kan Suh portion to Liao Tung, but some of the Tenduc tribe of North Shan Si became Christians, and, under the name of Ongku, married into Genghis Khan's family. Marco Polo, confusing Ongku with Wang Khan of the Keraïts, calls the former Prester John.

Some at least of the Shado must moreover have remained

in or returned to their old Kur-kara-usu territory ; for, during
the Cathayan dynasty (906–1120) which preceded the Nüchêns,
we find them a vassal tribe there. From other remarks by
Chinese authorities of weight, it seems probable that the
Tatan of the old T'ang history, and the *Tata* or *T'a-t'a* of later
records, must have been in some way allied to the eastern
Shado (cf. p. 97).

It is important to bear one thing in mind. When the
Hiung-nu fled westward, it was probably not the nation that
fled, but only the Jenuyes and the other three or four noble
clans ; for no nomad empire was ever more than an ill-digested
political conglomeration. So, when the Turkish Empires
above described came to an end, most of the people, being
unsympathetic tribes, would remain where they were : it
was merely the Assena family of masters that gave place to
another group. The broadly distinguishing feature in
Hiung-nu and Turkish, as distinct from Sien-pi and Cathayan
administration, which was more democratic, is the hereditary
and aristocratic organization of the state.

Before we dismiss the subject of the Turks we must take
a look at the Kirghiz and other obscure tribes.

CHAPTER IV

THE KIRGHIZ

THE history of the Kirghiz is traceable with almost perfect
clearness from the beginning of time to which man's
memory runs, and they seem to occupy, in part at least,
almost the same ground now that they did 2,000 years ago,
when the Jenuye Chirche (p. 40) overcame them and made
their ordo one of his capitals. Their race was much mixed up
with the Kankalis, and indeed both they and the High Carts,

whom we know to be Kankalis, or rather perhaps the ruling castes of each, are variously reported to have been the descendants of the same almost pre-historical northern tribes we have assumed to have been Kankalis. They never had any sustained intercourse with China until they were known by the name of Kirghiz ; but, previously to that, they were known from generation to generation by various names, all having a graduated resemblance to that word, and probably merely reflecting the change in dialect ; until finally we find the Tölös of the Orkhon inscriptions. East of them was a Turkish tribe called the Kurkan, who seem to have occupied both the north and south sides of Lake Baikal : the Chinese, noticing how unusually long the summer evenings were in these high latitudes, " the sun only setting during the period required to cook a leg of mutton thoroughly," imagined, in their ignorance of physical geography, that they were " near that part of the world where the sun went down." South-west of them were the Karluks, and Lake Balkash was undoubtedly in the Kirghiz domain. The word Kirghiz (Menander's χερχίς) is a corruption said to mean " tan-coloured faces " in the Ouigour language. Their proper designation was Kerkur. Chinese geographical descriptions are so vague and disproportionate that it is difficult to fix the relative bearings of any two countries, but it would seem that, towards the east, the Kirghiz must have had, at least at certain seasons of the year, certain Orotchi, Tupo, Mireka, and other Tungusic races on their farthest frontier ; for the descriptions given of birch-bark houses or huts, sledges propelled by poles, sable-hunting on long snow-shoes, feeding on the *Lilium spectabile* in lieu of grain, placing dead bodies in chests and hanging them on trees or exposing them on the hills, all point to Tungusic habits of life.

The description given of the Kirghiz themselves is very full and to the point. When first known through the Turks, they possessed 80,000 good soldiers. Their land was marshy in the summer and full of snow-drifts in the winter.

They were of tall stature, very active, with a reddish tinge of hair, white complexions (which peculiarity hardly accords with the " tan-coloured faces "), and a greenish iris to the eye. [It is to be noted that the nomads of Kuldja, who utterly disappear from Chinese history before the Turks are heard of, also attracted attention by their reddish hair and green or blue eyes. The Ungri or Hungarians who came to Hungary in the ninth century after the Goths, Huns, Gepidae, Lombards, Avars, etc., had in turn displayed themselves in that region, have never been satisfactorily accounted for,—in 1910 M. Kalman Nemati, a Hungarian, spent some time with me in his endeavour to trace the Asiatic origin of his people,— and possibly they may be the ancient Awsen, Wu-sun, or " nomads of Kuldja " of Hiung-nu times (p. 25) : the Wu-sun cannot well be the Kirghiz, for the history of the early Kirghiz or Kerkur is clear and connected ; and, besides, they are alluded to at the same time as, and are never mentioned in sympathy with, the nomads of Kuldja.] They think black hair is ominous of evil, and they regard those of their people with a black iris as being the descendants of the Chinese general who surrendered to the Hiung-nu in B.C. 100, and received a royal Tartar wife (p. 32). The women are more numerous than the men, and wear rings in their ears. The bravest men tattoo their hands. When the girls marry, they tattoo their necks. They live promiscuously, and are mostly lascivious. [Here follows a short description of their methods of time-keeping, which is unintelligible.] They keep count of the year by the use of the Twelve Beasts [the Animal Signs, or Duodenary Cycle, as developed by the Chinese] ; for instance, what the Chinese would call a " *yin* year " is with them a " tiger year." [Chavannes and others have published many learned papers as to the rival claims of Tartars and Chinese to originality in devising this Cycle.] The climate is mostly cold, and even the largest rivers are half frozen over. Of crops they have rice, millet, wheat, barley, and oats, which they triturate into flour with a machine worked by the feet, planting in April–May and reaping in October–November. They ferment a spirit out of boiled rice, but have no fruits or vegetables. [Rice so far north seems an anomaly.] They tend their horses until full-grown, when the best fighter is made leader of the herd. They also possessed wild horses. They own camels, cattle, and very many sheep, a rich man often owning several thousand. There were the *Antilope gutturosa*, the *Ovis argali*, and a deer like the *Cervus pygargus*, but larger and darker, with a black tail. Of their fishes the *mir* or *mit* was eight feet long, and the *moghen* was boneless and had its mouth below its chin. The birds were wild-geese, wild-ducks, crows, magpies, hawks, and kites. Of trees there were the birch, elm, fir, willow, and flag. Birch were the most plentiful, but some of the fir-trees were so high that you could not shoot an arrow up to the top. There is great plenty of gold, iron, and spelter. After the rains they always manage to secure some iron of a very hard quality called *kasa* or *gasha*, excellent for making weapons : they used to send it as tribute to the Turks. [Superior iron and knives offered by the Western Hu to the travelling Emperor Muh are mentioned by the Chinese about B.C. 960.] In battle they use bows, arrows, flags, and banners, and their cavaliers carve wood into shields for protecting the legs and feet : they also have a round shield to cover the shoulder and keep off darts and arrows. Their chief is called *Ajir* or *Ayet*, which is also used as a clan name ; and all of the clan hoist a standard, for which a red colour is preferred : others take their tribe names as a personal designation. For clothing they esteem most the sable and beaver. The Ajir in winter wears a sable hat, and in summer a pointed metal helmet with a turned up tip : all below him wear white felt caps, and they like to carry hones at the belt. The meanest merely wear skins, and no head-covering. The women wear a sort of frieze and embroidered silks from south-western China, which are sold or bartered to them by the Arabs at Kuche and Urumtsi. [The Abbassides sent troops in the year 800 to assist the

Tibetans in their wars with the early Shans or Siamese : the Chinese historians call them " Black-clothes Tazi."] The Ajir's ordo is surrounded by a stockade in lieu of a wall. They join pieces of felt together to make tents, which are called *mitichida*. The chiefs live in small tents. Whenever there is a summons to arms or a census of their vassals these have to pay a tribute in sables and martens or ermines. Their officials are six ranks : ministers, proconsuls, commissioners, residents, generals, and *dakan* [this is a Turkish title also, possibly the *daruga* or *darugachi* of Genghis Khan's time (see p. 131).] There are seven ministers, three proconsuls, and ten commissioners, all in charge of troops : of residents fifteen, of generals and *tarkhan* no fixed number. Every one lives on flesh and kumiss : only the Ajir has cakes set before him. Of musical instruments they have the flute, drum, Pandean pipe, horn, and tray of bells. Of sports they have camel, lion, and horse performances, and rope-dancing. They worship the unseen powers ; but if the pasturage fails they call in the services of a wizard. In marriages they give sheep and horses as betrothal presents, the rich often thousands at a time. At funerals they do not gash their faces, but parade thrice round the body, wailing ; they then burn it, collecting the bones and making a tomb when the year is out ; after which at certain intervals they utter lamentations. For winter habitations they provide roofs of bark. Their written character and spoken language are exactly like those of the Ouigours [which confirms the theory that the Kankali and Kirghiz are practically one stock]. The laws are very strict. For flinching in battle, failing in duty as an ambassador, suggesting mischievous state policy, or robbery, the punishment is decapitation. If a son commits robbery, his head is fastened to his father's neck and left there until he dies. When they came to court in 841–6, sketches were made of them as being such curious people, and every piece of information it was possible to gather about them was placed on record.

The Ouigour ordo was about 600 miles north-west of the

north-west corner of the Loop,and the Kirghiz ordo was 40 days more by camel. [Thus the one would be about Caracorum, and the other somewhere between Cobdo and the Black Irtysh.] The Turks were in the habit of giving wives to the leading Kirghiz chiefs, of whom there were three grades,—the *kisik*, *kushapo*, and *amei*. When first they attracted notice in China they were a subject state of the Seyenda, who had a *gherefa* over them ; but, in the year 648, when they heard the various Kankali tribes had submitted to China (see p. 175), the Kirghiz chief came to court, and the *gherefa* was made a Chinese prefect *in partibus*, subject to the control of the High Commissioner. Thus things went on for a century, when in the year 759 they were broken up by the Ouigours and totally cut off from intercourse with China : their only safety lay in joining caravans with the Arabs, Karluks, and Tibetans when they wished to escape the Ouigours : for instance, the Tibetans would remain in Karluk land until a Kirghiz escort should arrive to take them home. Their Ajir at that time held an official rank at the hands of the Ouigours ; but, as the power of the latter fell off, he assumed the title of khakhan, and in the year 841 killed the Ouigour ruler in battle, burning his ordo, and securing the person of his wife, who was a Chinese princess. He then moved his ordo south to a point [perhaps Uliassutai] only fifteen days' journey by horse from the Ouigour ordo : he was in the act of sending the princess loyally back to China when the Ouigours recaptured her. His ambassadors, who explained all this, took years to reach the capital, and the Emperor Wu Tsung (840–6) was delighted to see such remote visitors : he placed them on an equality with Puh-hai [the Manchurian state then and now known to the Japanese as Botskai : Botskai, or in older Chinese, Put-hai, was a highly civilized state which maintained itself in a condition of semi-independence from A.D. 700 to 900, when it was absorbed by the Cathayans. The Botskayans were the most civilized of all that pig-breeding race of hunters which subsequently produced the Kin dynasty of Nüchên Tartars and (later) the recently dethroned Manchu dynasty (1644-1912)]. It was for the moment resolved to invest the Ajir with the title of khakhan, and also with the inheritance (so to speak) of the Turks and Ouigours ; but, the Emperor dying, it was submitted to his successor that an obscure people like the Kirghiz were not fitted to treat with China on equal terms ; moreover, that the Ouigours had once served us faithfully, and had been in their times of prosperity invested with Chinese titles : so the matter dropped. A few years later the empty title was granted, but the Kirghiz never succeeded in obtaining the coveted birthright, and after sending tribute once or twice, they practically disappear from political history altogether. In Manchu times they have been known as the Buruts and Kaisaks, speaking the same language but suspicious of each other. Part of the Kaisaks belong to the Russian sphere as Kirghiz-Kaisaks.

CHAPTER V

MISCELLANEOUS TURKISH VASSALS

TO complete the subject, it may be well to merely mention a few other Turkish tribes. The most northerly were the Bukku, with 10,000 soldiers ; very rough and intractable : they were first under Gheri (p. 173), then under Seyenda ; after about the year 750 they seem to have been absorbed into China. West of the Bukku were the Telenguts, with 10,000 soldiers : they were east of Seyenda, on the Tongra River, and never had any intercourse with China until the great surrender of 648, after which their name disappears ; but the Kül-*teghin* inscription seems to mention them (see p. 160). The Bukku seem to take their name from the River Irtysh (p. 190). The Tongra were north-east of Seyenda, with 15,000 tents : they were at first under Gheri ; then submitted, but took to raiding ; and were at last broken up by the Ouigours. Possibly the River Tula is meant, though usually written (in older Chinese) Tuk-lo. The Baikals were east of the Bukku ; and a river, probably the Angara, 300 miles north-east of their land, had the property of petrifying wood in two years [the same thing takes place near the oil-wells of Burma]. Their language differed slightly from that of the other Kankalis : [it is possible Baikal may be a wrong guess, and that Marco Polo's Bargu, north-east of Caracorum, also called the Kara Mongols, are meant ; but the Russian Archimandrite Palladius has shown pretty clearly from modern Manchu history that a *butkha* (Chinese *pu-t'ê-ha*) tribe of " hunters " gave trouble in 1696, and are of Mongolian rather than Tungusian type]. The Ghuser and Adir were north of the Telenguts ; the Kibirs lay to the south. About 170 miles north-east of the Baikals, were a reindeer-keeping, moss-eating people called Kuk, herding pell-mell together in houses of timber ; and fifteen days east of them were the Ugai, with customs like the Baikals. Then, still eastwards, came the Sib, the Ghei, and the Cathayans, all hitherto mentioned in this book.

BOOK VI

THE EMPIRE OF THE OUIGOURS

BOOK VI

THE EMPIRE OF THE OUIGOURS

CHAPTER I

RISE AND FALL OF THE FIRST DOMINION IN THE NORTH

THE Hiung-nu conquered to the north a people called by
the Chinese Ting-ling, of whom they knew nothing
except that in Sien-pi times the Ting-ling occasionally fought
on the Chinese side. The Chinese were also puzzled to find
that there were also some Ting-ling in the West. As we have
shown (p. 186), their historians trace both the Kirghiz and the
High Carts, in a vague sort of way, at one time to the Ting-
ling, at another to the Kankalis, and we are distinctly told that
the Kirghiz and the Ouigours spoke exactly the same language.
Now, at a time when no more is heard of the word Ting-ling
or Tik-lik (p. 123), a new word Tchirek or Terek comes into
use, and all the tribes of the north-east, between the Turks and
the Cathayans, that surrendered to T'ang T'ai Tsung in 648
are grouped together under this one generic word (p. 186).
The Tereks are said to have differed in manners from the
Turks only in this, that in marriages the man visited his wife
as long as he liked, returning after a son was born. But the
forbears of the Tereks are said to have been the High Carts,
and it is quite clear that the Ouigours were at first a petty
tribe of Tereks, ultimately a great empire eponymously.
The Tereks also extended west to the Caspian, and even in
Mongol times we read of Kankali tribes there. Moreover
kunkly is Turkish for " a cart " (p. 40), and the Chinese sounds

k'ang-li used in Genghis' time for the Kankalis are the same as the Chinese sounds *k'ang-li* used in the 6th century for one of the *teghin* of the khakhan Sibir (p. 141). It may therefore be broadly stated that the cart-using Hiung-nu and Turks north of the Desert, Issekul, and Syr Daria, or Upper Jaxartes, were in ancient times called Ting-ling, then High Carts, then (another form of Ting-ling) Terek, and finally, when the Ouigour tribe became predominant, Ouigours and Kankalis. It is possible that the Mongol word *delegei* " earth " may have some etymological connection with Terek, in the sense of " autochthonous." In the early parts of this work as few uncouth names as possible have been used in order that the reader may obtain a preliminary grasp of the subject ; the word Kankali has been accordingly introduced, without much explanation, to facilitate the obtaining of a general bird's-eye view of the whole subject. But the reader has now become familiarized with certain ideas and expressions, and the matter may be gone into deeper without (it is hoped) causing weariness and disgust.

It may be shortly said, therefore, that the Ouigour tribes were those of the ancient Hiung-nu left behind, after the ruling castes migrated westward, which were not under the Assena Turks, and which were not Kirghiz : they were strong, daring nomads, great horse-archers, and fond of raiding ; as soon as the quite new name Turk (p. 129) became magical under the Assena family, they formed part of the Turkish dominion. It was under Chula Khakhan (p. 170), who forcibly annexed the Tereks and exacted heavy contributions from them, that the first bad blood was made ; dreading their resentment, he assembled and treacherously massacred a number of their chiefs. The Ouigours, Bukku, Tongras, and Baikals then revolted, and set up a *Djigin* of their own, with the national name Ouigour. [The Tongra are mentioned in Kül *teghin's* stone inscription.] The Ouigour's clan proper was called Yokraka, and they dwelt north of the Seyenda, on the River Selinga. Their horde numbered 100,000, of which total half were able soldiers: their land was mostly nitrous, barren desert; and their flocks consisted chiefly of large-footed sheep. The first *Djigin's* name was Ziken, but in Sibir's time his son Busat (the usual Chinese way of saying Bôdhisattva), who had been well-trained by a careful mother, made himself a great name. He joined the Seyenda in utterly defeating a force of 100,000 men under Gheri's lieutenant Duli (p. 147), and obtained the sobriquet of " Living Gherefa." He established his ordo on the River Tula. He first sent tribute to China in 629, when the first Turkish power had already collapsed and the Seyenda tribal chief alone was powerful besides himself. On Busat's death one of his chiefs named Tumed broke up (p. 154) and annexed the Seyenda, who appear, however, to have soon recovered themselves for a few years. Meanwhile the other Tereks, including the Ouigours, Telenguts, Baikals, Bukku, Tulas, Ghuser, Adir, Kibir, Ghei-Kir, White Sib, Sekir, Hun, and Kirghiz (the last now first grouped with the Tereks) submitted to China through their chiefs, who were entertained by the Emperor, and became mediatized officials of the Empire. At their request, good roads, provided with relay stations, were laid out from China to the Ouigour and Turkish political centres. Tumed, as has been explained, whilst outwardly conforming to the Chinese arrangements, was really a new khakhan, and in his own dominions was in fact so styled : he had twelve ministers, six for the interior with six for his outer dominions, and his ordo was organized in Turkish fashion. For some unexplained reason his (apparently adulterous) nephew murdered him, and the succession passed through Borun his son to Birut his grandson and Dukhetch his great-grandson.

Merchö's second Turkish Empire was now becoming formidable, and he seized upon the old Terek land (p. 160) : in consequence of this the Ouigours, Kibir, Sekir, and Hun tribes moved south (it will be remembered) to the old cradle of the Turkish race near Kan-chou Fu, where they did occasional service for China against the Tibetans. In the year 717

Dukhetch's son Vughteber assisted in the fighting which ultimately resulted in Merchö's death. His son, again being falsely accused of some offence by the Chinese proconsul, was banished to South China, where he died : the consequence of this was that the proconsul was murdered by an agnate of the clan, and the high road to Barkul was obstructed. This agnatic relative fled to the land of the Turks, where he died. But the Turks themselves were now once more in the state of political confusion already described as having followed the death of Mercrin. The son of the agnatic relative who had murdered the proconsul, by name Kurlik Bira, entered with vigour into the general tussle, in which the Basmyls and Karluks also took a part. It ended in the Basmyl pretender losing his head ; and Bira, who sent envoys to China to explain events, thereupon took the title of Kutluk Bilga Khakhan. The Emperor created him a Chinese prince, and removed him farther south to what had been the Turkish capital on the Orkhon : this must have been near Caracorum, for we are told it was over 500 miles north of the westernmost of the three Surrender Cities. The territory of the Nine Clans, with whose armies Merchö shortly before his death had fought such a bloody battle, was annexed by him. [It is unnecessary to give the uncouth names of all these clans ; but we may mention one, the Kazar or Khazar, who are also mentioned two centuries later as having joined in the invitation to Li Kwoh-ch'ang and his son,—the two famous Shado generals (p. 182). They would seem to have mostly migrated west, for the history of the T'ang dynasty gives a Khazar race north-west of the Arabs, i.e. the Caliphs, and we know that the Khan of the Khazars was, long before this, assisting Rome against Persia and the Avars, whilst Chinese history says that Persia is near the Turk Khazars (cf. p. 126).] The Karluks and Basmyls were also annexed, at least in part, and were always made to fight in the van. Bira was now formally appointed Khakhan through his envoy at the Chinese Court : he achieved several other victories over those Turks who were fighting in the interests of Kutluk's descendants (the Kutluk of Mercrin's time), received further imperial commendation, and gradually extended his empire from the Fish-skin Tartars in the east to the Altaï in the west, having the Great Desert on the south ; in fact, he once more conquered the old Hiung-nu domain.

Bira died in the year 756, and was succeeded by his son Mayen *chur*, otherwise the Bilga *chur*, or the *teghin* Kale. [Kale was the name of one of the Shado chiefs, too, and *teghin* was a Turkish title, at this time often used by the Affghan-Persian group of states, as, for instance, Alpteghin of the Ghiznee dynasty or the *teghin*-Shah of Gandhara.] His personal name was the Mayen *chur*, and he did good service against the famous fat Turkish rebel Amroshar, who, after conducting the war against the Cathayans as China's representative, in the end rebelled against his imperial master. [It is Amroshar who has left on record the remark that the Turks consider the mother before the father.] The Mayen *chur* also assisted as a lieutenant the celebrated general Kwoh Tsz-i, who is believed to have been a Nestorian Christian. The Tibetans were now in possession of the ancient Yüeh-chï territory, and both Chinese capitals were in the hands of rebels. Both were soon retaken, with the assistance of the Ouigours, who were at first allowed to loot the eastern capital, modern Ho-nan Fu, but were subsequently induced by a present of 10,000 pieces of silk, locally raised, to go away. For these services the Mayen *chur* was most handsomely treated by the Emperor, and received an annual present of 20,000 pieces of silk.

It is curious to read in the year 758 of the Abbaside Caliph's envoy and the Ouigour envoy struggling for precedence at the Chinese court. As in the case of the analogous diplomatic contest between Eastern and Western Turks, a compromise was arranged, and the rival envoys entered the presence room at the same time, but by different doors. Mayen *chur* received an imperial princess in marriage ; but he was inclined to be haughty when she arrived, and it was only after pressure that the envoy induced him to prostrate himself out of respect for the Emperor.

Kale did not live long. He was succeeded about the year 760 by his second son Idiken, who, finding that China was in a disorganized condition, allied himself with an adventurer, then setting himself up as a rival emperor, and advanced far into Shan Si with a view of plunder. By somewhat abject and humiliating diplomacy the Chinese managed to arrest their progress, but not until the haughty Ouigour and his *khatun* had caused one or two of the mission to be flogged to death for not " going through their postures " as demanded by Ouigour etiquette. This *khatun* was not the imperial princess, but only the daughter of General Bukku, a Turk in high Chinese employ, whose family had intermarried with both the Sui and the T'ang dynasties. The critical state of China precluded any idea of avenging the insult for the moment, and accordingly the imperial troops, assisted by the Ouigours, dispersed the rebels in a battle fought near the extreme south-west corner of Shan Si, and once more advanced upon the eastern capital. After that, they disposed of another rebel to the east, near Peking, "marching through a sea of blood for 600 miles," insulting the officials, plundering the people, kidnapping girls, and making themselves generally a curse. Yet they had to be rewarded as usual with titles and estates, and moreover, being staunch Manicheans, they insisted on having churches in even Central China. [On this subject MM. Ed. Chavannes and Paul Pelliot have published pamphlets of the highest historical and scientific value, showing the junction or contact point between Arab-Persian and Turko-Chinese civilizations.]

In the year 765 General Bukku rebelled on account of some fancied grievance, and arranged with the Tibetans and Ouigours to make a raid. But he died before anything serious was done, and Idiken arranged matters with Kwoh-Tsz-i, laying all the blame on Bukku, and offering to attack the Tibetans if Bukku's son, the *khatun's* brother were pardoned.

This *khatun* died in 768, and her younger sister was sent to replace her.   China was now so exhausted that the half-starved animals of the highest dignitaries of the state had to be impressed in order to convey her and the 20,000 pieces of silk sent as presents to the Ouigour khakhan.   The Ouigours, growing more insolent as they grew more indispensable, exacted forty pieces of silk for each horse brought to China, and they had brought 20,000 or 30,000 already : their envoys succeeded each other with wearisome rapidity, each expecting handsome entertainment ;   and now, as a culmination of misery, China was asked to take 10,000 more horses.   The unfortunate Emperor, unwilling to oppress his people further, had to effect a compromise.   In other ways the Tartars showed a domineering spirit which the Chinese durst not repress.   One Ouigour murderer was pardoned without trial, and another was forcibly rescued from prison by his comrades.   In 778 they made a raid, defeated the Chinese army sent to check them, and butchered ten thousand people. A second Chinese army was more successful.

The Emperor died the next year, and a eunuch was sent to announce the demise of the crown to the Ouigours.   The envoy met the khakhan with his whole army making for the Wall, but the haughty monarch neglected even to salute the envoy.   One of his ministers, apparently named the Tun *Baga*, remonstrated with him touching the unwisdom of this hostile policy : as the khakhan rejected his advice, the Tun *Baga* butchered him, his relatives, and two thousand other persons, setting himself up in his place as the "Alp Kutluk Bilga Khakhan."   In 780 an envoy was despatched from China to confirm the new ruler in his dignities.

The Ouigours proper seem to have considered themselves superior to the Nine Clans, who were the real guilty parties in the last raid, and of whom 2,000 had been massacred by the Tun *Baga* for giving Idiken evil counsel.   Shortly after this, a number of Ouigour and Nine Clan chiefs, who had been accumulating riches in the Chinese capital and were returning north, were discovered to have a cargo of girls cunningly concealed in their camel train ; the fraud was detected by one of the frontier officials poking each load with a long awl to see what the contents were. The guilty smugglers of the Nine Clan faction were afraid to go back when they heard of the Tun *Baga's* accession and massacres, and so they submitted to the Chinese frontier governor a plan for massacring all the Ouigour chiefs, who, they suspected, would not allow them to make their escape as they wished. The frontier officer approved this idea, and, as a preliminary, reported to the Emperor that the Ouigour power was really nothing if once separated from that of their vassals the Nine Clans. Meanwhile he sent a junior officer with instructions to behave rudely to the leading Ouigour chief,—one of the khakhan's uncles,—who of course lost his temper and raised his whip. The Chinese commander then marched up the troops he had lying by in readiness, massacred both the Ouigours and the other Tartars, and recovered 100,000 pieces of silk, with several thousand camels and horses. He then reported to the Emperor that the Ouigours had flogged one of the Chinese superior officers and had attempted to take the town,—the land of the modern Ulan-chap Mongols,—and that he had thought it his duty to anticipate their treacherous movement by killing them all, and now had the honour to return a bevy of maidens discovered, etc., etc.

The Emperor at once recalled and replaced the over-zealous frontier officer, and sent a eunuch to explain what had occurred to the Ouigour minister-resident. At the same time orders were sent to the special envoy who was on his way to confirm the khakhan in his titles to await further commands : he did not proceed onwards until the next year, when he took with him the coffins of the khakhan's murdered uncle and three other Ouigours of rank. The khakhan ordered his ministers to proceed with their carts and horses to meet the Chinese envoy, who was at once charged with conniving at the murder of the khakhan's uncle. He explained that the uncle had lost his life through getting involved in a quarrel with the frontier commandant, and that the Emperor had not ordered the massacre. For fifty days the envoy and his suite were kept in confinement without an opportunity of seeing the khakhan, and they had a very narrow escape from death whilst heated debates were going on in Ouigour circles. At last the khakhan sent the following message :—" My people " all demand your execution. I am the only exception. " But, as my uncle and his colleagues are now dead, to kill " you would simply be washing out blood with blood, and " making a dirtier mess than ever. I think it better to wash " out blood with water. What I say is this. The horses lost " by my officers are worth nearly two millions, and you had " better pay up this compensation sharp ! " He sent back the envoys with a mission of his own, and the Emperor, swallowing the leek, paid the money.

Three years later the Ouigours applied for a marriage alliance. The Emperor, still smarting under recent humiliations, said to his prime minister :—" Our descendants must fight out this marriage question. I can't stomach it." The premier asked :—" Surely your Majesty is not still thinking of the flogging of our envoys in the presence of Bukku's daughter ? " The Emperor said :—" Yes, I am : and it " was only the condition China was in at the time that " prevented her taking instant revenge." The premier argued :—" But that was Idiken, who, knowing your Majesty " would avenge the wrong, was just about to anticipate your " action and make war upon you when he was killed by the " present khakhan ; on the other hand the latter, notwith " standing the murder of his uncle, has made friendly advances. " I think the marriage should be conceded, and there can be " no harm done if we apply the rule, laid down for the Turkish " khakhans Mercrin and Sulu (p. 179) fifty years ago, limiting the " suite to two hundred and the number of horses to be brought " for sale to a thousand." The Emperor gave way, and the khakhan in his effusive gratitude for the princess (who lived to serve four other khakhans in succession) offered to lend his services, when required, against the Western Turks (some of which nation, it will be remembered, joined the Ouigours at this time when the Karluks became predominant at Sujâb, p. 178).

It was the khakhan Tun *Baga* who applied to China just now for permission to change the national designation in a more warlike sense ; that is, the Chinese way of writing it, which now became in Chinese signification *Houighour* or " swooping hawks." It is much as though the Germans, who call themselves Deutscher, had applied to the Roman Emperor to have their name changed from Germani to Germanes on account of their " cousinly " behaviour. [This leads to the consideration of another point. The Mahomedans of Tartary began to be called Ouigours some centuries after these events, and in Genghis Khan's time we find the term almost exclusively applied to Mussulman Tartars, whilst the new term Oui*wh*our (the difference in both syllables being merely a question of *afflatus* in the Chinese characters used) was applied to the then still existing Oui*gh*our states about Urumtsi and Pidjan, and also to the historical ancient race that emanated from the Caracorum region. In the 13th century we find the Karakitai (p. 108) calling the ruler of Samarcand the " Hui-hui King." This confusion in terms is apparently owing to the fact that, as we shall see, the Ouigours disappear from the Chinese ken for a century or two. There is no Chinese record as yet available showing when and how the Saracen influence grafted the Mussulman religion upon the Ouigours ; but naturally the Arabs and Persians would call all nomad Tartars within their sphere or ken by the old name of the only known dominant power lying between them and China, that is Turks ; whilst the hordes of Genghis, not finding them called Ouigours in the west until he carried that name west himself, would invent a new name to distinguish historically one particular race of Mussulman Tartars who were not idolaters (Shamanists) from the other. Thus the old word Oui*gh*our would come to mean

Mussulman Turks, whilst the new word Oui*wh*our would mean the ancient race which came from Caracorum, and the old families of which, though perhaps Mussulmans, were still found at Karahodjo. Even in 1915, under the Chinese Republic, we find the *Hwui* or *Hwui-tsz* princes of Hamil and Turfan coming to do vassal duty at Peking (as Turkish survivals). It is much like the word Frank, which, first meaning a petty tribe of Germans, is next applied to the Celtic inhabitants of the country ruled by that tribe : then by the Turks, under the name Fereng, to the whole family of Christian states headed by the Frankish empire ; then by all easterns to Europeans; then by the island Greeks to the Greeks of European mainland φραγκικος ; and finally by the Chinese to the first European comers, the Portuguese and Spaniards, until we get *Fa-lan-si* for France alone. Its last degradation is in the Tibetan and Nepaulese form P'i-ling, meaning " English."]

In 789 the khakhan died, and was succeeded by his brother Taras. Urumtsi and Barkul had fallen into Tibetan hands with the rest of modern Kan Suh between 751 and 766, and communications with those parts were only possible through Ouigour territory : of course the Ouigours charged exorbitant prices for their safe conducts. The Shado were consequently obliged, as already related (p. 181), to join the Tibetans, as there was no adequate Chinese protection to be got at Urumtsi, which place the Ouigours unsuccessfully endeavoured to rescue from Tibetan hands. The Karluks were now becoming so powerful, too, that the Ouigours had to fall back farther south. Taras was succeeded by his nephew Achö, who did good service against the Tibetans and Karluks. He died in 795, and, as he had left no issue, the Ouigours raised one of the ministers named Kutluk to the khakhanship. It is interesting to learn that this khakhan succeeded in obtaining a favourable reception in China for some Manichean missionaries, subjects of his : [two hundred years later Manichean temples served by Persian priests are mentioned in the Chinese annals as existing in the then Ouigour metropolis of Karahodjo. Important Manichean evidences were recently obtained from Tun-hwang (p. 117), and, as already stated (p. 200), were utilized by MM. Chavannes and Pelliot in 1911–1912.] In 808 another khakhan came to the throne, and applied for a new wife,—the old one's long services having been put an end to by death. Notwithstanding the representations of his ministers that it would be a politic thing to make friends with the Ouigours, so as to keep them hostile to the Tibetans and enable China the better to crush her rebellions, the Emperor would not give his consent. The request was renewed very pressingly in 821, and this time a new Emperor granted it ; but, the khakhan dying almost immediately, the envoy who had been sent formally to invest him did that duty for his successor instead. A splendid Ouigour mission, on an unheard of scale of magnificence, was sent to fetch the girl, who this time was a genuine daughter of an Emperor. There were 2,000 tribal chiefs, and as presents to China 20,000 horses and 1,000 camels ; but only 500 men were allowed to come into the capital ; the remainder had to stay behind at T'ai-yüan Fu in Shan Si. This khakhan rejoiced in the title of something like " Tängrida-ülük-bolmish-kutlug-bilga," to which the Emperor added Chinese words meaning " of exalted virtue." About this time the Cathayans were wavering in their allegiance, and seem to have perforce accepted the suzerainty of both the Ouigours and the Chinese : at that moment there were troubles on the Cathayan frontier, but on the whole it was thought more prudent not to employ the Ouigours again in China.

The Emperor and the khakhan both died in the year 824 : the successor and younger brother of the latter was murdered in 832 and succeeded by his nephew the Hu *teghin*. There seems to have been treason during this reign, for one of the Ouigour chiefs joined the Shado under Chuzia the Just (p. 182) in an attack upon his own sovereign, who committed suicide. Another outsider, the *teghin* Oyü, was raised to the throne : but the Ouigour power was now rapidly breaking up, added to which dearth, pestilence, and heavy snow-falls carried off the greater part of their live stock. One of the chiefs joined the Kirghiz, and the two, forming a united body of 100,000 men, marched upon the Ouigour ordo, killed the khakhan, and broke up the entire nation : one of the *teghins* with fifteen tribes took refuge with the Karluks, and the rest with the Tibetans or round about Barkul. The thirteen tribes which occupied the parts near the ordo moved south to the neighbourhood of Shan Si, and elected the *teghin* Oké to the khakhanship.

CHAPTER II

THE PERIOD OF WANDERING

WE have already narrated (p. 190) how the Kirghiz, during their attack upon the Ouigour ordo, obtained possession of the Chinese princess's person. Like the Hiung-nu, who claimed relationship with the Han dynasty because a Chinese princess had once been given to one of their ancestors (p. 65), so the Kirghiz now claimed to be of the same blood as the T'ang dynasty, because a Chinese general named Li (p. 35) had gone over to the Hiung-nu a thousand years ago, had married a Tartar wife, and had become the progenitor of the Kirghiz ! But Oké was too quick for them : he recaptured the princess, and advanced upon Kuku-hoton, or Tenduc as it had now begun to be called. His attack was repulsed ; but the Emperor, taking the advice of his ablest minister, resolved not to encourage the Kirghiz at the cost of his old allies the Ouigours, and sent envoys to the frontier with a mission to conduct a general inquiry. The princess also, who like all her predecessors seems to have had a healthy appreciation of at least one Tartar custom, sent a message to the Emperor suggesting that, as Oké was now khakhan, she might as well transfer her affections to him. [Possibly the custom of squeezing the feet, which began during this dynasty, had its origin in a desire to keep Chinese women from "running off to the Turks"; at any rate, no other more plausible explanation has ever been suggested.] Relief to the extent of a thousand tons of grain was sent to the impoverished Ouigours, but their application for the loan of the modern Tai Chou (between Tenduc and Peking) as a temporary residence was not conceded. Besides those under Oké, there were other parties of Ouigours under various chiefs who endeavoured to make terms with China on their own account. The negotiations were varied by occasional raiding, and several parties took refuge east amongst the Shirvi, Black Carts, [possibly Black Khirgiz] and other obscure tribes affiliated to the Cathayans. Oké established his ordo in the mountains north of Ta-t'ung Fu, where he still had a considerable force under him,—not far from a hundred thousand. Several Ouigour chiefs gave in their submission, received military titles, and undertook to guard the frontier. Oké now applied for the loan of Tenduc city, and, when this also was refused, vented his spleen by raiding the whole country round about. One of the Ouigour chiefs named Umuz was granted the imperial surname, and co-operated with the Chinese with a view of crushing Oké. An attack was made upon his ordo during the night, and the person of the Chinese princess was secured, together with 20,000 or 30,000 prisoners. Oké succeeded in effecting his escape, and took refuge with the Black Carts, who were subsequently bribed to kill him. The miserable remnants of his force, under a new khakhan called Okner, now reduced to 5,000, obtained food from the chieftain of the Ghei; but the Ghei themselves, who had lately been giving trouble, were broken up by the Chinese in the year 847, and shortly after that found themselves obliged to throw in their lot with their powerful kinsmen the Cathayans, who were now carving out an organized empire of their own.

The Ouigours in this part became gradually extinct, only about 300 of the noble class remaining : these took refuge with the Shirvi. As the Chinese demanded the surrender of the khakhan from the Shirvi, Okner left his people in the lurch, and fled with his wife and son and nine other cavaliers to the Karluks. The Shirvi now made slaves of the remaining Ouigours ; but the Kirghiz seem to have thought that they had a prior claim, and marched an army of 70,000 men against the Shirvi, from whom they recovered all the Ouigours. They were taken back to the north of the Desert, whence, after skulking about for a time and picking up a precarious livelihood by preying upon other tribes, they at last found their way in small parties to the other branch of their tribe, which had taken refuge in the old Turkish birthplace around Kan-chou Fu.

CHAPTER III

THE LATER OUIGOURS OF THE WEST

WHEN the power of the Western Turks was broken up, it will be borne in mind that some of Buchin's horde joined the Ouigours ; and when the Ouigours were dispersed by the Kirghiz, these particular people took refuge around Barkul (pp. 177, 205). They seem to have occupied Harashar for a time, and at last to have worked their way down under the *teghin* who acted as chief to the region of Kan-chou. The Emperor Süan Tsung was kindly disposed towards these refugees, and sent envoys to arrange matters with them and to confer a khanish title upon their chief. In the year 866 a General Bukku, with a force of Ouigours and others, acting on behalf of China, drove the Tibetans out of Kan Suh and the Kuche group of cities, and sent the head of the Tibetan *blon* or general as a trophy to the Emperor. But not very long after this the great Chinese dynasty of T'ang itself began to fall to

pieces, and the visits of the Ouigours became so irregular
that history records very little of their doings. Towards
the end of the ninth century they proffered military assistance,
which it was thought more prudent to decline ; but they
occasionally came with a stock of horses and precious stones
to exchange for tea, silks, etc.

During the Five Dynasty period of the tenth century
(p. 183), which may be described roughly as that during which
the Shado Turks ruled the northern part of China as Emperors,
the Ouigours occasionally came to pay their respects to China,
of which they always spoke as " uncle," on account of the
T'ang dynasty having often given them girls in marriage.
There appear to have been two distinct Ouigour centres at
this time : one at Kan-chou, and the other in the Pidjan
region ; and the Ouigours of the former, naturally, as being
the nearer, were the most frequent visitors. The short-lived
dynasty of Liang received a visit in the year 911 ; but although
titles were conferred upon the envoys, no record was kept of
the names and titles of their masters. During the reign of
the founder of the Chuzia dynasty of After T'ang, an individual
bearing a Chinese name, who styled himself " acting khakhan,"
sent an envoy with tribute of jewels and horses. A return
ambassador was despatched to invest him with the title of
khakhan ; but the latter died the same year, and was succeeded
by a younger brother, whose somewhat curious name appears
really to represent the Turkish word *teghin* : he again was
succeeded by one Aturyuk in 926. The following year another
" acting regent " with a Chinese name (apparently a relative
of the supposed *teghin*) sent an envoy, and was invested by
Maokire, the second Shado Emperor Ming Tsung, with
a khanish title, which title was added to by the founder of the
second Shado dynasty of After Tsin ; but it is distinctly
stated that no one ever knew if Aturyuk was a relative of
Teghin, and if so, in what degree ; nor did it ever appear how
and why he succeeded, and how he ceased to reign ; but the
acting regent, although nothing further is known of him,

certainly went on reigning until about 960, and frequently
sent tribute. In 961 his son and successor (bearing a Chinese
name) sent an envoy to the Sung court.

It is evidently during this dark age of China that the
Ouigour name by imperceptible degrees became transformed
in its signification (p. 204). It is interesting to know what the
Chinese could glean concerning these later Ouigour kingdoms,
which may be said to bear the same relation to the old nomad
empire that the Christian Ostrogoth and Visigoth kingdoms did
to the wandering Gothic powers previous to the 4th century.
The territory of the last-named Ouigour ruler is described
as producing yaks, precious stones, wild horses, single-humped
camels, antelope horns, sal ammoniac, castoreum, diamonds,
red salt, hair-rugs, cotton, and horse-skins. [The single-
humped camels must have been brought by Arab merchants,
as only the Bactrian camel is found in Tartary.] The country
is suited to the growth of various wheats and barleys, yellow
hemp (abutilon), onions, scallions, carraways. The land is
sown with seed after being ploughed by camels. The khakhan
usually lived in a storeyed edifice, and his wife was styled the
" celestial princess." Their ministers of state were qualified
by the word *meiluk*, and when they had audience of the khakhan
etiquette required them to remove the hat and enter with
dishevelled hair [something akin to the old Hiung-nu custom
mentioned (p. 28) in the first book]. The women bound up
their hair in a sort of top-knot five or six inches high, and
gathered it into a red silk bag. When they married they
used to add a felt cap. One particular race, styled the Dragon
Family, differ in customs slightly from the Ouigours. [No
further trace can be found of this tribe.] In the year 933 the
Ouigours presented a cast of white pigeon-hawks, but the
After T'ang emperor Ming Tsung ordered the birds' fastenings
to be undone and their liberty to be given to them. From
this time and onwards they often brought horses to China
for sale. The rule used to be that all the precious stones
they brought were to be sold to the officers of government,

and any other persons discovered dealing in such were liable to punishment ; but the first After Chou Emperor, about the year 952, removed this prohibition, and threw the trade open, the result being that prices went down by one-half. [According to Marco Polo, in Kublai's time the rule was re-established that no gems should be sold to any but the Emperor.] His successor declined a present of gems on the ground that, however precious, they were useless. In the years 964 and 965 they sent an envoy to the Sung court [China was now once more in Chinese hands], bringing tribute of jewels, amber, yaks' tails, sables, and such like things. [The mention of yaks is remarkable, for the Tibetans held the Koko-nor region for many centuries after they were turned out of Kuche (pp. 178, 205), and the later Ouigour power— at least that part of it which had its government at Karahodjo —never seems to have gone far west of Harashar or south of Lob-nor.] During the next decade they sent tribute several times, and their ministers of state also brought presents of horses. In the year 977, on the arrival of the Ouigour envoys, the Emperor ordered that " the Ouigour Khakhan of the " Kan-Sha Chou (sic), son-in-law to the Emperor, should " be presented with a sum of money and various objects, " and that he should be called upon to send fine horses and " gems for the imperial use." [It is evident from these words that this particular Ouigour power extended between but north of Koko-nor and Lob-nor, over Kan Chou and Sha Chou, the ancient Yüeh-chï domain.] In 981 and 984 tribute was brought. In 988 a few Ouigour families, under a royal prince named Mara and another high official, settled at the foot of the Alashan Hills (Marco Polo's Calachan). They had no horde, and the various tribes that came with tribute used to pass that way. The prince explained that his road had been previously blocked by a certain military adventurer, but that now he wished to belong to China : he and his friends were all presented with robes and girdles. In 996 the Kan-Chou khakhan offered military assistance against the kingdom of Hia. [A well-organized state of this name, the Tangut of Marco Polo, was founded in the Ordous region by a family of Toba Sien-pi extraction (see p. 134), and was ruled by them almost independently from the year 890 until the final conquests of Genghis Khan in 1226–7, shortly before which time it had annexed the southern Ouigour dominions of Kan-chou: Polo's Campichu. There are Hia inscriptions extant; but, so far, no one has been able to decipher them. I believe there is a lengthy one in the Nan-k'ou Pass (p. 61). The histories of the Cathayan, Nüchên, and Sung dynasties all contain lengthy descriptions of this country. Li was the T'ang " surname," and Chao that of Sung, presented as a compliment in turn to the early " Emperors " of Hia.] He was thanked for his offer. In the year 1001 the Kan-chou khakhan sent an envoy with tribute, and said that his kingdom extended eastwards as far as the Yellow River and westwards as far as the Snowy Mountains [east of Issekul]; that he had several hundred petty principalities under him, and possessed troops of veteran quality : he would be glad if the Emperor would send a commander-in-chief for his army with a view to capturing the person of the Tangut ruler and delivering up his person to China in chains. The Emperor sent his best thanks for this doughty offer ; it was probably from the Bogra Khan Harun (of Abulfaradj), a Turkish ruler who is said to have resided at the old Western Turkish capital of Sujâb or Belasagun, and reigned over Kashgar, Khoten, etc., up to the frontiers of China. Pelliot says it was he who converted Kashgar to Islam. In 1004 these same Ouigours sent tribute, and again in 1007 : on this last occasion a bonze accompanied the mission and prayed for permission to erect a Buddhist monastery in the Chinese capital, in order that prayers might be offered up for the long life of the Emperor, who would doubtless be pleased to present the dedicatory door-slab. This request was not conceded. [The earlier Sung Emperors did not encourage Buddhism. The Cathayans had now a powerful empire in Mongolia, Manchuria, and

North-east China : their history mentions that in the year 1001 a " Sanskrit bonze," who was also a distinguished physician, was sent by the Ouigours to the Cathayan court. This incident evidently inspired the 16th century author of a very celebrated Chinese novel with a basis for one of his grimmest characters, a " Sanskrit bonze " who dealt in love philtres ; the events described in the novel took place about a century after those here recorded, at a time when the Nüchêns were clamouring at the gates of China, held by the Sung dynasty.] In 1008 the Ouigours sent tribute, and in 1011 they applied for permission to erect a place of worship at the modern P'u-chou Fu in Shan Si. [We have already alluded (p. 205) to the Manichean temples at Karahodjo ; it is evident that a religious wave was now overspreading the whole Turkish race. At this time the Western Turks, whether politically Ouigours or not, were rapidly becoming a mixed race, and were continually at war with the Ghaznavids, Samanids (902–999), and others in the Perso-Samarcand regions, as to whom, however, we can only speak second-hand, in the absence of intelligible Chinese record. The owl-like and beardless Mongols, so familiar to those who have lived in North China, are almost as far removed in appearance from the Turk of Europe as is a Chinese from a Spaniard.]

It appears that the minor Ouigour chiefs used to send tribute to the Sung or South Chinese Court independently of the central power, be it Sujâb or elsewhere ; but probably the so-called " tribute " was very often a mere mercantile speculation. In 1008 we are told that the Ouigours of Ts'in Chou (which is in Kan Suh province, almost on the Shen Si frontier) sent a jewelled belt : there were three clans living at this place, and the chief bore a name which looks like Armil or Amir. Later on a certain Eroghut sent to report a victory over Tangut, and rewards were conferred upon his generals. Eroghut seems to have been the Kan-chou ruler and to have had a difficulty in reaching China, for his missions required the convoy of a Tibetan tribe which had some reason or other to be grateful to the easy-going China of those days. The next thing we hear is that one Kuksara, a native of Karahodjo, was at enmity with the Ouigour khakhan because the latter would not give him his daughter in marriage : the result was that the road to China was again blocked, and the khakhan sent to request that the same Tibetan tribe might be politely asked by China to keep the road open, which was done. [*Kuk* is said to mean " Buddha," and *sara* " son " in the language of Tangut ; but as Kuksara was always at war with Tangut he cannot well have been a Tangut. Moreover, although the rulers of Tangut were of Toba origin, the population would seem to have been largely of Tibetan stock.] In 1018 and 1021 further envoys came, on the latter occasion in company with the khakhan of Kuche, who sent some fat-tailed sheep. The Cathayan Empire of North China was now in its prime, and the Sung dynasty of Central and South China, which in its luxurious effeminacy resembled nothing so much as the Byzantine Empire at Constantinople, really knew very little of Tartary : in both cases the nominally superior power or Empire was practically tributary to the roving Hun, Avar, Turk, or Tartar. The Cathayans must have driven some of the Ouigours farther west, and probably possessed all the old Hiung-nu and Turkish Empires north of the Desert. Kur-kara-usu and Pidjan certainly belonged to the Cathayans, who on their own fall did not hesitate (see p. 180) to found a new empire at Sujâb, and even at Kermané near Bokhara ; from which it is evident that they must previously to this have had a thorough knowledge of Turkestan. That partly explains why, at the time of which we are now treating, there were so many petty Ouigour khakhans (anxious to be on good terms with South China and Cathay alike) existing on sufferance along what is called the Southern Road to the West. During the 11th century there were at least three of them, and upon two were conferred pompous Chinese titles. They continued to assist China against the Tanguts, and we may form an idea of what sort of states they were from the answer of one of their envoys, who estimated the number of capable men in his master's country at 200,000. During the 12th century they began to settle almost permanently in trading parties all about the province of Shen Si : they always had to pass first through the dominions of Tangut. The Cathayan history claims the Ouigours of all Kan Suh, i.e. Kan-chou, Sha-chou, Ho-chou, and Arslan, as being dependent upon their empire. The position of Arslan is uncertain : it is not likely to mean the Affghan Alp Arslan (1029–1072) ; probably the Arslan mentioned as being under Mercrin (p. 161), or possibly the Abulmodhaffer Arslan of Belasagun (about 1020) ; but here we are getting beyond our depth as a chronicler of Chinese matters, and " throw up the sponge."

BOOK VII

THE EMPIRE OF THE CATHAYANS

BOOK VII

THE EMPIRE OF THE CATHAYANS

CHAPTER I

THE KINGDOM OF THE FOUNDER APAOKI

THE Cathayans or Kitans (whose name still exists in Marco Polo's word Cathay and in the Russian word Kitai, see p. 184) were of the same race as the Kumok-Ghei, and of both tribes it is said that they used to place corpses amongst or hang them upon trees in the mountains (p. 150). Of the Cathayans it is added that the bones were collected and burnt after a lapse of three years, when a libation of liquor was offered and the following prayer uttered :—" In winter at noon may " I eat towards the south, in summer towards the north, and " always find plenty of swine and deer in my hunts." This mention of swine at once recalls what we have said touching this differentiating feature of the Tungus or " pig " races. The Cathayans and the Ghei were both descendants of the old Sien-pi, and were found in the old Sien-pi haunts. The Ghei were originally the eastern branch of the Jumen tribe which, as we have seen (p. 105), gave a dynasty to North China during the 6th century. But before that the Mujung Sien-pi had driven both the Ghei and Cathayan tribes north-wards to the region north of the Sira Muren between the Sungari and the Desert (p. 149). The first Toba Emperor had occasion to punish the Ghei for raiding in the year 388 ; and in 479 the Cathayans, who with the Ghei had brought regular tribute of horses since the year 440, moved under their chief Bagatur Murkan southwards to the Loha River, a tributary of the Sira Muren in modern Tumet Mongol country. In 493 the Ghei committed the offence of raiding; but they were repulsed, forgiven, allowed to trade within the Wall, and afterwards sent tribute of horses and sables regularly. The After Wei dynasty of Tobas towards the middle of the 6th century found it necessary to punish the Cathayans, in consequence of which the latter separated from the Ghei for twenty years, and went back north of the Sira Muren. The Ts'i dynasty of Tobas built a new stretch of Great Wall 300 miles in length from the Nank'ou Pass near Peking westwards to Ta-t'ung Fu (p. 105) in order to keep them off. Thus we see that China proper had as yet no knowledge whatever of these people except through their congeners the Toba and Jumen dynasties of North China, who were simply the more civilized tribes of one and the same race. Just in the same way with the more eastern Tunguses, whose hunting habits were totally different from those of their kinsmen, the Ghei and Cathayans, we first find the more or earlier civilized Murkors or Blackwaters founding the kingdom of Botskai (as narrated, p. 190); then the less or later civilized founding the Empire of the Nüchêns: and finally the most obscure and uncleanly tribe of all rearing its head over both its predecessors, and developing into the great Manchu Empire of to-day. The Manchus when they conquered China and Mongolia considered (p. 106) the Solons of the Amur to be the descendants of the ancient Cathayans. It is important to keep this feature of Tartar vicissitudes well in mind. As with the Mongols, Turks, and Hiung-nu, so with the Manchus, Cathayans, and Sien-pi, in each case " horse-back forms the state " (as the Chinese historians say), and it is always a petty tribe which, under some impulsive hero or some great provocation, takes the lead and gives a new name to a kingdom or an empire: otherwise there is no idea of " nationality," and things always remain much the same; until at last

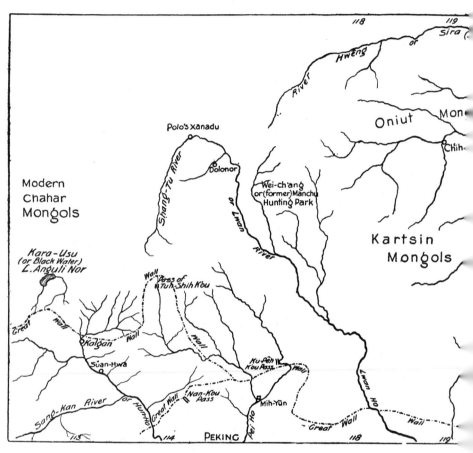

Sketch map largely based upon His Excellency Ch. Waeber's map of N.E. China (1893).

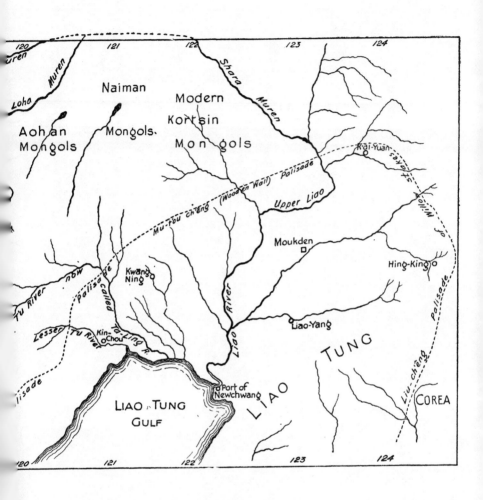

Buddhism and the use of writing gradually leaven and civilize the whole mass. Chinese statesmen of the 19th century asked themselves whether it would not be possible to turn Christianity to similar uses, and emasculate the fierce nations of Europe in the same way that Buddhism has emasculated the degenerate Tibetans and Mongols. Hence the *hubilhan* and golden urn hocus-pocus, subject to the Manchu Emperor's fiat, " I won't have any souls found and reborn (in such and such a disgraced Mongol family)."

The Turks were now beginning to press upon the Ghei and Cathayans, 10,000 families of the latter emigrating to Corea rather than become Turkish vassals, and 4,000 offering to submit to China with the same object. All the Ghei submitted to China. This was rather awkward for the founder of the Sui dynasty, who was most anxious to keep on good terms with his neighbours the Turks : he tried to induce the Cathayans to go back, and ordered the Turks to be kind to them. However, those near the Chinese frontier positively refused to go back, and banded together in company with the Ghei for mutual protection. They killed the Turkish *tudun* who had been despatched by the khakhan Shaporo to govern them, and sent tribute to the mad Emperor Yang Ti (pp. 106, 140). Several of their chiefs came to court during the reign of Li Yüan the founder of the T'ang dynasty ; but they used notwithstanding to make raids occasionally. It will be recollected (p. 148) that Gheri offered to surrender a dangerous rebel to T'ai Tsung if the latter would abandon the Cathayans to him ; but the Emperor was generous enough to refuse to do this. In 648 he made a new proconsular province of Sung-moh, appointing the Kitan chief, who was given the imperial clan name of Li, as proconsul, having ten divisional governors under him : practically speaking this was the vast country now known as the Jêhol Superintendency. At the same time a Chinese High Commissioner for the Eastern Barbarians generally was established at modern Yung-p'ing Fu. This went on all well until 696 when the great-grandson of the

first appointee raised the standard of revolt, murdered the
High Commissioner, and styled himself Khakhan. [See
p. 181 for a Shado Turk of exactly the same name.] Army after
army sent to quell the rebellion met with utter defeat, until
at last the services of the Turkish Khakhan Merchö were called
for against the rebels, and he annexed them to his dominions
(p. 156). As Merchö's power began to fall off, the Ghei and
Cathayan chieftains once more came to China and received
(more or less royal) ladies in marriage. Then the Cathayans
went over to the Turkish interests and tried to force the Ghei
to do likewise. For some years after this there is a succession
of revolts, raids, pardons, marriages, tribute missions, etc.,
of too obscure and uninteresting a nature to be followed out
in detail with any satisfaction. The Ghei began to intrigue
with the Shirvi and Ouigours with a view to raiding, and
finally both they and the Cathayans found it convenient
to keep in with the Ouigours. In 842 the Ouigours chastised
the Cathayans, apparently for coquetting with the Chinese,
who now once more granted them an imperial seal and took
them under protection. The Chinese dynasty of T'ang was
by this time falling into decrepitude, and the Cathayans,
who had all this time been gaining in strength, took the
opportunity to annex the Ghei, Sib, Shirvi, and all the other
smaller tribes in their locality (p. 149).

The Ghei, who were west of the Cathayans, must have
been rather more Turkish in manners than the Cathayans :
they are mentioned in a way which does not separate them
either politically or ethnologically from the Turks so distinctly
as it does the Cathayans. The pasture-seeking habits of
the Ghei are said to have been those of the Turks without
much difference. At the same time the ways of the Ghei
were very foul, which is never said of any Hiung-nu race
except the Jwen-jwen, whose " Hiungnuism " is in any case
not quite certain ; and the Ghei kept pigs, and placed corpses
on trees, which were both Tungusic characteristics. They
possessed great numbers of black sheep (or goats), and their

horses were a very hardy and active breed. One branch of them, disgusted with Cathayan tyranny, moved westwards to the region of modern Kalgan, where they lived by shooting and by collecting ginseng and musk for sale to the Chinese : these latter gave them a certain amount of countenance, and allowed them to develop their aptitude for tillage by cultivating the spare land along the frontier. The Shado Turkish dynasty of After T'ang found them useful soldiers; but the Shado Turkish dynasty of After Tsin ceded parts of Shan Si and Chih Li within the Wall to the Cathayans, and with them these western Ghei : of the other Ghei the Chinese had lost sight altogether, so far at least as being in any way distinct from the Cathayans was concerned.

The Ghei and some at least of the Cathayans cannot well be anything but the ancestors of the various Mongol tribes that now occupy their old quarters ; and it is also difficult to imagine what the Eleuths or western Mongols can be other than the fragments of the old Hiung-nu and Turkish Empires dished up, so to speak, in a new shape, after having been reduced or raised by Genghis Khan and his successors to one monotonous level bearing a Mongol tinge, and after having their originally fierce character softened by the influence of Buddhism. There was, it is true (p. 150), a Shirvi tribe called Mungwa, and there was the petty tribe, more akin to the Tunguses than the Turks, called Tatur, from either of which the Mongols proper may possibly have sprung (p. 97). But extensive nationalities must either immigrate, annex, or breed : they cannot suddenly spring into existence. We know that the tribe of Genghis Khan (which, along with the Keraits, Merkits, etc., paid regular tribute to the Nüchên dynasty) did not come in large bodies from the north, south, east, or west ; but, beginning in the humblest way, grew (after his revolt in 1211) as it rolled over the plains like a huge snow-ball, absorbing almost everything in its way. Anyone who has lived amongst the modern Mongols must see that they correspond exactly in appearance and very much in manners to the descriptions given of the ancient Hiung-nu and Huns ; off their horses they are lubbers. In other words, things remain largely as they always were, so far as not unmanned by Buddhism. But where is the line to be drawn between the Hiung-nu and the Sien-pi element ? How is it the eastern and western Mongols are almost exactly the same in language and habit; whilst the Manchus, who are closely connected so far as language goes with the Cathayans and Ghei, are and were totally different in manners from the Mongols ? The answer probably is that some of the Hiung-nu have gone off west, mixed with Sarts, Persians, Albanians, and Circassians, and totally lost their old individuality. The easternmost of the Tunguses in the same way have been absorbed or coloured by the Chinese. The Hiung-nu, Sien-pi, Jwen-jwen, Ouigour, and Turkish tribes that remained in their old country have mixed with the Keraits, Mongols proper, etc., and become the modern Mongol " Leagues " or Confederations. The same " horseback " hordes have from time immemorial assailed China, Persia, Mesopotamia, Syria, Babylonia, and even Egypt, always introducing a new " horse " era, and sometimes even forming a semi-permanent, but always unproductive, empire, as in the case of the Parthians, Hyksos,—and Turks as we still see them,—leaving no " works " behind.

After the Cathayans had unified themselves into an independent state as above described, they called it *hiaolka muri*, referring to its position on both sides of the *muri* or " river " (Sira Muren). There were eight tribes, each with a chief ; but a head chief was elected at intervals and invested with a drum and standard as a symbol of his authority, just as in old Sien-pi times ; yet he was deposed if a dearth or pestilence afflicted the country, or if the flocks and herds fell off seriously. Horse-breeding seems to have been one of the chief resources of the Cathayans, as it is now of the Eastern Mongols ; and the Chinese, when at war with them, used to set fire to the prairie grass in order to starve or destroy the horses. At the beginning of the 10th century, when the T'ang dynasty had given way to the Shado Turks, a man of obscure origin named Apaoki was elected President of the Eight Tribes, and a great many Chinese sought safety from anarchy with him. He received them hospitably and built towns for them, and for his prisoners too, one at or near the modern Dolonor. Apaoki now learnt for the first time that the elective system was considered an anomaly by the Chinese ; he had already been President of the Cathayan Republic for nine years, and there were murmurs on account of his alleged Cæsarism making themselves heard. He proceeded cautiously, first obtaining the sanction of the Eight Tribes to his forming a tribe of his own out of the numerous Chinese his policy had induced to immigrate. Then he took the advice of a shrewd Chinaman in his employ and instructed his people in polite manners. He made what was called " Chinese Town " as much like a real one as possible, with shops, houses, and markets, all on the plan of the provincial metropolis occupying the site of modern Peking,—as it then was. The position of Chinese Town was selected on account of the plentiful arable land, iron, and salt in the neighbourhood ; and Chinese merchants and cultivators were made so comfortable that they had, under Apaoki at least, no idea of going back to their own country. His wife next persuaded him to claim compensation from the other chiefs for the salt which they used to obtain from the pools in his territory. This claim was thought reasonable, and all the other chiefs, bringing oxen with them for a feast, assembled at the pools. After having made them all drunk with liquor, Apaoki summoned the soldiers he had ready lying in ambush, and massacred the whole of his visitors. He then proceeded to resume power as permanent supreme chief without being further troubled with the prospect of re-elections or the claims of vice-presidents.

Apaoki was now so powerful that the Shado Turks representing the coming After T'ang dynasty were only too glad to make an alliance with him with a view to getting rid of the After Liang dynasty. But for some unexplained

reason he changed his mind, and, declaring himself a vassal to Liang, proceeded to raid the country between Kalgan, Jêhol, and Peking, then forming part of the territory in the nominal possession of the Shado Turks. He was unsuccessful, and suffered several crushing defeats ; at the same time he had advanced so far into the great Peking plain, and had seen so much of the rich prospect of plunder in the numerous Chinese cities, that it was from this moment that he and his people began to harbour serious designs upon the Chinese Empire. But even at this date the Early Manchu organized state of Botskai, which lay between them and Corea, and the as yet unorganized Manchu communities known as Juchên or Nüchêns, which lay to their rear, were sufficiently formidable to make the Cathayans pause before venturing too far into China. It was therefore resolved to secure unfettered action by first conquering Botskai ; and, lest the Shado Turks, then reigning at modern Chêng-ting Fu in Chih-li, should seize the opportunity to invade Cathay, Apaoki exchanged several friendly missions with the Shado ruler. Meanwhile the latter had transferred his capital to Ho-nan Fu, had been killed there in a popular tumult, and had been succeeded by his excellent adoptive son Maokire, better known, as already stated, as the Emperor Ming Tsung. Maokire sent an envoy formally to notify the Cathayans of his accession. Apaoki, turning his eyes to Heaven, wept aloud, saying :—
" Alas ! your emperor's grandfather and I had agreed to be
" brethren : it therefore follows that the father of the present
" Ho-nan Emperor was my son. When I heard of the tumult,
" I was on the point of marching with 50,000 men to my
" son's assistance, had it not been that Botskai was not yet
" extinguished, and that I was unable to fulfil my heart's
" desire. But, my son being dead, how can a new Emperor
" set himself up without asking my advice ? " Maokire's envoy replied :—" The new Emperor has held for some time
" the military dignity of Field-Marshal, having led armies
" in person during the past twenty years : he has 300,000

" seasoned troops under his command, so that Heaven and
" Man alike have conspired to place him where he is. Who then
" is going to oppose him ? " Apaoki's son Turyuk, who was
standing near, said :—" Envoy ! do not talk so much ! You
" know the saying in the parable, (and a reasonable one too
" it seems to me), that a cow is liable to seizure for her trespass ! "
The envoy rejoined :—" How can an old parable about an
" obscure peasant apply to God's Anointed and Man's Choice ?
" For instance, when your august father appropriated the
" Cathay throne and abolished election, who would charge
" him with trespass ? " As usual Chinese diplomacy (for
the Turkish Emperor's envoy was a Chinese) won the day.
Apaoki modified his tone a little. He went on :—" I under-
" stand my son had 2,000 women with 1,000 musicians and
" mummers in his palace ; that he spent his time in hawking
" and coursing, and indulged freely in the pleasures of wine
" and women, employing worthless persons, and showing
" consideration for no man, all which brought on his fall.
" Since the news of his collapse I and my family have given
" up dram-drinking, set our hawks and hounds at liberty,
" and dismissed all our musicians except those few required
" for public banquets : otherwise I might share my son's
" fate." Later on he said :—" I can speak Chinese, but I
" never utter a word of it before my own people, lest they
" should imitate the Chinese and become timid and feeble.
" You had better go back and tell the Emperor I will meet
" him with 20,000 dragoons somewhere between Peking and
" Chêng-ting Fu, and will make a treaty with him there.
" If he will cede me the Peking plain I will not make any
" further attacks."

Apaoki after this marched on the Botskai, took their
capital, (the modern K'ai-yüan), and changed the name of
the country to " Eastern Tan." [This seems to show that
the second syllable in the word Kitan must have had a meaning
distinct from the first, though the Coreans pronounce it
Kyöran which is equivalent to *Kyöl-an*, or Kit-an.] He placed

his son Turyuk in charge as king, and from that time the Botskai state was extinguished, except in so far as occasionally the Chinese Sung dynasty intrigued to secure its assistance with a view to making a demonstration against the Cathayans. The Japanese, however, who had diplomatic relations with Botskai, declined to recognize the words *Tung Tan* and Turyuk's royal status. Apaoki died very shortly after these events in the year 926. The After T'ang Emperor Maokire seems to have inspired the Chinese in Cathay with more confidence than the successor of Apaoki, who was besides not the rightful heir : at any rate 100,000 of them found their way back to China. During Apaoki's reign the old Sien-pi system of conveying orders by wooden tallies had been abandoned in favour of writing, and certain Chinese had invented for him a very simple and at the same time ingenious form of written character consisting of Chinese hieroglyphs and ideographs mutilated or re-pieced: [no one has yet made a successful attempt to decipher the few inscriptions which are known still to exist in this artificial language. Colonel Yule gives a specimen in his Marco Polo, and M. Gabriel Devéria in 1898 discussed the question of the Nan-k'ou Pass inscriptions (Kitan and Tangut) in his paper upon the Tangut inscription of 1094 found at Liang Chou]. Apaoki had also assumed the imperial style as " Celestial Imperial King," which he evidently intended to be as high if not higher than that of the Emperor of China. His first reign-period began in the year 916, but it was from 922 that his celestial pretensions dated. His ordo, *napo*, or chief encampment, called also " western shooting box " (a place on the River Taling, just within Mongolia, and north-west of Kwang-ning in modern Manchuria), was made his Upper Capital : this, which seems to have been also the old Mujung seat of government, became the Central Capital of the fifth Cathayan Emperor. His " eastern box " was 300 miles further east, which would be somewhere near either Moukden or Hing-king. The " northern box " was a hundred miles north of the western, and the " southern

box," where the first tombs were, was some distance to the
south of the western. The gates and doors of all four hunting-
boxes faced eastwards (p. 84), and at all great functions to
face eastwards was considered the most dignified and solemn
proceeding. On the 1st day of every moon they turned east
to worship the sun, and they were great believers in the unseen
powers. The notes of a Chinese who spent several years
with the Cathayans have been preserved ; but, though he
gives a pretty vivid description of the country through which
he passed, and the names of many places, it is quite impossible,
owing to the total absence of proper compass directions with
the distances, and of precise information of any sort, to do
more than guess where any particular place was, and how the
country was organized for administration. The Upper Capital
was a regular town with houses and market-place. No coins
were used ; only cloth. There were silk factories, priests,
and nuns (Buddhist and Taoist), brothels and houses of
pleasure, artisans, wrestlers, students, doctors of learning,
and various officials. All the above were Chinese, chiefly
from the four prefectures of Shan Si and Chih Li just within
the Great Wall. It was thirteen miles from this Upper Capital
eastwards to the Palisade, and here the Chinese traveller
for the first time found some vegetables. The land grew more
elevated as he advanced eastwards : looking back westwards,
he thought the country seemed like a dense fir forest. In
a short time they reached a level well-wooded meadow country,
and found water-melons there, the seeds for which the
Cathayans had obtained from the west when they defeated
the Ouigours : they were grown in beds of cows'-dung covered
over with mats, and were large and very sweet. Continuing
eastwards through a lovely meadow country, they saw their
first willow trees, and a peculiar kind of fine rich bulky grass,
ten blades of which would make a good feed for a horse.
After this the traveller gives no direction of any kind for his
journeys, but it seems he travelled at the rate of 20 miles a day,
probably in the direction of Moukden, and got to a place

where there was no grass at all, only spiky tares like the feathers of an arrow. Wherever this locality was, the Cathayan monarchs occasionally "pitched their cart-tents" here. [It is then explained that the Cathayans learnt the use of these tents from the Black Cart tribe, at the time they conquered the Ouigours, so that we may conclude that in this particular at least the Northern Hiung-nu or Kankali tribes differed from the Sien-pi.] Thence they travelled seven days south-west to the Imperial Tombs enclosure, which seems to have been approached by a narrow pass : it contained houses, and there was a stone slab inscribed [it is presumed in Chinese] with the word " Tombs." No Chinese were allowed to enter, and no Cathayan chiefs either, unless they carried sacrificial objects with them ; nor would they tell the Chinese anything about what went on inside. A walled town 700 miles north-east of Peking is also mentioned, where there were 3,000 Chinese captives : the town had been built for their benefit. East of this, towards the sea, the country was inhabited by hunting tribes living in skin tents. It is easy to recognize from the description given the various Nüchên and then still barbarous Manchu tribes. It is also evident that the traveller worked his way down to the modern Shan-hai Kwan, where the T'ang dynasty had once had flourishing military colonies. Then he came to the Southern Ghei, already described, who were "rather like the Cathayans, but more murderously disposed." Then the traveller speaks from hearsay of the Turks, Ouigours, Kirghiz, and Kankalis all lying to the west. This particular Chinaman was a secretary in the employ of a Cathayan general of rank, apparently viceroy of the extreme east, and that is how he came to see and hear so much of the country. When he got back to China he wrote a book called "Among the Caterans." The above is as much of main fact as can be ascertained at present touching the Cathayan dominions of Apaoki's time and that of his immediate successor, but there is a considerable amount of further detail for specialists.

CHAPTER II

CONQUEST OF THE TURKO-CHINESE EMPIRE BY CATHAY

ON the death of Apaoki his eldest son Turyuk, " King of Eastern Tan," i.e. Botskai, ought to have succeeded ; but the queen-mother's favourite son was the second one, who possessed an unpronounceable native name ; he is usually known by his adopted Chinese name of Têh-kwang, " Brilliancy of Virtue." Apaoki seems to have died directly after installing Turyuk in the Botskai capital. At any rate his wife managed to keep the death secret until she could get her second son back safely to the western shooting-box, where she at once had him proclaimed successor : the Turko-Chinese envoy above-mentioned was with her all the time. Of course this proceeding was very distasteful to Turyuk ; but, as his brother was a brave man of remarkable ability, and as all the great men had supported the mother's choice, he was unable during several years to assert his rights ; consequently he took a junk and sought refuge in the year 930 with China, i.e. with Maokire. That After T'ang Emperor presented him with the imperial T'ang clan name of Li (which Maokire's own Turkish ancestors had long ago adopted), and also gave him a military command. China's prestige was now almost entirely re-established under these Shado Turks, who not only beat the Cathayans in the field, but felt strong enough utterly to ignore their envoys. One ambassador who came to demand the surrender of certain Cathayan prisoners was simply decapitated for his pains.

Since the garrisons which used to keep out the Tartars from the Shan-hai Kwan passage had been allowed to fall into desuetude, the Cathayans had begun to choose that way as the most convenient one for raiding, and the Peking plains lay entirely at their mercy. All Chinese communications in those parts had to be protected by strong convoys. But the Shado Turkish dynasty had now remedied this in a great measure, and the people were able to resume their cultivation. Têh-kwang therefore moved east to a place which sounds like Bola Nor, evidently north of Shan Si, and made that the centre of his raiding operations. Maokire was so troubled about this that he sent his son-in-law—afterwards the founder of the Later Tsin dynasty—to protect East of the River (as Shan Si was then called), and to take supreme command of the four frontier armies : the whole neighbouring country was denuded in order to keep him supplied with the necessary stores. But the son-in-law rebelled against Maokire's worthless successors, sent envoys to the Cathayans, declared himself their vassal, and promised to cede to them in return for their recognition all those parts of modern Shan Si and Chih Li which lie north of the 39th parallel of north latitude. The Cathayans emerged from the celebrated Goose Gate Pass, (the scene of so many events in old Hiung-nu history), their carts and cavalry extending over a distance of seven miles ; the armies of T'ang were defeated, and Shih King-t'ang, son-in-law of Maokire, was created Emperor by the Cathayans under the most humiliating conditions as to status, subsidies, cession of territory, and general dependence. Maokire seems to have been one of the purest characters in Chinese history : he was quite an old man when he died, and one of his last prayers was :—" I am a poor simple Tartar, elevated to the " throne by the acclamations of a fickle multitude : my only " prayer is that so long as Heaven is pleased to preserve me I may " be guided to do the best for my people." Peking was now made a district metropolitan city of the Cathayan Empire, which from this time was called Liao, a word said to mean " Iron." [In connection with this subject it may be mentioned that the successors of the Cathayans, the Nüchêns, called their empire Kin or " Golden." It is by no means unlikely that the word Mongol, Mungu, or *munku*, which is said to mean " Silver," was adopted by Genghis Khan in imitation of his predecessors, and that the people or tribe then first called *munku* cannot be shown with certitude to have had any other ethnic origin. This, however, is conjecture, see p. 150.]

The Cathayan Empire, which was never very extensive so far as China proper was included in its limits, now embraced sixteen Chinese departments south of the Great Wall, Manchuria, and North Tartary : from first to last the Cathayans appear to have adhered to one fixed principle— never to abandon their ancient wandering habits of life. At the same time Têh-kwang now organized his empire on the Chinese system, for that was apparently the only way to keep Chinamen in it. The Shado Emperor had to send 300,000 pieces of silk a year, besides jewels, curiosities, dainties, and liquor. It was agreed, however, that the relation of " father and son " should be officially substituted for that of " suzerain and vassal." Shih King-t'ang, whose Tartar name, if he had one, does not appear, kept his bargain faithfully throughout his reign ; but on his death in 943 Têh-kwang professed great indignation because the event was not announced before the successor—a nephew—presumed to write a letter as " grandson," taking it for granted that he also was no " vassal." In the year 944 the irate suzerain marched in three columns to invade China. The column which advanced through Goose Gate was repulsed by the Shado Turkish general Liu Chï-yüan, who afterwards founded the dynasty of After Han (p. 183) : [it is probable, to judge by his name, that he professed to be connected in some way with the ancient Jenuyes and with the Han dynasty, or at least with the Liu Yüan dynasty of the fourth century (p. 65) : but that also is mere conjecture]. The eastern column advanced as far as the Yellow River in Shan Tung, whilst Têh-kwang himself, at the head of the central column, marched upon Ta-ming Fu and the northernmost point of Ho Nan province. Here a great but indecisive battle was fought, both sides losing half their men. The Cathayans withdrew after dark in two bodies, one going by way of the Grand Canal towards the Tientsin of to-day.

The next spring Têh-kwang invaded China with the whole available forces of his dominions, taking city after city in modern Chih Li province, and advancing right up to the old Toba capital (p. 105) of Chang-têh Fu in Ho Nan, as it is now called, destroying and looting everything in his way, setting fire to houses and mulberry trees, and massacring people right and left. On the approach of the Chinese army the Cathayans retreated, but the Chinese generals were too cowardly to pursue. The Tsin Emperor, although ill, now took command in person, and the Cathayans, who had already got pretty far on the way home, at once turned back to give him battle. Têh-kwang is represented as travelling in a Ghei wagon from which he exhorted his men to do their very best, as there was now a chance of engulfing the whole Tsin army and putting an end to their Empire. The Tsin men, amongst whom we may fairly assume there were some Shado Turks, fought with desperate resolution ; the Cathayans were totally defeated, and Têh-kwang, abandoning his cart, fled on a white camel to Peking, where he had all his generals flogged, with the single exception of a certain Chinese commander whom he had forced to join him in Maokire's time.

As that part of the Chinese Empire under the Shado Turk rule was suffering from a plague of locusts and from drought, the war with Cathay pressed very hard upon the people, and it was accordingly decided to make peace proposals to the Cathayans, submit the respectful address demanded, and declare China a vassal state. Têh-kwang's behaviour to the envoy was very rude, but the Cathayans themselves were getting tired of war. His mother took up the reply as follows :—" Does our Chinese sonny of the southern dynasty " think he can wrest from us a corner to repose in ? Well, " from ancient times it has always been China that made " proposals to the foreigner ; we never hear of foreigners " going to make peace with China. If our Chinese son has

" really come to think better of it, we have no objection to
" making friends." However, the Tsin people did not send
any further mission, but contented themselves with trying
to induce the above-mentioned able Chinese general—who
was aiming at empire on his own account—to desert back to
the Shado side. This general pretended to fall in with the
proposals, but, seeing that his true interests now lay on the
Cathayan side, he betrayed the secret, and laid a trap to catch
the Chinese armies who were to come and co-operate with him.
The plan succeeded, and Têh-kwang, in order to gain further
confidence, sent back all his former prisoners to China with
the following words tattooed on their faces :—" Life spared
"by imperial command." The armies which had now
surrendered were conciliated by being placed under their
own commanders, and a march was made on the capital,—
the modern K'ai-fêng Fu. The Tsin Emperor and Empress-
Dowager lost no time in submitting a humble address of apology,
to which the following autograph reply was received :—
" Don't feel too sad, grandson ; just find me a place to dine
"in." As Têh-kwang was approaching the capital, the authorities
sent out an offer to place the imperial state carriages at his
disposal, but he replied :—" I have put on my armour to
"conquer China, and have no time for ritualistic gew-gaws."
The Emperor and Empress-Dowager came outside the walls
to receive him, but he declined, saying :—" How can two
" Emperors meet on the high road ? " Early the next morning
Têh-kwang made his official entry into the Tsin capital :
all the official body, civil and military, after bowing northwards
and taking leave of their own Emperor, prostrated themselves
before the conqueror, who took up his position on horseback
upon an elevation outside the city, clad in his armour and
wearing a sable cap. He then entered the gates, mounted
the watch-tower, and ordered an interpreter to proclaim as
follows :—" I am but human. You need not fear. It was
" not I that wished to come : the Chinese troops brought me."
[This word Han cannot here refer to the dynasty created by

Liu Chï-yüan in 947, but it must mean " Chinaman " in the
old sense, still used.] Then he entered the palace. The
women of the seraglio were all there to receive him, but he took
no notice of them whatever. In the evening he came out and
passed the night upon a red hillock (cf. p. 86). The Emperor
was created " Marquis of Ingratitude," and sent to one of the
Cathayan capitals near modern Jêhol. On the 7th day after
his arrival, Têh-kwang took up his residence in the palace,
placing all the gates in charge of Cathayans : at the main
gate and in all the court-yards in order to discourage
independent feeling he had caused to be hung up the skins of
dogs that had been hacked to pieces. The next day he held
a court, he himself wearing Tartar attire. The following day
he held another dressed in Chinese clothes, except that he had
on a felt cape buttoning, in Tartar fashion, on the left side.
[Confucius once said :—" Had it not been for Kwan-tsz, China
" would have had to button on the left."] All the Tsin officials
were present in full dress, and in front of the pavilion Ghei
wagons and Tartar horsemen were drawn up in line. Three
weeks after that, Têh-kwang held another grand court on
the first of the second moon (somewhere in March). The
six regiments of metropolitan guards, the lictors and attendants
of the palace, the imperial musicians, mummers, etc., were
all drawn up in the court-yard. Têh-kwang wore a high
imperial dragon crown with a brown crape robe, and held
a sceptre in his hand. There was a general pardon, the
" Tsin Empire " [ends A.D. 947] was changed to that of
" Great Liao," and the year 947 was declared to be the 10th
of Têh-kwang's second period, or the 22nd of his reign :
[Apaoki died in 926, and Têh-kwang was *chosen* in 927].

Now, the Chinese renegade who decoyed the Tsin armies
into a Cathayan trap had been promised the southern empire,
in consequence of which he led the van in the march upon
the capital, and moreover brought into hotch-pot all the
booty he had taken ; but now Têh-kwang decided to leave
him as he had recently been created, that is, Prince of Yen

(around modern Peking) and viceroy of the central capital, now Chêng-ting Fu. On the 1st of the next moon Têh-kwang held another grand court, and, looking proudly round, said :—"Surely I am the true Emperor, seeing that I have the " power to seat myself in this magnificent hall, and command " all these Chinese ceremonies ? " Cathayan governors with interpreters were sent to take up posts in all the cities and provinces, and these men simply raked in all the wealth of the Empire in order to satisfy the demands of their men. The Cathayan armies being short of food and forage, Têh-kwang sent out flying columns in all directions and looted the country over an area east and west of nearly a thousand miles, to the great misery of the people.

Whilst all this was going on in the south, the Shado general Liu Chĭ-yüan was striking out a line for himself in Shan Si, where nearly all the Cathayan military governors were soon killed. This news greatly alarmed Têh-kwang, besides which the weather was already growing uncomfortably hot in China ; so he left his brother-in-law in charge of the Tsin capital and himself hastened north, taking with him the whole of the Tsin bureaucracy, skilled artisans, palace women, and army officers, several thousand persons in all. Crossing the Yellow River, he approached Chang-têh Fu : as he was surveying the country from an eminence he observed to one of his Chinese officers :—"At home I took pleasure in " surrounding big game and eating the meat thereof, but since " I entered China my spirits have been depressed. If I can " but see the home of my ancestors once more I shall die " content." The officer remarked to his friends :—"The " cateran is dying." The Cathayan military man in charge had already been killed by a Chinese officer, and the city had to be taken by storm, every living soul in it, except a number of women who were carried off, being ruthlessly butchered ; so that a few years later, when a viceroy of the Shado Han dynasty took over charge, he counted over 100,000 human skulls, which he buried in one huge barrow. As

Têh-kwang was approaching the modern Kwang-p'ing Fu and saw the utter ruin prevailing, he said jokingly to the captives :—" Your renegade general the Prince of Peking " has done most of this." Turning to another Chinese general he added :—" You have not done badly either." When he reached Lwan-ch'êng, a few days' journey farther north (a city still bearing that name), he fell sick and died. The Cathayans disembowelled him, filled his carcase with salt, and carried it with them up north : the Chinese of the party used to derisively call the load " corned emperor."

His nephew Uryuk, son of Turyuk, succeeded (947), and conferred posthumous titles as *divi* in the Chinese style upon his uncle and grandfather. Uryuk had not accompanied his father to China (p. 231). He was of cruel but convivial temperament, fond of liquor, a good artist, and fairly well-read. When the Cathayans assisted Maokire's son-in-law to the throne (p. 232), Maokire's successor (an adopted son and a Chinese) had Turyuk put to death. Uryuk had accompanied his uncle Têh-kwang to China, and was with him at the time of his death. The renegade Chinese general of whom we have spoken attempted to establish himself as Protector, but he was too undecided to make use at once of the 10,000 Chinese troops at hand. Meanwhile Uryuk sent for him to drink wine, got him into a quiet corner, locked him up, and placed all his belongings under arrest or embargo. He then proclaimed Têh-kwang's testament, which was to the following laconic effect :—" You may mount the imperial throne at " the central capital." Messengers were sent in all directions to notify the sad news. When the Cathayan viceroy of the Tsin capital heard of the event, he at once abandoned his charge and went north, and it was this man who took with him the secretary to whom we are beholden for the scant description of Cathay given above (cf. p. 230).

When Uryuk had mounted the throne he sent the first news of it to his grandmother, who said angrily :—" Why " should the son of Turyuk who went over to China succeed ?

" My boy who is dead had the glory of conquering China,
" and it is *his* son who should succeed." She thereupon
marched out an army to dethrone Uryuk. It is not clear
where the battle was fought, but most of her troops went over
to Uryuk, who interned her in the northern part of his
dominions, at a place where Apaoki's remains were interred
and his relics kept. This place can be almost exactly identified.
It was in the Barin Mongol land of to-day, on the upper course
of the Sira Muren [*Sira* means " Yellow," but of course this
is not *the* Yellow River]. The old woman had always disapproved of Têh-kwang's conquests, although she was none
the less proud of him. She once said to him :—" Do you
" think our country would put up with a Chinaman ? " " No."
" Then, even if you take China yourself, you will never have
" a successor, and disaster is certain to overtake you when
" it is too late to repent." She did not shed a tear when his
corpse was brought for her to see, but patted it affectionately
saying :—" You shall be buried, my lad, so soon as our people
" and our herds shall have recovered their former condition."
She died in strict confinement at the Mu-yeh Tombs reserve
(p. 230).

The Cathayan general Matar, Têh-kwang's cousin, whom
Uryuk had left in charge of the central capital, was a monster
of the most ferocious type. In addition to plundering the
people, he used to move about with an assortment of tweezers,
chisels, and other implements of torture, and took a pleasure
in flaying Chinamen's faces, gouging out their eyes, plucking
out their hair, and chopping off their wrists. He had his
sleeping apartment hung with men's livers, shins, hands,
and feet, whilst at the same time he talked and laughed to
those about him as though quite indifferent to the ghastly
spectacle. It is not to be wondered at therefore that the
Chinese generals rose against him and drove the Cathayans
out, or that the Tsin officials went back to join the new Shado
Han dynasty of China.

In the year 948 Uryuk at the head of 10,000 horsemen

made a raid upon and took the city (still bearing that name) of Nei-k'iu in Shun-têh Fu, but he lost half his men in the operation. On this occasion the Cathayans were discouraged because their horses did not neigh as they approached, and they were in the habit of attaching a superstitious importance to such omens. Moreover there was an eclipse of the moon, and their spears glistened to an unusual degree,—both inauspicious signs. After Uryuk had reigned five years, he assembled all the tribal chiefs to deliberate concerning another raid : they were all unwilling, and as Uryuk pushed the matter he was murdered : further murders took place to avenge his. In the end Djurrut, son of Têh-kwang, was elected. As this prince bore the same name as his grand-mother, perhaps the old lady gave it him out of particular affection : at any rate it is curious to find men and women bearing the same names. In his case it was a peculiarly apt coincidence, for, though he was able to hunt, and was a great drinker, he possessed some congenital defect which made it impossible for him to approach women as a sire. He paid no attention to public affairs. For this reason, and from his habit of boozing through the night and sleeping during the day, he received the nickname of the " Sleeping King." Uryuk had sent envoys to the Han court, but on arrival there they found a Chinese general and ex-minister of that short-lived house just on the point of entering the capital to found a dynasty of his own. The founder of this Chou dynasty accepted the mission as addressed to him, and sent one back as a return compliment ; but his envoys in turn only arrived in Cathay in time to find that Uryuk had been succeeded by Djurrut. No further raids were made southwards into China.

In the summer of 959 the second Emperor of the Chou dynasty (the adopted son of the first), travelling by boat, himself conducted an expedition to the Cathayan frontiers ; it is not clear why, for, as stated, there had been no raiding in Djurrut's time. Several Kitan officers at once surrendered their charges. The object seems to have been to assert the

Chinese right to Hiung Chou and Pa Chou, as both cities are still called. The Chinese operations appear to have been impeded by want of water in the river or canal. Orders had been given for an attack on what is now called Peking, but the Emperor, falling sick, thought better of it and went back to his own capital. Djurrut does not seem to have been much disturbed at this Chinese demonstration : in fact we may assume from a remark of his that the Cathayans who thus surrendered had themselves been encroaching, for he said :—" This used to be Chinese territory, what matter " therefore if they recover it ? " In the year 960 the highly literary and very distinguished Sung dynasty was established and it was the early policy of the founder to do justice to the Tartars. He ordered the return of all stolen horses, and forbade the frontier people from making raids beyond the Wall : it had been the custom for many years to kidnap frontier Cathayans and draft them into Turko-Chinese cavalry regiments. The Cathayans do not seem to have properly appreciated the purely Chinese Emperor's sentiments, for they lost no time in making raids in the good old style. This went on for several years, and the Emperor himself led one of the expeditions sent to punish them. In that same year 969 Djurrut was murdered, and succeeded by Uryuk's son Ming-ki. From this time the Cathayan Emperors are known by Chinese names only. Ming-ki called his empire " Great Kitan " instead of " Great Liao."

CHAPTER III

PERIOD OF COMPARATIVE PEACE

IN the autumn of 970, 60,000 Cathayans made a raid upon the country around the present provincial capital of Chih Li (Pao-ting Fu), but 3,000 Chinese, under a competent general specially instructed by the Emperor, managed so to manœuvre that the Cathayans got distinctly the worst of it though numbering twenty to one. The Emperor now found it expedient to change his earlier policy should raids continue, and offered 24 pieces of silk for every Cathayan head, calculating that with some two and a half million pieces he could purchase the whole of their effective force. This estimate is not unreasonable, for the total effective force even of the Manchus, who over-ran China with ease in the 17th century, was never much over 200,000 men; and indeed 100,000 men of any civilized country, if given a free hand and properly supplied, could have conquered and held China at any moment up to the year 1860.

From 975 and onwards began a series of friendly missions, and resident envoys with regular international relations date from this period. Cathay was now sufficiently advanced in the arts to be able to send imperial robes as presents to China. Her envoys used to attend the Emperor's hunting parties, and on his death in 976 she sent a special mission to condole and sacrifice in good Confucian form. [And here may be mentioned an amusing incident in reference to the Cathayan ideas of Confucius (which took place, however, sixty years later). The descendant of Confucius in the 45th generation happened to be the Chinese Resident Minister at the Cathayan court, and the rough Tartars, by way of entertaining him, gave a theatrical performance, in which Confucius the Great was introduced in a comic capacity. Confucius the 46th very properly left the theatre at once, and obtained an official apology.] In the year 979 war broke out, and the new Sung Emperor temporarily occupied Peking in person, besides several towns near it: the Cathayans lost 10,000 heads in this campaign. The following year 100,000 of them made raids between the line of the Shan Si and Chih Li Great Walls, and the Emperor again marched north as far as Ta-ming (still so called). He was for taking and occupying Peking permanently, but he found the surrounding country so ravaged and exhausted by generations of war that the question of supplies forced him to abandon the notion. Raiding, always repulsed, went on until Ming-ki's death in 983. He was succeeded by his son Lung-sü, then barely twelve years of age. His mother, Dame Siao, acted as regent. Raiding and war went on : nothing is said of the causes ; but, as strict orders were circulated not to rob the Cathayans, and to return all objects stolen from them, it may be assumed that the Chinese were often themselves the first offenders.

In the year 984 it was discovered that the Cathayan regent had, much to the disgust of her people, formed a liaison with (amongst other paramours) one of her Chinese marshals, who did what he liked with her. It was suggested that advantage should be taken of Cathayan disunion to recover the Peking country east of the (still) well-known river Hun Ho as far as Yung-p'ing Fu. The Emperor approved the suggestion, and in 986 a large Chinese army marched through the Great Wall (the southern line of it of course) between Goose Gate and Peking. Bounties were offered to " privateers," and so much a head was promised for each Cathayan officer. The Emperor's strategical plan was that one column should march on Ta-t'ung whilst the other with 100,000 men should make a leisurely feint on Peking, so as to attract all the Cathayan forces in that quarter ; and then outflank them and co-operate with the first column in their rear. The territory forming a loop between the two Great Walls was duly taken by the first column, whilst the second took several large towns south of Peking in very brilliant style, resting at the (still) well-known Choh Chou. The Emperor was very nervous lest this column should advance too quickly and have its supplies cut off ; and indeed, after spending a fortnight at Choh Chou, the general had to come back some distance in order to convoy his own supplies. His soldiers, hearing of the other column's success, murmured at this retrograde movement, and so to appease them he took only five days' provision with him and once more marched on Choh Chou ;

but they had to fight every inch of their way, and it took them twenty days to get there. The season was now getting very hot, and the men, insufficiently fed, were utterly exhausted, so there was no alternative but to fall back once more upon Yih Chou, at which place the half-starved and defeated remnants of the force at last arrived after crossing the river at night. The officers were all degraded. Arrangements were made to remove the population of the conquered tract within the two Great Walls into China. There were 50,000 households, besides three tribes of Tukuhun (p. 110) and Turks with a few other odd clans. Raiding still went on, and the commanding officers of the column whose blundering had spoiled the Emperor's last combination were given another chance to distinguish themselves. The year 987 was a bad one for China : the fighting was around the Pao-ting Fu neighbourhood as before, but all the Chinese generals were badly defeated : Yih Chou was stormed by the Cathayans, and taken with great slaughter and plunder, so that in 989 the Emperor had to issue a sorrowful manifesto, calling for more troops. Meanwhile the Wall Loop region was retaken, and the Chinese set themselves to work to prevent any further advance by erecting block-houses and planting willow trees in such a way as to prevent large bodies of Cathayan horsemen from moving freely about the country. Hitherto the Chinese had had much better success in the Ordous region, where a number of frontier tribes had deserted the Cathayans ; but now the latter induced an Upper Yellow River Tibetan tribe to join them. The result was unsuccessful for the Cathayans ; the Tibetans, seeing them fly, turned upon them with great slaughter, and the total result was that innumerable tents came over to the Chinese side of the Yellow River, and the Sung dynasty secured at least ten thousand heavy cavalry by way of allies. This was in the year 995. In the year 999 the third Emperor Chên Tsung took the field in person, and from this time onwards for five or six years the Cathayans received pretty rough handling.

In the year 1003 a Chinese official who had been employed by the Cathayans deserted to the Chinese side, and gave the Emperor some account of what was going on in Cathay. It appears that the Cathayans had as many as 18,000 Chinese cavalry at Peking. The armies of their own Eight Tribes and of the four chief garrisons north of the Wall numbered about 180,000 cavaliers, 5,600 of which were always employed as the monarch's personal guard, whilst 94,000 were raiding troops. It was (here of course we use modern names) 180 miles from Peking to Yung-p'ing Fu, whence another 180 miles to Kin-chou Fu (p. 101), the frontier of their eastern metropolitan district. Two hundred miles north of that was the capital of a state where the Chinese method of writing was in use,—apparently (from other evidence) the Sib (p. 149) or else Botskai is meant,—north of which were the Nüchên, and south-east Shinra, or Sin-lo (a Corean state).

In the late autumn of 1004 the Cathayan monarch and his mother invaded China with all their available forces in three columns. The attacks on North Shan Si and Pao-ting Fu were unsuccessful, and afterwards the unsuccessful columns united to attack modern Ho-kien Fu, where the most obstinate and desperate fighting took place day and night without intermission. The Cathayans used a sort of artillery worked by a spring called " bed-frame cross-bows." Carrying planks on their backs and torches in their hands, they drove the Ghei men up the city walls, from which the defenders rained down huge stones and blocks of wood. Over 30,000 of the assailants were slain in the attempt to carry the town by storm. Another party was equally unsuccessful at Ki Chou (still so called) farther south. There were still 200,000 of the enemy to deal with, and desperate efforts were made to raise army after army, surround them, and drive them out. But the Cathayans managed so to manœuvre as nearly to surround the main Chinese force just north of modern K'ai Chou in Ta-ming Fu ; and it might have gone ill with the latter had not a lucky shot (fired from a cover commanding the narrow road where a number of crossbow-men lay in ambush) struck the Cathayan prince and commander-in-chief Taran in the head. He was carried into camp and died that night. This event seems to have discouraged the Tartars, who shortly withdrew. They now made peaceful overtures through a Chinese general whom they had taken prisoner, and who, like most of his countrymen, was as ready to serve one master as the other, if his personal interests required it. He made the unpleasant condition that the first envoy should come from China, a point which the Emperor at first declined to concede, but which he ultimately did concede under pressure. The chief point discussed at the negotiations was whether the territory south of parallel 39 ceded by the Shado dynasty of Tsin (p. 223), and, as the Chinese claimed, subsequently recovered by the second Emperor of Chou, should remain with Cathay or with China. The result was that the Chinese kept the territory they actually had, and received the barren honour of being called " elder brother," whilst the Cathayans were to receive an annual subsidy of 200,000 pieces of silk and 100,000 ounces of silver. Besides this, the queen-dowager sent her own special envoys, who explained that this was because she was the practical ruler; so that extra annual presents of silk and silver had to be sent to her in consideration of her reverent care for the Emperor's health.

In the spring of 1005 Hiung Chou, Pa Chou, and Pao-ting Fu, or rather three suitable points in the frontier passes under each of them, were thrown open to trade by imperial decree, and custom-houses were established there. It was also ordered that all Cathayan deserters subsequent in date to the first overtures for peace should be sent back. A friendly mission was sent to Cathay to congratulate the queen-mother on her birthday: she was in summer residence at the time, but she sent her son to receive the ambassadors at modern Peking, where they were most handsomely fêted. They received valuable presents, and were accompanied outside the gates by the monarch himself, who drank a stirrup-cup with them.

Envoys representing mother and son came during the winter, and this amicable exchange went on for several years. One Chinese envoy on his return said :—" The cateran ruler when " he receives the Chinese envoys makes a shift to figure in hat " and robes, but so soon as ever the function is over he gets " into easy costume, and, mixing promiscuously with his " cavaliers, goes out hunting followed by his ministers ; but " there is no purveyance ; he provides his own arms, cooking " utensils, and provisions." The laws he described as being barbarously severe :—" Those condemned to death are always " hacked to death in a fearful manner. The cateran ruler " once said to me that his people were like wild animals, " and not to be ruled by civil laws in Chinese fashion." In the year 1008 another envoy (who had been received at a specially prepared hotel just north of the river which was the scene of the disastrous night retreat to Yih Chou in 986) came back and reported that the Cathayan central capital was now removed to a place north-east of Peking. [It may here be explained that a place in Aokhan or Kartsin Mongol land, possibly Jêhol, Ch'ih-fêng, or some locality between them, is certainly meant ;—in fact the old Upper Capital. Owing to the word Ch'ang-li having been used both for the ancient Sien-pi capital here, and for the later Sien-pi capital at Yung-p'ing Fu, the Chinese historians themselves have got hopelessly muddled on the subject of Cathayan capitals, and are frequently wrong (cf. p. 228).] The walls and ramparts were very mean, and the inhabitants were very few. As a rule bare walls lined each side of the streets. There were two large edifices occupied by the monarch and his mother respectively, but there was great boorishness and looseness of etiquette when banquets were given.

At the beginning of the year 1010 the queen-mother died, and shortly afterwards her paramour (p. 243) the Chinese premier died also. His rule had been nearly absolute ; he was remarkably shrewd, and the Cathayans had learned to esteem him very highly. From this time the Cathayan ruler, deprived of his best counsellors, became incompeten and unpopular. The Nüchêns at this time formed part of the Cathayan dominions : twenty years previously they had offered China military assistance, which was declined ; in consequence of this they ceased to send tribute, and for a time had to throw in their interests with those of Cathay. The Cathayans now sent word to China that they were about to attack Corea, which, formerly a triple dominion like England, Scotland, and Ireland, had since 930 become a united kingdom, quite independent, but tributary to China. In 986 Corea had attacked Cathay at China's request on account of Cathayans having passed through part of Corea in order to raid the Nüchêns, who had complained of Corea to China, thinking that Corea was an accomplice. The Coreans also complained to China in the year 1000 that ever since the Shado Tsin had (p. 223) given the Peking plain to Cathay, Corea had been exposed to Cathayan exactions. Corea, finding nothing but fine words could be got from China, now built six frontier citadels for her own defence, and it was to take these that Cathay now declared war. The Cathayans called upon the Ghei, the Shirvi, and the Blackwater Nüchêns to furnish men and carts for the campaign. But the Nüchêns, having discovered the evil ways of Cathay, joined Corea, and the Cathayans led by their own king received a thorough thrashing, losing nearly the whole of their army and half their nobles. They were now obliged to recruit soldiers from the Peking plain. The Cathayan system of recruiting was very oppressive and wasteful. They used to send round orders to those summoned to prepare their own weapons, horses, camels, food, and provender, and to rendez-vous at a certain place ; the result was that the share of plunder obtained rarely compensated the soldier for his original outlay. They used also to force all Chinese in their dominions guilty of any offence to act as scouts or skirmishers for them.

A pretty exact account of the journey *via* Hiung Chou, Choh Chou, and over the well-known Lu-kou Bridge to Peking

is given. The earlier envoys got no farther north than this.
A short description is also given of Peking as it then was.
There was, amongst other sights which the Chinese envoys
were taken to see, a monastery erected in the 7th century
by T'ang T'ai Tsung to the memory of those killed in the
Corean campaigns (p. 153). Then, as now, the wealthy used
to retire from the city to the hills during the summer season.
The ruler used to occasionally pass the winter in the neighbourhood of modern Mih-yün.   Most places on the roads were then
called *tien* or " meadows " (as the well-known Hai-tien of
to-day), and *kwan* or " hostelries."   The Ku-pêh K'ou Pass
so familiar to Europeans at Peking was then known by the
same name, and this, before the Cathayans had it, was
considered the most important pass to hold in keeping off
the Ghei from Peking. Our travellers in Cathayan times
noticed a shop just outside the pass where bows were strung
for passers-by. The journey past Lwan-p'ing to Jêhol is
easily recognizable : the first-named place was then called
Lwan Chou, and at the second, which was probably a mere
village, there was a smithy worked by Botskai men. It is
not very clear if the " Sleeping Buddha " of those days was
the Putolá Temple of to-day, a few miles north of Jêhol.
The Botskai custom was to assemble for rejoicings and dancing
at the new year, lads and lasses singing in turns to a " following
dance."   The description given of houses built in the mountain
side corresponds exactly to the appearance of those we see
to-day between Jêhol and Ch'ih-fêng.   Some of the inhabitants
lived in carts.   The " hills to the east where hunting in a circle
goes on " is evidently the Wei-ch'ang or imperial hunting
ground of our days (1870), whence it was a good day's journey
to the " Central Capital of Ta-ting Fu " [in modern Kartsin
Mongol land].   The city walls of Ta-ting were low and mean,
forming an oblong of about a mile and a quarter round :
the gates were surmounted merely by an extra storey, there
were no elevated watch-towers or citadels. The houses or
hotels seem to have been of the caravanserai description,

but there was a bazaar with storeyed houses near the south gate. Northwards from this the habits of the people began to change. The people lived in thatched huts with plank walls, and engaged in agriculture. The oak-mulberry was planted in rows along the ridges as a protection from sand-drifts. The forests were full of tall firs, and in the mountain valleys were people engaged in burning charcoal. The most usually met with were herds of dark sheep (or goats) and yellow pigs, but occasionally also oxen, horses, and camels. From the central capital it was 170 miles to the crossing of the Sira Muren and the capital of the native proconsulate established (p. 152) by the T'ang dynasty [in modern Ongniod Mongol land], occupied at the time of which we write by Botskai men. Then 63 miles to Apaoki's temple and the dynastic shrine : his boots are preserved as a relic : they were four or five feet in length. Thence 13 miles to the Upper Capital [in Aru Korchin Mongol land]. The old Cathayan land lay north of a line 100 miles south of the Sira Muren. South of that were the Ghei. The northern capital had east and west gates, and the palaces inside faced east. The felt tent habitations also faced east. About 65 miles north-west of this capital were the " Cool Meadows," with plenty of rich grass, where the ruling family used to go to avoid the heats of summer. The Ghei did not speak the same language, nor had they the same customs as the Cathayans : they are good agriculturalists and foot archers, and magnificent horse-men, being as it were glued to their beasts (cf. p. 224).

It appears that Apaoki's remains were first placed in the hill cemetery lying to the east, a trifle north of the central capital (Ta-ting Fu), the place where Heaven and Earth are worshipped. " There is a felt house facing east here with " a suitable inscription. There are no steps leading up to " the shrine, but the ground is spread with felts, and there are " two large felt tents behind. There are several tame leopards " here used in hunting. They also have a way of fishing, " by putting a felt tent on the ice, boring a hole, and keeping

" up a bright light inside : the fish collect at the hole and are
" speared in great numbers."

According to their laws, the queen-dowager and native
officials all wore Tartar costume : the ruler and the Chinese
officials all Chinese costume.   Lung-sü's nephew was viceroy
of the central capital.   The native officials wore felt hats,
the top of which was ornamented with a golden flower ; or
sometimes they had a pearl jewel or kingfisher's feather ; this
hat being the lineal representative of the hat adopted by the
Mujung Sien-pi [and which (p. 99) furnished one of the fanciful
derivations for that word] : the hair was gathered inside it,
and a sort of woven band with ornaments hanging behind
enclosed the head.   A purple robe with a kind of petticoat and
saddle-belt made of leather embroidered with red or yellow
braid was worn.   They also wore civilian official caps with
flaps as in China.   [The rest of the description is vague and
of no particular interest.]

Such are the scant features of Cathayan life which attracted
the attention of the Chinese envoys : doubtless numerous
Chinese residents in Cathay could have furnished much more
exact and interesting accounts of the northern realm ; but
there is reason to believe there was great mutual jealousy,
and that the frontiers were very closely watched for spies.
Besides, the classes that sought a living or were compelled
to gain one in Cathay were certainly of the most illiterate ;
and, even if it had been possible to smuggle information out
of the country, the persons most competent to give it were
probably incapable of recording it.

CHAPTER IV

General Description of Cathay in the Eleventh Century

THE Chinese (Sung) Emperor Chên Tsung died in 1022 and Lung-sü expressed his sympathy in the most effusive way. He himself died in 1031 and received his full equivalent in the shape of wails, mourning, sacrifices, and so on. It is difficult to see why the Chinese should first describe him as "incapable" after his mother's death, and yet add that he kept his engagements with China faithfully and never once gave trouble. He was succeeded by his eighth son Tsung-chên, whose Tartar name in his own family circle was Mukpuku : in his case also, the mother, a concubine in rank, managed things for him. China was having considerable trouble with the Ordous state of Tangut or Hia, the ruler of which had in 1028 captured the Ouigour city of Kan Chou. Tsung-chên thought this was his opportunity, so he massed troops in the Peking plain and wrote a letter to his "elder brother" the Emperor reopening the question of the ten districts recovered by the Chou Emperor, and complaining of the unprovoked attempt of the Sung Emperor T'ai Tsung to conquer the Loop and the Peking plain in 986 (pp. 223, 246), and the fact that two of the conquered districts still remained in Chinese hands. Also of the action of a frontier governor in making strategic use of the water of a river near Pa Chou. The Cathayan envoys, whilst ostensibly putting in a claim for territory, were not sufficiently skilful to disguise from the Chinese that larger annual subsidies were really what they wanted. A return envoy was sent to Cathay, supported by a strong body of troops, to take the Emperor's reply. This was to point out the advantages which had accrued to both sides from the forty years' unbroken peace, and how unreasonable it was for one dynasty to be expected to undo what its predecessors had arranged. It was explained that the war of 979 had broken out (p. 242) owing to the Cathayans having assisted an enemy of China. As to Tangut, China is quite competent to deal with that power satisfactorily. The river works are to prevent floods, and are not strategic ; nor are there more troops on the frontier than are necessary for ordinary routine purposes. The letter concludes with an exhortation to preserve neighbourly good feeling, and not to make the above petty matters pretexts for demanding a cession of territory.

The envoys found Tsung-chên at his *napo* or shooting box on a certain river, where he was living in a travelling tent. He repeated his complaints, and said that " the country " had wanted immediate war, but that he had satisfied himself with demanding " compensation " in the shape of territory. The wily Chinaman reproached the monarch with having forgotten the goodness of the Emperor, who, contrary to the advice of his generals, had allowed the Cathayans to withdraw unmolested after Taran's death (p. 246) ; and added that Tsung-chên himself was the only one to lose by war and to gain by peace. On being asked for further explanation, he went on to say that, during the reign of the last Tsin emperor, China was reduced to a very small area ; prince and people were at loggerheads, and thus Cathay was able to take her capital. With what result ? The Cathayan monarch, who himself perished in the end, lost the larger half of his best troops and horses before he secured his object, and the only gain was that the survivors had their pockets filled of valuables, and their residences stuffed with plunder. China has now recovered her thousands of miles of territory and possesses millions of seasoned troops. In the event of war, therefore, the question of victory is at any rate uncertain, whereas further loss of Cathayan life is a matter of complete certainty. On the other hand, in the event of peace being preserved, not only will the monarch not lose his soldiers' lives, but all the subsidy goes to himself alone, whilst his ministers get nothing but what they can make out of being occasional envoys. Thus it is plainly the interest of the counsellors to have war and plunder, the ruler losing his men and his subsidy ; and therefore great circumspection is necessary : and so on. Observing the effect these words had upon the Tartar, the Chinese envoy went on with well-acted frankness to explain :—" We have closed the " Goose Gate in order to keep out the ruler of Tangut (p. 213). " The damming up of the reservoirs on the Cathayan frontier at " Pa Chou dates from the year 997. The new drafts of soldiers " and the repairs to fortifications are only the inevitable " restorations required by decay. We have done nothing " contrary to standing treaty. True, the Shado founder of " the Tsin dynasty bribed Cathay with cessions of territory ; " but the second Chou Emperor re-conquered part of this, " both events having occurred before our present Sung dynasty " came in. If you are to annul the act of Chou, then surely we " may annul that of Tsin, and China will thus be the gainer. " The Emperor has instructed me to say that in his opinion " your desire for the land is at bottom a desire only for the " profits on that land, and he is quite resolved that not " for a mere question of profits will he cause valuable lives to " be sacrificed. He therefore increases the subsidy by the " amount of taxation leviable on the disputed territory. " If Cathay insists on having the land itself, she evidently " puts this forward as a pretext for overturning the treaty " of 1005 ; and if war be desired, his Majesty cannot refuse " to accept it." Tsung-chên was visibly impressed, and proposed a marriage alliance ; but the observant Chinese envoy, seeing his advantage, said :—" Marriage connections " easily give rise to disputes, and are not so durable as subsidies. " A hundred thousand ounces of silver is the dowry given " with a first-class princess, which is immeasurably below " the value of an annual subsidy." Tsung-chên said :— " Well, anyhow, go back, and on your next arrival I will tell " you which I will have : but bring your full-powers with

" you." The envoy on his return to China counselled the
conceding of the following points : first, China will not flood
the Pa Chou frontier too readily ; second, she will not add
troops to the number now on the boundaries ; third, she will
not receive deserters. The prime minister, who was a private
foe, tried to play a trick on the envoy when his second mission
took place by falsifying his full-powers ; but the envoy, who
had already started, suspected some treachery on the part
of his personal enemy, and was too sharp for him ; for he secretly
opened the cover, discovered the ruse, and confidentially
sent the document back to the Emperor to be altered. On
his arrival in Cathay, the envoy had to object to the use of the
word " submit " which the Tartar demanded : the word
" pay " was substituted, and the subsidy was raised to " half
a million " : this seems to mean that the 200,000 pieces of
silk and 100,000 of silver of the last treaty were each raised
by 100,000. Just then, as a matter of fact, Cathay was
anxious for peace ; but China was so worried with the Tangut
trouble, and was in the hands of such a weak and corrupt
premier, that she had to pay through the nose for Cathayan
neutrality.

In the year 1044 the Cathayans declared war against
Tangut for the offence of harbouring deserters, and announced
the fact to China : they were victorious, and in 1049 announced
that fact too. In official documents the words " Great Sung "
and " Great Kitan " were insisted upon by China in preference
to the expressions " Court of the North " and " Court of the
South." In 1054 Tsung-chên sent an envoy to say that he
was so gratified with the 50 years of peace that he would like
to possess the Emperor's portrait. A tame elephant was
sent to him as well. The next year he sent his own portrait
in return, and shortly afterwards died, after a reign of 25 years.
This monarch was characterized by great levity of character :
he had his " Jack Falstaff " in the shape of a low-born boon
companion, with whom he used to go about in various dis-
guises to the pot-houses, circuses, monasteries, and other resorts

of his capital. He was also a favourer of Buddhists, many bonzes holding high positions in his government. He was succeeded by his son Hung-ki, and there was the usual exchange of sympathetic missions between the two Emperors, and, again, of portraits.

Of course the name Tientsin did not exist then, but none the less Tientsin salt seems to have been manufactured in those times very much as now. In 1006 it seems to have been agreed that the Cathayans should not make use of the frontier streams; but for some time past their subjects had been in the habit of clandestinely fishing and gathering reeds in the river; sometimes also of taking a short cut by way of Pa Chou and Hiung Chou in China to their own town of Choh Chou. The Chinese officials had hitherto been too timid to do anything but occasionally remonstrate : but now there was an active governor at Hiung Chou, who shot several of the trespassers and broke up their boats. China's weakness in increasing the subsidy had made the Cathayans grow overweening, and a Chinese renegade in their employ suggested to them that the subsidy might be best maintained as a permanent in- stitution by keeping China in a state of worry, and by wrangling over small matters. Consequently all Cathayan envoys were instructed to make as much fuss as possible about points of etiquette; trespasses across the frontier were instigated; and a small town near the northern boundary of the Chinese district of modern Chêng-ting Fu was walled in so as to annoy the Chinese garrison opposite. Cultivators were encouraged to encroach, and night parties used to steal forth and cut down the willows which had been planted with a view to impede cavalry movements. However, China bore all this " with a friendly shrug," and simply increased her watchfulness.

In the months of February and March the Cathayans used to sally forth for a 60 days' hunting expedition, after which they went to fish in a watercourse called the Taru River through holes in the ice : then came the hawking season, when they took ducks, geese, etc. In the summer they used to go to the Charcoal Hills or the Upper Capital to avoid the heat ; and in the autumn they went deer hunting in the mountains : beaters were sent out in the middle of the night to blow horns in imitation of deer cries. There were two clan names of distinction, none of the others being thought of much account. One of the clans, that of Siao (p. 243), seems to have represented the royal Ghei family ; the other, that of Yerut or Yelüh, the royal house of Cathay. Of the public offices, the Privy Council, Executive, and Headquarters Staff were styled " south-siders," because south of the ruler's place, and intended for the administration of Chinese affairs. Their *teghin* (cf. p. 210) were what in China are called " members of the ruling family " ; their *ilipir* were " assistant ministers "; their *linya* " doctors of learning " ; their *iligin* " provincial governors." [*Lin-ya* was a form of the Chinese *Hanlin*, or "Wrangler," and the founder of the Karakitai Empire at Kermané (pp. 108, 293) is often spoken of simply as "the *Linya*."] Most of their other officers bore titles similar to those of corresponding officials in China. There were special departments or officials for the Ghei, Shirvi, Nüchêns, and Botskai men. All persons between the ages of 15 and 50 had to serve in the army ; and, when about to start on a military expedition, they used to sacrifice an ash-coloured ox and a white horse (p. 146) to Heaven, Earth, the Sun, and the genius of the ancestral hills in Kartsin land. They used to cast metal tallies resembling gold fish as warrants to raise troops or horse (cf. 9, 174). For impounding animals on post service silver plaques were used. Wherever an army was encamped they had a number of foraging scouts on specially trained horses, which at nightfall would reassemble by recognizing distant sounds and carry the plunder to one spot. When a king died, his image in molten gold was erected in a separate tent, and on the 1st and 15th of each moon sacrifices of food and wine were offered to his *manes* : each mausoleum had its glebe, with serfs to furnish soldiers and horses. According to the Cathayan military system each free soldier had to provide himself with three horses, and with saddle, saddle-cloth, and horse-armour of iron or hide according to his means ; one servant for foraging, and one to look after his kit ; four bows, 400 arrows, long and short spears, ax, hatchet, hammer, awl, a small flag, flint and steel, jug, ration-bag, hook, piece of felt, and umbrella ; also 200 feet of rope, and a peck of parched grain. He had to come south about November, and in February they withdrew in scattered bodies, cutting down mulberry trees and orchards, setting fire to dwellings, and carrying off the women, children, old, and helpless persons. When they were unable to take a place, they used to announce that they were shortly coming back with reinforcements, so as to keep the people inside in a state of alarm and prevent pursuit. Small parties would attack each gate first, and if overpowered, at once retire for reinforcements. Whenever they came to a ford or narrow road, they would throw out scouts to protect the passage. In storming towns, they drove their captives in front, and made them fill up the moat with earth and brushwood, so as to form a passage for those behind. Their system of fighting was to form themselves into battalions of from 500 to 700 horsemen, according to the topography of the road or frozen river they were passing ; each ten of such battalions advancing in turn, one after the other, one body rushing wildly on with howls, and retiring when exhausted to take rest or refreshment, whilst others came on in turn, so as to keep up an incessant attack : the foraging servants were made to raise the dust and shout by their masters' side. The monarch was always surrounded by a body-guard of veterans. The Chinese troops, being mostly infantry, and having to carry their own provisions and armour, were liable to be taken at a disadvantage if they took their kit off, whereas if they kept it on for several days in succession they naturally felt exhausted and unrefreshed.

CHAPTER V

INSOLENCE, TYRANNY, REBELLION OF THE NÜCHÊNS, AND COLLAPSE

IN the year 1066 the Cathayans once more styled their empire " Great Liao "; (see pp. 232, 255). In 1067 they sent the usual friendly missions on the occasion of the Emperor Shên Tsung's accession, but notwithstanding this they increased their fortifications at Choh Chou and Yih Chou, besides adding to their stores of grain and weapons, and massing more troops on the frontier. China also had frequent skirmishes with trespassers on the frontier rivers, and with scouts who advanced beyond the military line agreed upon. Steps were therefore taken to dig trenches and dam up the water in the neighbourhood of modern Pao-ting Fu, so as to further impede cavalry movements, and corresponding additions were made to China's armies and fortifications too. Hung-ki tried several times to get up a dispute on some petty question, so as to test China's mettle, and at last in 1074 he sent envoys to formulate regular complaints, and demand the dismantling of certain strong places, besides a general rectification of the frontier. The Emperor offered to send a delimitation commission to see that the frontier previously agreed upon had not been transgressed, and to stop further works ; although, he said, they were as a matter of fact only necessary repairs. The officer who had destroyed boats and shot certain Cathayans (p. 255) had already been degraded, " but the true responsibility " for the late skirmishes must be fixed before anyone can " be punished on that score, as the Cathayan scouts seem to " have come too far." Thus spoke the Emperor. A return mission was sent, and some time was consumed in preliminaries. The following year the same Cathayan envoy returned with a positive demand for a certain watershed as the boundary in

Shan Si. All the precedents and correspondence showed clearly that the demand was unjust, and even the most peacefully disposed of the ministers and ex-ministers were of opinion that it would be impolitic to give way. However, the celebrated reformer Wang An-shih was then in power, and he persuaded the Emperor (as Cathay was evidently going to take it whether China gave way or not) to issue a decree conceding the line demanded, no matter what the evidence of the records might be. What really was conceded seems to have been practically the line of the more southerly Shan Si Great Wall, as still existing, for over 200 miles : formerly the Chinese possessed the heights looking down upon the modern Süan-hwa Fu, westwards to Shoh Chou ; whereas now the Cathayans could look down upon Tai Chou and Hin Chou. Notwithstanding this important concession, the Cathayans committed further aggressive acts, such as crossing the frontier to arrest spies. It seems that both sides guarded the frontier with extreme jealousy at this time, and deserters or spies were often sent back blindfolded, with their ears plugged.

Hung-ki is described as being an able and firm administrator, possessed of an amiable disposition ; quiet, and not to be flurried : the only thing was that he allowed himself to be guided too much by a favourite. Whilst the monarch had his Robert Carr, his mother had her Rienzi, and the result of court jealousies was that the heir-apparent and his mother both fell victims to the favourite's machinations, after which he himself and a thousand others perished at the instance of Hung-ki's able prime minister. The grandson, whose name was Yen-hi, now became heir-apparent, and succeeded in the year 1101, his grandfather having enjoyed a long reign of 47 years.

The Chinese Emperor Chêh Tsung had died a year before. China was again at war with Hia or Tangut, and the Cathayans sent a mission to mediate. Guessing their object, the Chinese premier (the corrupt rascal whose doings are so vividly portrayed in the Chinese novel previously mentioned) fore-

stalled their arrival by hastening off a counter mission asking
for military assistance. Yen-hi at once saw through this
move, and was very angry. Four years later he again sent
a mission to interfere in the question of Tangut frontiers.
He was a grasping, violent, unconscionable man, and the result
was that all the vassal states in his empire became disaffected.
Amongst others Akuta, chieftain of the Nüchêns, rebelled,
whilst Yen-hi was engaged upon his autumn deer hunt, and
took the district around modern Ninguta in Kirin, defeating
the Botskai troops sent against him (that is, the more civilized
half of the nation to which the Nüchêns themselves belonged),
and possessing himself of the city. There used to be
a periodical fair held there, to which the Nüchêns brought
their gold, pearls, honey, and wax for sale, and the Cathayans
had for long been in the habit of making purveyances, beating
the Nüchêns and paying insufficient prices. All these old
wrongs now welled up again in the breasts of the local Nüchên
people, who proceeded to massacre every Cathayan in the
place, secured 3,000 suits of armour, and retired towards the
mountains either of Corea or of the Lower Amur,—it is
uncertain which is meant. A Cathayan general with 5,000
Ghei and Cathayan troops was hastily sent against the revolters.
For a long time there had been no trouble in these parts,
and therefore there was no difficulty in obtaining further
volunteers for the service. Confident of victory, and neglectful
of every precaution, most of the men had brought their wives
and families with them, when suddenly the Nüchêns, who
seem to have crossed the Sungari (cf. p. 103) by stealth and
taken the Cathayans in the rear, fell upon the advancing
column before it had time to get into fighting array. There
was a complete stampede, and all the children, cattle, sheep,
and treasure were captured. The enemy also pursued the
retreating force for 30 miles, taking a few prisoners, besides
killing a small number.

It was not the Cathayan custom to let their Chinese
subjects take part in great affairs of state, at any rate in

military matters ; but after these two reverses they decided to place the conduct of the eastern campaign in the hands of two Chinese ministers. Like most of their race, they were mere paper strategists, and had no idea of real generalship, as is here, in fact, distinctly stated. They represented that the recent defeats were due to hastiness of preparation, but that, if 200,000 Chinese soldiers were employed to march upon the enemy by different roads, success would be certain. Yen-hi placed 100,000 men at their disposal, and ordered a property-tax to be levied in the four chief provinces at the rate of one soldier for every hundred pounds sterling worth of property owned, as by survey to be made under commission. The result was that rich families had to furnish sometimes as many as 200 men, and this draft was a very exhausting demand upon the country. The men had to be ready in January, but their weapons and armour were of a most heterogeneous character, not more than two per cent possessing a proper regulation equipment of bow, cross-bow, and iron cuirass. They marched forth in four columns, and with them were contingents of native troops. A Cathayan general, in every case belonging to one of the two leading clans, Siao and Yerut, commanded each column. Only one of the four columns came up with the enemy. Receiving a slight check at the outset, the 30,000 Chinese gave way a little, when the general, Yerut Wolito, thinking they were going to run, at once galloped off with all his Ghei and Cathayans, leaving the Chinese completely in the lurch. The latter now elected their own general, but were beaten in two subsequent battles which they fought. The other three columns, hearing of this, retired upon their respective bases, all of which were taken by storm within a few months by the victorious Nüchêns. Yen-hi was afraid to punish anyone lest he should further discourage the soldiers, and the consequence was that the latter thought it better in future always to run away rather than to risk death for no adequate reward. This was all in the year 1114.

In 1115 Yen-hi announced his intention to take the field

in person. Meanwhile one of his barons was conspiring to dethrone him, on account of his unconstitutional behaviour, and to substitute an uncle : for this he was executed : the uncle was in no way molested. Yen-hi was defeated in all his encounters with Akuta, who now assumed the imperial title, taking the style Kin, or " Golden," in imitation of the Cathayan " Iron " (p. 232). The Chinese envoys went and came as before to Cathay, but found a difficulty in obtaining audience. The Botskai contingent now revolted, and murdered the Cathayan viceroy of the eastern metropolitan province, where the rule had been extremely tyrannical. They proclaimed their own general (whose name has rather a Corean look) Emperor of Botskai. Nearly all Liao Tung fell into his hands, only the modern Moukden remaining untaken. One of the vapouring Chinese ministers who had failed so miserably hitherto was a native of this place, and he offered to march against the Botskayans with 20,000 men : he was successful, and they had to take to the sea ; their leader was decapitated. In 1118 Cathay suffered so much from dearth that people actually ate one another.

All these troubles in Cathay land were gradually discovered and reported to the Emperor by the frontier officers, who received repeated instructions not to show too much zeal so far as action went. But there was a eunuch in power, nicknamed the " prime grandmother," who was in favour of a forward policy, and it was only through persistent counsels not to provoke the Cathayans, so long as they were united and able to maintain the government, that the Emperor was restrained from giving the bellicose eunuch a free hand.

Yen-hi now appointed his uncle commander-in-chief : all the starving riff-raff of Liao Tung, to the number of 20,000, were enlisted and jocularly called the " pauper army." The uncle had just become a very popular viceroy at the modern Kin-chou Fu, and it was entirely through his influence that Moukden was not taken. The pauper army soon broke into mutiny because insufficiently clothed, and the uncle had first to check this mutiny and then advance to meet the Nüchêns. He was defeated and compelled to fall back with the small force of Cathayan cavalry under his immediate command, whilst the victorious Nüchêns advanced up to the Taling River, taking city after city. Yen-hi was in his Central Capital (in the Jêhol region) when the staggering news of these successive defeats reached him. He gave private orders for 500 bags of jewellery and other valuables to be put up, selected 2,000 of his best horses, and prepared for flight. He expressed to his entourage the conviction that his brother Emperor of Sung and his connection by marriage the ruler of Tangut would give him an asylum if necessary ; his only regret was to think of the massacre of his people which would take place if the Nüchêns really came. However, the Nüchêns had to go back for a time to rest their worn-out horses, so Yen-hi was able to pluck up a little courage. Meanwhile the Nüchêns conquered the whole of the Liao Tung promontory, besides occupying the line west of the Palisade. They sent a list of ten demands, one of which was for the immediate recognition of their ruler as Ta Kin, or " Great Gold " Emperor (p. 232). This was conceded at once, and a special mission was sent, with chariot, crown, and regalia complete, to " confer " this dignity upon Akuta. But the qualifications attached thereto were not what he wanted, and the Cathayan envoys had a narrow escape of being sawn in two : as it was they each received a hundred lashes.

In the year 1120 the Nüchêns took the Upper Capital and destroyed all the imperial tombs, both there and north-east of the Central Capital between Jêhol and the Palisade, leaving no wrack behind. Family squabbles now took place regarding the Cathayan succession (p. 257). Yen-hi had four sons, at least three of which were by different mothers. The mother of the second son, who was a youth of high promise, was murdered by opposition intriguers, and the result was that her two sisters' husbands went over with a thousand cavalry to the Nüchêns. The armies of the latter had now all crossed the River Liao, and these men came in very useful as guides. In 1121 the Central Capital was taken, and Yen-hi (evidently retiring south by way of the Ku-pêh K'ou Pass) passed through the Nan-k'ou Pass to the " Mandarin-Duck " Lake, north-west of Kalgan. Here the popular and much-respected second son of Yen-hi was induced to commit suicide ; really, in order not to stand in the way of his younger brother, whose mother's sister had married Yen-hi's counsellor, but, nominally, to prevent the two renegade uncles from accomplishing their purpose of setting him upon the throne. The young man sacrificed himself without a murmur, and his unselfish action excited much sympathy. But the dastardly behaviour of Yen-hi in thus allowing himself to be persuaded by a crafty counsellor completely alienated his people from him.

From the Duck Lake Yen-hi fled west to Ta-t'ung Fu. Nearly all his 5,000 men had dropped off by the time he arrived there. But his eldest son with 300 cavaliers stood by him. Yen-hi left word hurriedly with the viceroy at Ta-t'ung to prepare for the enemy, and himself passed on to Tenduc. Fearing lest the presence of his unpopular counsellor should attract the enemy, he ordered him to go away, reproaching him at the same time with the murder of the queen, and with having brought on all this trouble in consequence. The counsellor had not gone three miles before he was despatched by Yen-hi's attendants. When the Nüchêns came up to Ta-t'ung Fu the viceroy at once surrendered the city.

Yen-hi had left his uncle and one of the Chinese ministers in charge of Peking, and now the uncle suddenly found himself, much against his sincere wish and the advice of the Chinese minister, invested with the purple by the governor of that town and his party. When he found that he must perforce accept the position, he issued a decree degrading his nephew to the rank of prince. His government extended over the whole of the Cathayan dominions (not in the hands of the Nüchêns) except the parts north of the Desert and lying towards

the West. From this time the Liao Empire may be said
to have been split up into two parts, the *linya* Ye-lüh Ta-shih
proceeding west to found an empire in Persia. Meanwhile
the Nüchêns entered into negotiations with China, and received
the subsidy which used to be paid to Cathay. Akuta would
tolerate no " mandates " from the Chinese Emperor, who was
told he must treat as an equal or not at all. The Emperor
accordingly addressed him an autograph letter as " His
Majesty the Emperor of Great Kin." Tientsin and Peking
were claimed for China, but the Nüchêns were told that they
might keep Yung-p'ing Fu and the Central Capital. The
enormous herds of horses which the Cathayans used to feed
in the plains south of Tientsin also fell into Nüchên's hands.
The celebrated Yelüh Tashih just mentioned, a kinsman of
the royal house, afterwards founder of the Karakitai or Black
Cathayan dynasty in West Asia, was viceroy in the north-
eastern provinces, the old Cathayan habitat between the
Sungari and the Desert when Yen-hi left the Peking plain ;
but he seems to have subsequently come south and formed
one of the party who placed the uncle on the throne.
Ambassadors were sent to China, but the Emperor declined
to receive them, on the ground that the legitimate monarch
was yet alive.

Now that the Cathayan power was thoroughly broken,
the Chinese thought it would be a good time to step in and
give the dying lion a parting kick. Accordingly they eagerly
availed themselves of the proffered services of an adventurer,
who had been filibustering on his own account, to co-operate
with the Nüchêns and march on Peking from the south.
The attack failed through the cowardice of the Chinese.
The Chinese governor who had been instrumental in placing
the uncle on the throne commenced to intrigue with both
China and the Nüchêns, being quite prepared to sell his new
master to whichever side should give him the best terms.
The Nüchêns on their part knew that the Chinese would wriggle
out of their subsidy if they were suffered to get into Peking.

Indeed the Chinese were already beginning to increase their demands : at first it had been the territory given by the Shado Tsin as a reward for Cathayan assistance, but now they also demanded the Yung-p'ing Fu plain, which had for some reason been given to Apaoki in or about A.D. 900 by a Chinese military satrap then in possession of the Peking plain. The Nüchên general informed the Chinese that if they did not discontinue increasing their demands they should not have even Peking, and that in any case the rents of the six districts belonging to that department must be paid to the Nüchên dynasty. Meanwhile Yung-p'ing Fu was made the Southern Capital of Kin. The result of the negotiations was that in addition to the 400,000 strings of money which used to be paid to the Cathayans, the Chinese had to pay to the Nüchêns annually 1,000,000 strings for " rent," besides an immediate present of 2,000,000 peculs of grain ; in exchange for which they received the Peking plain up to the Great Wall and the three well-known passes of Nan K'ou, Ku-pêh K'ou, and Tuh-shih K'ou. It is presumed that the Pêh-t'ang River to the east of Tientsin must have been the boundary between the Yung-p'ing and Peking plains.

The Cathayan Emperor-uncle (p. 265), who considered the Chinese had broken old treaties, beheaded the messenger sent by the eunuch (p. 263) demanding his submission to China. He also sent Yelüh Tashih to occupy Choh Chou and to call upon the Chinese forces either to retire or fight. Tashih ultimately drove them as far as Hiung Chou. Dying shortly after that, the uncle was succeeded nominally by his widow acting as regent, the real power being in the hands of one of her generals. But when the Nüchêns had secured the Nan-k'ou Pass it was evident that Peking was no longer tenable. The Empress-regent and her chief generals took to flight, and the only question was now what direction to take. It ended in one of the generals, who was a Ghei man and wished to return to his native land, taking all the Ghei troops with him in one direction, whilst the Empress and Yelüh Tashih, taking with them the

Cathayan troops, rejoined the fugitive Emperor Yen-hi at Tenduc. The Emperor, who could not forgive her for being instrumental in raising his uncle to the throne, had her put to death at once, but Tashih for some reason got off with a reprimand. Meanwhile the other or Ghei general captured several cities in the Ho-kien Fu plain and styled himself " Sacred Holy Emperor of the Great Ghei Empire," but he was soon defeated by the Chinese and killed. The Chinese Emperor, hearing that Yen-hi was gaining a little strength at Tenduc, seems to have behaved rather well—supposing that he was acting in good faith. He sent a Tartar bonze to him, assuring him of a welcome at the Chinese capital and honourable treatment as " brother," besides placing palaces at the disposal of other Cathayan princes. It is not stated, but it may easily be imagined, why the Cathayan monarch did not throw himself into his Chinese brother's arms.

Meanwhile Tashih, who had justified his conduct at Peking on the ground that the Cathayan Emperor's own precipitate flight had left no other dignified course open, thought it would be more prudent to place the desert between himself and his pusillanimous sovereign. Akuta was now (1123) dead, and had been succeeded by his brother Gukimai. This caused the Nüchêns to withdraw from Shan Si for a time. Yen-hi had, with Tashih's reinforcements, 30,000 cavalry at his disposal, and thought he might with these regain his ancient patrimony, but Tashih considered that a monarch who could not win a single battle when Cathay was yet intact was hardly likely to win one now that she was falling to pieces, and declined to join in the enterprise. He decamped with his own men at night, declared himself a sovereign, travelled for three days until he crossed the Karagol or Blackwater north of Shan Si, received considerable assistance from the White Tartars in the neighbourhood (a tribe mentioned from the most ancient times always as living in that neighbourhood), and made the best of his way to Urumtsi. There his eloquent harangues seem to have attached the fragmentary tribes of Ouigours,

Merkits, Djadjerats, Tanguts, etc. (who had already for many generations formed part of the Cathayan empire, or at least been on visiting terms with it), to his interests and person. With the assistance of Bilga Khan of the Ouigours (whose capital seems to have been at Karahodjo or Pidjan, and who had never been actually a vassal of Cathay), he equipped his forces and fought his way step by step to Samarcand, and thence to Kermané, between Samarcand and Bokhara, where he assumed the western title of Gurkhan (pp. 108, 169), at the same time keeping up his Chinese reign style and dignities concurrently.

Whilst Yelüh Tashih was adventuring in the West, Yelüh Yen-hi, the fugitive Emperor of Cathay, taking with him his queens and two sons, marched south from Tenduc and reduced one of the Shan Si cities. The Nüchên general in those parts soon out-manœuvred him, and at last succeeded in capturing the whole of his family. Yen-hi now sought asylum in the Ordous kingdom of Hia or Tangut; but the Tanguts were afraid to give him asylum, and he took refuge with an obscure Tibetan tribe. Early in the year 1125, when he still had a thousand cavaliers with him, he was surprised by the Nüchên general charged with that duty and taken. He had with him an image of Buddha in gold sixteen feet long, and many other valuable things to match it: as he retreated, these were abandoned one after the other in order to facilitate his flight. The Nüchên general very gallantly got down from his horse, knelt before his captive, and presented him a cup of wine, after which he was taken to Manchuria and interned by Gukimai in the neighbourhood of modern Vladivostock with the title of "Coast Prince." Thus ended Cathay.

Shortly after that the Nüchêns, disgusted with the paltry treachery of the Chinese, who had as a last act connived at the betrayal of Yung-p'ing, took that city by storm and demanded the cession of all China north of the Yellow River. Tangut meanwhile hastened to declare herself a vassal of the Nüchêns. In 1126 the Nüchêns under General Warib crossed the Yellow River in small boats without opposition and invested the Chinese capital at modern K'ai-fêng Fu. The confusion and misery of the times is well described in the Chinese novel to which allusion has already been twice made (pp. 214, 260). Their "indemnity" demands were now 5,000,000 ounces of gold, 10,000,000 of silver, 1,000,000 pieces of silk, and 10,000 head of cattle; the recognition of the Nüchên Emperor as Uncle, the restoration of all northern Chinese in the Sung Empire, and the cession of certain territory. The Emperor hastily got together 200,000 ounces of gold and 4,000,000 of silver as an immediate instalment, and promised all the rest: his brother and one of the ministers were given as hostages. The Chinese had no sooner got rid of immediate danger than they began to wriggle out of their bargain. The Nüchêns thereupon determined to read them a lesson they would not soon forget. After defeating them in several pitched battles— in which, by the way, military engines were used—they took the capital by storm, and the Emperor placed himself in the hands of General Jemugor. Their demands now were 10,000,000 ounces of gold, 20,000,000 "shoes" of silver (say 100,000,000 ounces), and 10,000,000 pieces of silk. The Emperor, the Emperor-Abdicate, together with a vast number of Empresses, imperial concubines, relatives, etc., to the number of 3,000 in all, were carried off to Tartary, and official China (or Manzi—"Southern Barbarians"—as Marco Polo calls it) had to migrate once more across the River Yangtsze. The Nüchên dominions now included almost the whole of the modern Shan Si, Shan Tung, and Chih-li, with part of Ho Nan provinces. After Warib's death that same year the feeble Nüchên Emperor Gukimai fell under Jemugor's sole influence.

In 1127 Tashih got tired of his Kermané surroundings, and leading his army east to a spot near Issekul founded a new capital called Ghuz Ordo, near the old Sujàb of the Western Turks. During his stay there he made one unsuccessful effort to regain his old dominions north of the

Mongolian desert, and died in 1136. The term " Ghuz Turks " (at the end of Book III) seems to have been an Arab expression indicating the Uzes or Alans, also called Comans (Russian Polovtsi), who once occupied Tashih's territory. Comana had been one of the six divisions of Justinian's " Third Armenia"; it seems to be mentioned (under a very similar name) amongst the conquests of Tiglath Pileser the First, as recounted by Maspero. The Karakitai dynasty, which was a mere dominant tribe over a total population of 85,000 families, lasted until 1203, when it was destroyed by the Khan of the Naimans, which people in turn, together with Manchuria, Nüchên land, China, Tangut, Persia, Russia, etc., were gradually conquered by the Mongols, originally (p. 223) a petty tribe north of the desert. From 1368 to 1643 China was once more ruled by pure Chinese. Since then she has been in the competent hands of the Manchus, as already explained (pp. 220, 230), an obscure tribe affiliated to the Nüchêns, who spoke a similar language. It will thus be plain that with the exception of the Han dynasties (B.C. 200 to A.D. 200) and the T'ang dynasty (600–900) no native ruling house has ever held North China for long : even the Ming dynasty (1368–1643) was worried by incessant Mongol raids, and one Emperor was carried off prisoner by Essen the Eleuth Mongol.

INDEX

The object of this unconscionably long index is to enable readers of all classes to refer, compare, and (it is hoped) understand, without having to move from the arm-chair. Comparatively few "general" readers take notice of foot-notes, and still fewer are willing—if indeed able—to consult the foot-note references to original authors ; many of whom, again, have written in languages and books inaccessible to the exceptionally favoured individuals who might (if willing) take the trouble to hunt them up.

THE AUTHOR.